L. W. NIXON LIBRARY
BUTLER COUNTY COMMUNITY
901 SOUTH HAVERHILL ROAD
EL DORADO, KANSAS 67042-3280

W9-AGV-719

362.2     Kane, Geoffrey P., 1
KAN       Inner-city
1981      alcoholism : an
          ecological analysis
          and cross-cultural

BCCC

a31111000898567n

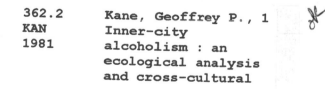

# INNER-CITY ALCOHOLISM

# INNER-CITY ALCOHOLISM
## An Ecological Analysis and Cross-Cultural Study

## Geoffrey P. Kane, M.D., M.P.H.

*Department of Social Medicine,*
*Montefiore Hospital and Medical Center,*
*Albert Einstein College of Medicine,*
*Bronx, New York*

**HUMAN SCIENCES PRESS**
72 Fifth Avenue    3 Henrietta Street
NEW YORK, NY 10011  ●  LONDON, WC2E 8LU

Copyright © 1981 by Geoffrey P. Kane, M.D.
72 Fifth Avenue, New York, New York 10011

All rights reserved. No part of this work may be reproduced or utilized in any form or by any means, electronic or mechanical, including photocopying, microfilm and recording, or by any information storage and retrieval system without permission in writing from the publisher.

Printed in the United States of America
123456789 987654321

Editorial/Production Services
by *Harkavy Publishing Service*

**Library of Congress Cataloging in Publication Data**

Kane, Geoffrey P        1944–
  Inner-city alcoholism.

  Includes bibliographical references and index.
    1. Alcoholism — New York (City) — Case studies.
  2. Alcoholism — New York (City) — Prevention — Case
  studies.   3. Alcoholism — Treatment — New York (City)
  — Case studies.   4. Cross-cultural studies — New York
  (City) — Case studies.   5. Bronx (Borough) — Social
  conditions.   I. Title.
  HV5298.N5K36        362.2'97
  ISBN  0-89885-023-1

362.2
KAN
1981

Kane, Geoffrey P., 1
Inner-city
alcoholism : an
ecological analysis
and cross-cultural

*To My Wife*

If nobody can learn from the past,
then there's no point in raking it up.

— Billie Holiday
from her autobiography
*Lady Sings the Blues*

# CONTENTS

9

## List of Figures

## List of Tables

13

# FOREWORD

Ale, man, ale's the stuff to drink.
For fellows whom it hurts to think.

— Alfred Edward Housman (1859–1936)
*A Shropshire Lad*

Like many an ethnic restaurant on New York's East Side, this book offers the reader more sustenance than its title suggests. The first few chapters greatly clarify the confusing array of terms, theories, and disciplinary biases so rife in this field. The last few chapters paint large the critical issues now facing us with regard to treatment and prevention. Data from inner-city New York are sandwiched between the former "where we've been" and the latter "where we must go" sections.

Geoffrey Kane's first three chapters are much more than a mere review of relevant terms and concepts. They comprise a philosophical treatise, an epistomological critique of what the finest minds have brought to the alcoholism field over the last half century. Kane deftly, respectfully, exposes this one's oversight, that one's academic limitations, the datedness of older hypotheses uninformed by new and unexpected data. He does not shrink from such herculean tasks as considering the composition of "disease," characteristics of the "medical model," or criteria for "alcoholism." Such pluck is unexpected in one able to discourse so cogently on the philosophy of science!

It is evident that we as readers must acknowledge—and thank—Alvan R. Feinstein, mathematician-turned-physician, for his early influences on the author. Dr. Feinstein's efforts "to champion better logic and more precise description in medicine" certainly find fruition in this book. We also benefit from Geoffrey Kane's training in both medicine and public health. Unlike many who have turned their research skills to this field, the author has an appreciation of disorder-within-an-individual as well as disorder-within-a-population—a subtle, but very powerful distinction reflected in Kane's repeated references to "clinical medicine" and "social medicine." Public health models for alcoholism are well explicated. You will appreciate the well-recognized medical aphorism—often lost on careful researchers as well as the lay public—that causal relationships (even when elucidated, as they seldom are) infrequently produce obvious solutions to problems.

After such masterful overtures in the first chapters, the reader will very likely arrive at the data section with great anticipations indeed. The reader's appetite will be further whetted by the careful historical/political/sociocultural background provided in Chapter 4. The extensive data presented in Chapters 5 and 6 do add appreciably to our knowledge regarding the cross-cultural similarities and differences among people with alcohol-related problems. Yet the data do not clearly guide clinicians, community leaders, policy planners, or others toward resolution of inner-city alcoholism. If this is disappointing, so be it. That is the state of the field.

Running lightly through these middle and later chapters is an emphasis on education, training, employment, social competence, hope, social deviance, poverty, and escapism. Relatedness of these factors to alcohol abuse is not a new observation. Bishop John Still (1543–1608) wrote four centuries ago:

> Back and side go bare, go bare,
> Both foot and hand go cold;
> But, belly, God send thee good ale enough,
> Whether it be new or old.
>
> *Gammer Gurton's Needle*, Act V

Such observations are unlikely to bring massive infusions of federal or private monies into the South Bronx in the name of stemming alcoholism. Especially from vantage points outside the South Bronx, such investments would seem likely to be diluted by increased migrations from Puerto Rico and the rural South. The theme provides an example of the typical distance between most causal theories and interventions for alcoholism.

What, then, are the alternatives in the South Bronx? This brings us to the general issue raised in the last two chapters: more effective treatment and prevention. Enhanced efforts in these endeavors would help not only the people of the South Bronx, but all areas of the country. Kane supports approaches that have been widely suggested by others: identifying sub groups, matching treatment to patients, looking beyond the "alcoholism" to the individual, screening and early diagnosis, need for evaluation and research. He calls for more "social experimentation," stronger leadership by the National Institute of Alcohol Abuse and Alcoholism, new institutions such as social "field stations," and the need for social action and broad social policy. It is not so much that any of these ideas are new or worthy that is of interest. Rather, the striking fact is that yet another careful thinker has stepped forward to enunciate them! And despite their reiteration, they continue to be ignored by our political leaders and our leaders in the health and alcoholism fields.

Why such continued, downright foolishness? Set against the background of Kane's logic and clarity, the absurdity of the field's position calls out for explanation. A useful analogy may be to consider this field as the black and Hispanic drinkers of this volume are considered. This field and the people in it have a history, values, and attitudes. These involve people, power, incomes, personal commitment, status, and prestige. Change from current activities and directions — along the lines described in the last two chapters — would involve social action, reassignment of priorities, and attitudinal change from the status quo. Careers would be made and broken, jobs lost and gained, values reaffirmed and destroyed.

In a highly politicized field such as this one, it seems unlikely that risks in this order of magnitude will be run — especially by those leading the field. Although such a revolutionary social movement might conceivably originate outside the field, such alternatives are always difficult to predict and certainly cannot be relied upon. More likely is an evolutionary change, as new thoughts are conceived and old thoughts (along with their owners in many cases) simply die out. While Geoffrey Kane calls for the former revolutionary approach, it is more likely that his thoughts will guide us along evolutionary lines. Whatever your own preferences for the field, I am sure you will find yourself the richer for availing yourself of his lucid thinking.

Joseph Westermeyer, M.D., Ph.D.
Department of Psychiatry
University of Minnesota
Minneapolis, Minnesota
January 1980

# ACKNOWLEDGMENTS

This study could not have begun or come to completion without conscientious efforts by many people. Though the writer must be the focus of any criticism regarding what appears here, any credit must be widely shared with the people mentioned below. Essential encouragement, advice, and patient endurance of inconvenience have come not just from those named, but also from numerous other friends, relatives, and associates.

Arlington Garris, formerly Director of the Alcoholism Unit of the Martin Luther King Jr. Health Center (MLKHC), was responsible for the primary collection of the data used in the case study. He developed the Information Sheet as the basic component of MLKHC alcoholism treatment records in 1971. The rest of the Alcoholism Unit staff—Jennie Avila, James McKeller, James Molyneaux, David Romero, and Elizabeth Rubero—helped collect and maintain the data studied here. The Alcoholism Unit staff also assisted in the preparation of the case histories included with the statistical information in Chapter 5.

Steven Athanail, then a student of the Sophie Davis Center for Biomedical Education of the City College of New York, reviewed the Information Sheets and coded the data items. Steven also coordinated data processing. Two other Biomedical Education students, Leza Gallo and Gregory Vazquez, contributed to these efforts, as did Janice Charles, then of the MLKHC Data Processing Department.

This project owes a fundamental debt to Harold Wise for

founding MLKHC and for sharing his conviction that the South Bronx can again become a desirable place to live. MLKHC administrators William Lloyd, Eleanor Minor, Deloris Smith, and Gloria Perry consistently supported this project. Phillip Dawes of the Special Projects Branch of the National Institute on Alcohol Abuse and Alcoholism mobilized funds for computer time from the MLKHC alcoholism grant.

Without the capable (and invariably cheerful) help of library personnel, the literature review could not have progressed. Katharine Gardner of the Albert Einstein College of Medicine Library, Dinah Reitman formerly of the Department of Social Medicine Library at Montefiore Hospital, and Margaret Roche of the Montefiore Medical Library deserve special mention. Technical publications that were very useful but do not appear in the references are Turabian's *A Manual for Writers* (Chicago: University of Chicago Press, 1973), Swinscow's *Statistics at Square One* (London: British Medical Association, 1976), Balkin's *A Writer's Guide to Book Publishing* (New York: Hawthorn Books, 1977), and Crawford's *The Writer's Legal Guide* (New York: Hawthorn Books, 1977).

Elizabeth Bellis of the Yale University School of Medicine Department of Epidemiology and Public Health reviewed this book in draft form. Her comments guided revisions in Chapters 2, 3, 5, and 6 that more adequately attuned the material to readers' needs. Victor Sidel of the Montefiore Department of Social Medicine provided thoughtful comments on a draft copy and, over a five year span, helped the writer manage sundry situations that might otherwise have slowed this work. John Docherty of the Yale Department of Psychiatry read a late version and suggested changes that strengthened the final manuscript.

Beverly Anderson and Anna Salabarria of the MLKHC Office of Professional Affairs typed most of the tables and drafts of some chapters. Suzanne Kane, the writer's wife, typed the text of the final manuscript. Suzanne's most significant contribution, however, was resolutely freeing time for the writer to pursue his own work on this project by temporarily carrying more than her share of parental and other domestic responsibilities. Barbara Jeckell, the writer's secretary, helped prepare, and then typed, the index. Norma Fox of Human Sciences Press generated Human Science's commitment to publish the book and made suggestions that helped the writer improve the balance of the material included. Karol Lightner of Human Sciences and Michael Harkavy of Harkavy Publishing Service skillfully directed the transformation of the work from typescript to its present form.

Financial support for this study came from Grant No. 5H84 AA01440-04 from the National Institute on Alcohol Abuse and Alcoholism and from MLKHC's U.S. Department of Health, Education, and Welfare, Public Health Service Basic Grant No. 02-H-000 319-04-1.

## CREDITS

The writer is grateful to the following for permission to quote passages from copyrighted material (quotations are identified in this list by authors' last names and by the page numbers of the quotes in this volume — complete references for each chapter appear on pp. 220–241; the page numbers in parentheses throughout the text indicate the locations of quoted or cited material in the original sources):

Fabrega - pp. 34n, 35, 40 - Copyright 1974, the Massachusetts Institute of Technology

Clark - pp. 34, 35, 37–38 - Copyright 1967, Little, Brown and Company

MacMahon and Pugh - pp. 38–39 - Copyright 1967, Little, Brown and Company

Feinstein - p. 42 - Copyright 1967, The Williams & Wilkins Co., Baltimore

Jellinek - pp. 46–47, 47–48 - Copyright 1960, Hillhouse Press

Glatt - p. 51 - Copyright 1974, B. Edsall & Co. Ltd.

Seixas - p. 52 - Copyright 1976, Human Sciences Press

Gitlow - pp. 52–53 - Copyright 1973, Academic Press

Cahalan - pp. 57, 113–114 - Copyright 1970, Jossey-Bass, Inc.

Susser - pp. 64, 65, 67n - Copyright 1973, Oxford University Press

Keller - pp. 73–74, 82–83 - Reprinted by permission from *Journal of Studies on Alcohol*, 1975, *36*, 133–147. Copyright by Journal of Studies on Alcohol, Inc., New Brunswick, NJ 08903

Roebuck and Kessler - pp. 80–81 - Copyright 1972, J. B. Roebuck and R. G. Kessler

Friedman - p. 82 - Copyright 1974, McGraw-Hill, Inc.

Dylan - p. 83 - Copyright 1965, WARNER BROS., INC. All Rights Reserved. Used by permission

Harper - pp. 91–92, 93 - Copyright 1976, Douglass Publishers, Inc.

Torres de Gonzalez - p. 111 - Printed by courtesy of Blanca Torres de Negron

Lewis - pp. 159–160 - Copyright 1965, Random House, Inc.

Trice, Roman, and Belasco - p. 177 - Copyright 1969, Marcel Dekker, Inc. (*International Journal of the Addictions*)

Sugerman, Reilly, and Albahary - pp. 184–185 - Copyright 1965, American Medical Association (*Archives of General Psychiatry*, 1965, *12*, 552–556)

Hill and Blane - pp. 191, 193 - Reprinted by permission from *Quarterly Journal of Studies on Alcohol*, 1967, *28*, 76–104. Copyright by Journal of Studies on Alcohol, Inc., New Brunswick, NJ 08903

Straus - p. 214 - Copyright 1973, Insight Publishing Co., Inc. (*Psychiatric Annals*)

National Council on Alcoholism - p. 219 - Copyright 1972, the American Psychiatric Association.

*Chapter 1*

# INTRODUCTION

## WHERE *IS* THE ACTION?

Alcoholism is not among the health and social problems that generally get better if left alone. Present efforts to decrease the ill effects of alcohol are insufficient. Mass media and scientific communications provide an almost constant reminder of the rising "tide of alcoholic casualty"[1] (p. 320). The counted victims include large numbers of men, women, and adolescents who are sick or dead because of their experiences with alcohol. They include the families of alcoholics; often, abused spouses and children. They include others injured or killed by intoxicated persons through violence in homes, barrooms, or on highways. Counted also are government and industrial organizations, who pay the price of alcohol-related illness and absenteeism with incomprehensible sums.

Society's once-reassuring belief that skid-row men predominate among alcoholics has been almost completely eroded by waves of information revealing the diversity among people with serious alcohol problems. The extensive alcohol problems among the employed, women, teenagers, and even among the unborn* now regularly receive public attention. As the real extent of alcohol-related suffering becomes apparent, societal concern or worry increases. This response is appropriate since virtually every member of society, whether already touched by such suffering or not, remains somehow vulnerable in the future. Society's uneasiness is heightened by changing patterns of alcohol use and abuse that seem to many to be beyond control. College students, for example, after following the trend toward polydrug abuse that characterized the early 1970s,[2] now appear determined to go "Back to the Booze"[3] (p. 71).

Action is needed. But those uninformed about alcohol problems don't know what to do. Those more informed often hear so many conflicting suggestions and come to see so many competing possibilities that they don't know where to begin. Conflicting suggestions often come from scientists who study alcohol abuse and alcoholism and who might justifiably be regarded as among those most informed about alcohol problems. It is recognized, however, that these scientists have generally been unable to establish mutual relevance even among the scientific domains of their research;[4, 5] it should not be surprising that direction society receives from them is fragmented and discordant.

This book may help. Chapter 2 isolates and neutralizes issues that impede scientific understanding and communication about alcoholism. Chapter 3 offers a conceptual scheme that accommodates not only the complexity of alcoholism but also the multiplicity of views people have of it.

A provocative recent article by Kendell[6] helps illustrate that the approach presented here fosters clearer thinking about alcoholism and facilitates more effective action planning. Ken-

---

*Authoritative discussions and references pertaining to many of the victims of alcohol abuse and alcoholism, such as Smith's chapter on the fetal alcohol syndrome, are conveniently collected in *Alcoholism: Development, consequences, and interventions*. Estes, N. J., & Heinemann, E. M., eds., St. Louis: C. V. Mosby, 1977.

dell, who questions the efficacy of the medical treatment of alcoholism and generally accepts the hypothesis of Ledermann [6, 7] that "the proportion of a population drinking excessively is largely determined by the average consumption of that population" [6] (pp. 368–369), concludes that the most promising means of reducing the consequences of alcohol abuse is legislative action "to increase the price or restrict the availability of alcoholic beverages" [6] (p. 370). Such an intervention might prove beneficial. It could be gradually undertaken and repeatedly evaluated. Kendell, however, allies the issue in question — that society should perhaps take political action to reduce alcohol problems — with questionable issues, leaving his paper likely to confuse some readers and alienate others, perhaps with the result that his suggested intervention will obtain too little support to elicit an actual test of its merit.

In his arguments Kendell assumes that alcoholism must be regarded as *either* a medical *or* a political problem and he feels "that it is no longer appropriate to regard alcoholism as a medical problem" [6] (p. 371).

> Until we stop regarding alcoholism as a disease, and therefore as a problem to be dealt with by the medical profession, and accept it as an essentially political problem, for everyone and for our legislators in particular, we shall never tackle the problem effectively. [6] (p. 370)

Though somewhat inconsistent with these statements, Kendell encourages medical professionals to continue trying to help alcoholics and even to take initiative in the political sphere. The article's internal inconsistency seems to arise because of Kendell's medical/political dichotomy, which artificially restricts notions of alcoholism and of disease. Kendell's rhetoric thus promotes reader confusion because it inaccurately approximates reality. His rejection of alcoholism as a disease promotes alienation of readers whose concerns with alcoholism are disease oriented. Though perhaps influential politically, these readers might totally overlook Kendell's central message as they hasten to defend alcoholism as a disease.

Such difficulties in comprehension and persuasion might be avoided if readers or author, or ideally both, were equipped with sets of assumptions about alcoholism and disease that better represent reality. For example, they could adopt the assumption that multiple, diverse factors contribute to the development of *all* disease. In that framework every disease, to some extent, may be seen as inextricably *both* a medical *and* a political (or social) problem. Further, they could assume that the responsibility for dealing with disease is shared both by the persons affected and by society, and that only a portion of society's responsibility can possibly be discharged by medical personnel. Applying assumptions like these, readers might quickly recognize the pitfalls in various arguments; authors might avoid needlessly competitive or ultimately untenable positions.

The alternative assumptions just mentioned and others that may assist thinking and communicating about alcohol problems are developed in Chapters 2 and 3. These ideas are already used by many health scientists. The writer believes they deserve increasing exposure and acceptance in the alcoholism field.

Alcoholism in the inner city is the focus of this book. The preceding discussion suggests a broad relevance of Chapters 2 and 3 to alcohol studies, but here these chapters serve primarily to provide perspective on the special problems and treatment needs of alcoholics who live in a deteriorated urban environment. Analogous to the possible general applicability of Chapters 2 and 3 to alcohol studies, alcoholism research in the inner city — where human problems are magnified and causal relationships may therefore be more obvious — may lead to knowledge applicable throughout society.

## BACKGROUND: THE SOUTH BRONX

Here, *inner city* refers to run-down urban areas inhabited primarily by indigent minority groups. In these areas, alcohol problems are both more visible and more extensive* than else-where. The writer worked as a physician in one such area, the South Bronx, for more than six years, primarily at the Dr. Martin Luther King Jr. Health Center (MLKHC). As metropolitan New Yorkers—and perhaps by now most people in the United States—know, the South Bronx is a part of the city where dwellings pass from habitation to abandonment to ruin in a matter of weeks. The landscape features rubble and architectural skeletons. South Bronx residents are chiefly blacks and Hispan-ics, the latter mostly Puerto Rican by birth or parentage. The ethnic composition of the population served by MLKHC changes continuously; at the time of this study it was roughly half black and half Hispanic.

People in the South Bronx are poor.** They experience a disproportionate share of death and disease.***

MLKHC is a neighborhood health center that provides comprehensive care through eight interdisciplinary (nurse prac-titioner, internist, pediatrician, family health worker) teams. The center has offered alcoholism treatment services since 1970.

*New York City Health Services Administration estimates of alcoholism prevalence by health district reveal the highest rates in the city's three major inner-city or ghetto areas    Central Harlem, Bedford/Fort Green, and the South Bronx (Morrisania/Mott Haven). In some comparisons these rates are over twice those of other districts.

** Bureau of the Census data summarized by the Department of Community Health of the Albert Einstein College of Medicine indicate that the median family income of blacks and Puerto Ricans living in the Bronx is about 70% that of whites in the Bronx and about 60% that of whites throughout New York City. In 1970, over 25% of Bronx families had an annual income below $5,000 and these families are presumably concentrated in the South Bronx.

***MLKHC is in the Morrisania health district. In 1970, the age-adjusted death rate for all causes was 8.7 (per 1,000) in Morrisania compared to 7.7 in the Bronx and 7.5 in New York City; the infant mortality rate (1974) was 24.3 (per 1,000 live births) in Morrisania compared to 20.9 (Bronx) and 19.7 (N.Y.C); new cases of tuberculosis (1974) were 37.8 (per 100,000) in Morrisania com-pared to 25.4 (Bronx) and 25.6 (N.Y.C.). (These figures also from Department of Community Health summaries.)

The clinical data used in this study were collected within the period from mid-1972 through 1975, when the MLKHC alcoholism program was based in a walk-in center—the Alcoholism Unit—at 507 East 171st Street, about two blocks from the main health center. The alcoholism treatment approach of the Alcoholism Unit staff is described in Chapter 7. An abandoned structure adjacent to the unit was the site of at least two fires during the study period. Typical of the availability of alcohol in black neighborhoods (see Chapter 4), liquor stores were located at either end of the unit's block. Within a one-block walk from the unit were six alcohol outlets, either bars or liquor stores. When the unit relocated in January 1976, the next tenant at the East 171st Street address promptly opened an after-hours club.

## STUDY OVERVIEW

*Clinical medicine* refers to a variety of medical-scientific disciplines and activities that help *individuals* identify and treat their health problems. *Epidemiology* is a nonclinical medical-scientific discipline that probes why people develop their health problems. In contrast to clinical medicine's focus on individuals, epidemiology focuses on *groups* of people, or populations. Epidemiologic research frequently leads to better understanding of the factors that contribute to the causation of particular health problems—knowledge often then applied in preventive activities. In an essay that examines "the possible relevance of epidemiological research to the planning of response to alcoholism"[8] (p. 29), Edwards points out

> that however much the need for epidemiological information as the basis for planned response may have been a subject of comment, the actual linking of the epidemiology and the action has seldom been attempted.[8] (p. 29)

The core of this book (Chapters 5, 6, and 7) represents a modest attempt to establish such a link in the context of the

MLKHC alcoholism treatment program — "modest" because
the logical and feasible initial study was to examine the information
already on hand in the treatment records of the Alcoholism Unit.
The result is *descriptive* epidemiology, a characterization of the
group of people using the program, the treatment population.
Such studies of aggregated cases* have inherent limitations.
The members of the study group in effect have selected themselves for investigation by entering a program for treatment.
Conclusions drawn from a particular study apply only to the
actual study group and, with caution, to groups defined in a very
similar way. This study of MLKHC Alcoholism Unit patients,
therefore, can not generate valid general statements about
alcoholics in the South Bronx or even in the MLKHC neighborhood. It can, however, generate statements about the people
who use this program and thus it can be applied, as it is here, to
internal program planning.

As this investigation progressed, the alcoholism literature
carried pleas for more advanced, longitudinal research. [5, 11]
Longitudinal studies are relevant where there is sufficient preliminary knowledge to generate research hypotheses and where
there are sufficient resources to conduct the research. In the
inner city, neither condition has been well satisfied. Chapter 7
discusses what may be a realistic plan for transition from this
study to a longitudinal mode within the MLKHC alcoholism
treatment program.

The black and Hispanic ethnic composition of the treatment
population permits cross-cultural comparisons. Westermeyer[12]
reviewed a group of recent studies that describe cross-cultural
similarities and differences in alcohol-related problems. The
studies were drawn, like this one, from clinical settings. Only
five of the studies dealt with outpatient alcoholics. None seem to
have provided information on similarities and differences between blacks and Hispanics.

*Distinct from case-control studies, which are *analytic* epidemiology.[9, 10] To
some, "population" as above may be more statistical than epidemiological —
they might call Chapter 5 descriptive research rather than epidemiology.

## COMMENT ON THE LITERATURE REVIEW

Literature used in this study is eclectic. Many references were obtained, however, from thematically organized sources. A National Library of Medicine MEDLARS II search was conducted in April 1975 and it provided numerous citations related to alcoholism in ghetto areas. In efforts to expand and update these references, National Clearinghouse for Alcohol Information bibliographies and *Journal of Studies on Alcohol* abstracts were particularly helpful. When priorities turned to making sense of what had already been found—epidemiologically as well as in the library—the systematic inclusion of new material ceased.

In the cross-cultural area, it was often difficult or impossible to compare studies because of unstandardized data collection and data presentation. To ease the burden on future reviewers, Chapter 4 organizes studies on alcohol problems among blacks and Hispanics in ways that convey the particular information available in each study. To avoid contributing more than necessary (use of existing records precluded influencing the primary data collection) to this lack of comparability, data presentation in Chapter 5 includes many *counts* of black and Hispanic men and women with particular characteristics. If the numerical and verbal summaries here do not meet a reader's needs, access to these counts allows the reader to explore alternatives.

A variety of scientific disciplines contribute to understanding alcoholism in the inner city or in any other environment. Throughout this book studies having diverse disciplinary origins are cited. The writer struggled to present the interrelationships of these studies coherently. Yet if planned movement toward better health in our communities, as sketched in Chapter 8, is to occur, members of diverse disciplines must themselves interrelate and generate more than just coherent discussion—they must generate coherent action.

*Chapter 2*

# UNDERSTANDING ALCOHOLISM

## RESOLVING TAXONOMIC CONTROVERSY

People who repeatedly consume large amounts of beverage alcohol frequently develop serious physical and/or social problems. This statement alone would not evoke earnest criticism from anyone even remotely connected with alcohol studies. Couple it, however, with a remark that gives a name or label to the people afflicted with alcohol-related problems, thereby establishing a classification scheme or taxonomy, and one immediately enters the realm of a longstanding, wordy, and many-sided dispute. Christie and Bruun,[1] surveying the written substance of this dispute, call its perplexity and inconsistent word use "the great confusion" (p. 65). Bacon[2] offers a more descriptive summation of the same literature: "The participants seem to be talking about different things under the same label and talking about the same things under different labels; they seem to have brought different languages, methodologies, and philosophies

31

to bear upon whatever the label might be . . ." (p. 59).*

Reviewers[1, 2, 7] seem agreed that thinking in this field needs clarification and that their own efforts do not adequately provide this. There is ample reason to continue striving for clarity. Christie and Bruun,[1] for example, point out that an ordered conceptual framework would greatly improve communication. This would make possible two reaching benefits: better communication among scholars—to maximize the impact of interdisciplinary scientific effort on alcohol problems—and better informed and more communicative lay people—to reintroduce valuable lay power to decision making on important ethical and policy issues.

This chapter proposes to make more clear why there is so much controversy in the literature of alcohol problems and how acceptance of a few scientific concepts can help resolve at least a portion of it. The chapter centers on a question that reverberates throughout the taxonomic controversy: Can people with alcohol problems be thought of as diseased? Conceptual tools basic to epidemiology can facilitate understanding and responding to this recurrent issue, perhaps to the satisfaction of most of the interested parties.

## A NEGLECTED SCIENCE

It is fair to inquire why, if epidemiology has such useful tools, the job of resolving this controversy is still not completed. One reason is epidemiology's traditional lack of influence. Relative to other medical sciences such as anatomy, physiology, or

*Any reader who has not encountered the competition of terms and formulations under discussion here might look at the first chapter of Mann's *New Primer on Alcoholism*;[3] Jellinek's exhaustive *Disease Concept of Alcoholism*;[4] the first chapter of Cahalan's *Problem Drinkers*;[5] Larkin's[6] review (pp. 5–15) of recent studies relevant to the loss of control and abstinence emphasized by Jellinek; and the discussions of models of alcoholism by Siegler, Osmond, and Newell[7] and by Pattison.[8]

biochemistry, epidemiology has not been widely studied, understood, or utilized. Friedman's statement "that most students of medicine and other health sciences regard epidemiology as a boring and irrelevant subject which they study only because they are required to"[9] (p. ix) can be quickly substantiated by talking with a small sample of physicians — or epidemiologists.

The segments of epidemiologic knowledge applicable here include the meaning and appropriate use of "disease" as a medical term and, in Chapter 3, a model that depicts disease causation or etiology. Since epidemiology "may be defined as the study of the distribution of a *disease* or a physiological condition in human populations and of the factors that *influence* this distribution"[10] (p. 3, italics added), notions of disease and of disease causation are obviously fundamental to the discipline.

Presumably in part because epidemiologic thinking penetrates the medical community so poorly, physicians and others are prone to making statements about alcohol problems that violate logical, basic epidemiologic assumptions about disease. These statements do not go unchallenged, but the protestors — also insufficiently influenced by epidemiology — fail to isolate the fallacy underlying the statements they oppose, even though their own clinical experience with diseases helps them avoid the same error. Students of alcohol problems who enter the taxonomic controversy without a background in medicine are hindered by not having the clinician's practical experience with sick people to guide their thinking. Epidemiologic knowledge could probably help them, but unfortunately no one is likely to direct them to it.

## No Such Thing as Disease

Rooted in Old French, the word *disease* suggests negated comfort, a troubled or painful state. The word has been, and is, viewed from many perspectives and used in many ways. The orientations of social scientists, physicians, and lay persons do share general features, however, and notions of disease* can be formulated that are potentially both widely acceptable and useful. Such formulations succeed when they offer a reasonable representation of reality.

A notion of disease, if it is to have the practical value of representing real human experience or reality, must stay close to the root sense of the word. For a *state* of negated comfort to exist or be real, some organism must actually experience the dis-ease. This restricts *real disease* to the context of *the disturbed individual*. Outside this context; considered of itself, there is no such *thing* as disease.

Definitions of disease that can serve as models clearly state their dependency upon particular instances of illness. Clark's reference here to ''an organism'' provides the needed restriction.

> *Disease* . . . may be defined as a failure of the adaptive mechanisms of an organism to counteract adequately the stimuli and stresses to which it is subject, resulting in a disturbance in function or structure of some part of the body. . . .
> . . . It is possible . . . to conceive of disease manifestations and causes at any level from the molecular to the social.[12] (p. 4)

Fabrega[11] manages the issue by first developing a representation of persons and then specifying that a disease is ''person-centered'':

*No attempt will be made here to review the many semantic and syntactic functions of the term disease, which have been ably dissected by Fabrega.[11] Readers interested in pursuing this detail are referred to his book, especially pp. 119–141 and 205–222. The present discussion is confined to what Fabrega calls the *biologistic* perspective, wherein ''the term *disease* signifies a medical concept whose meaning or intention involves an abnormality in function and/or structure of any part, process, or system of the organism. The framing of the organism's 'normal' functioning or structure is accomplished by means of the concepts, findings, and premises of Western biological science. The range of application of the term or the class of things to which it applies—its extension—would include such things as appendicitis, schizophrenia, hypertension, depression, or diabetes. In any particular instance of its use, the term might refer to one of these items'' (pp. 132–133, italics in original).

A. Persons can be represented as though they were constituted of a hierarchic array of open and interconnected systems (molecular, chemical, physiological, psychological, social, etc.).

B. A disease is a person-centered, time-bound, undesirable deviation in the way a person functions (or is characterized by himself and/or others) in any of these systems. (p. 298)

## The Fallacy of Reification

These definitions protect against an error that is common within as well as outside of the medical community. Clark[12] emphasizes:

> In focusing on the person who is sick, one who has experienced a failure in his adaptive mechanisms, disease is more clearly established in this definition as not something unto itself. As has been emphasized many times, "there are no diseases, there are only sick people." Nevertheless, the impression is still widely extant that disease is something "with a life of its own," something that "attacks" man from the outside. This understanding originated in primitive medicine through reliance on the role of magic and supernatural forces. It also persists in folk medicine, which draws upon a repository of traditional belief based on lay experience. Even within scientific medicine, specific disease states are often described as if they had lives of their own. (p. 4)

No two sick people—that is, no two occurrences of disease—are exactly alike. People do, however, frequently have *similar* illnesses. Some of the characteristics that make the illnesses similar, such as a tendency to benefit from a particular therapy, have practical importance and need to be reliably recorded and communicated. For convenience, disease names are used to refer to groups of sick people with similar problems and similar biologic responses to intervention.

These disease names or categories are, because of individual variability, artificial. Yet disease descriptions, each of which is no more than a summary of characteristics shared by members of a group of sick people, are often regarded as independent standards. Persons taking this view can be said to *reify* the disease category, that is, they fallaciously think of an abstract as a real thing.

## Accommodating Variability

People with drinking problems emerge from different backgrounds, they experience different combinations of symptoms, and they develop different types or degrees of social and/or physical dysfunction. Particularly frustrating for those trying to help these people is the additional fact that they do not consistently respond to any one means of treatment. While such variability creates difficulties, there is really no alternative but to accept it and the constraints it imposes; for variability is the rule rather than the exception among biologic phenomena.*

Virtually every disease category is affected by similar problems arising from variability. For example, a substantial proportion of the patients referred to medical specialists for diagnosis and treatment have illnesses that are "atypical" or "borderline" with respect to conventional disease categories. Even the reasoning process physicians learn to follow to determine the most appropriate disease name or diagnosis for a given patient is an accommodation to variability. In this process the particulars of a case are used to generate a written or unwritten list of disease names, referred to as the patient's differential diagnosis. The patient would have one or more characteristics in common with each of the groups of sick people referred to by the diagnoses in the list. The logical clinician then

> tests each hypothetical diagnosis in turn, trying to disprove the incorrect and to prove the correct. He does this by asking two questions: Does the diagnosis explain all the findings?, and, Are the expected findings present?[13] (pp. 90–91)

*Foregoing a discussion of molecular genetics and of contemporary life science's understanding of the uniqueness of organisms, it is relevant to simply quote the writer's venerable freshman biology professor who would intermittently remind his students, "Variation is the law of life!"

Partly because there are few clinical findings that are uniquely attributable to one diagnosis and to no other disease, diagnosic thinking is not an easy process.[13] Nor is it, because of the limitations of our knowledge, a certain one. Very often the diagnosis accepted as the basis for treatment is simply the most likely diagnosis, not one that has been logically proved. A failure to respond to treatment could indicate that either the diagnosis was inappropriate or that the patient is one of those within the disease group not helped by the therapy in use.

Another example of how clinicians adapt to the kindred but heterogeneous membership of disease groups is their isolation of *clinical subgroups*. These subgroups are based, like the disease groups themselves, on shared patient characteristics that have practical significance. Among patients with rheumatoid arthritis, for example, "aspirin-responders" are an identifiable subgroup whose drug management generally would be distinct from other rheumatoids.*

## NOSOLOGY EVOLVES

The classification of diseases is called nosology. Nosologic activities include selecting names for groups of sick people and ordering these into more general categories such as *infectious diseases* or *diseases of the digestive system*. This work is embodied in various compendia or coding manuals such as the World Health Organization's International Classification of Diseases (ICD), which of late has been revised every ten years.

In nosology, diseases are treated as "entities" and caution is needed during conceptual manipulations to avoid reifying the diseases under consideration.

> Although diseases do not exist apart from sick individuals, there
> is a narrow sense in which disease may be considered as an

---

* More examples of clinical subgroups and a systematic discussion of the topic may be found in Chapters 10 and 11 of Feinstein's *Clinical Judgement.*[14]

entity. A group of ill persons, classified by the attributes of the disorder they possess in common, is said to be suffering from *a* disease to which a name is applied for purpose of communication. In this sense, disease is an entity, and different diseases are viewed as being distinct from one another.[12] (p. 4, italic in original)

Feinstein[14] is among those recognizing the need for a nomenclature and classification scheme that reaches beyond disease entities and more adequately classifies "the complex natural phenomena occurring in diseased people" (p. 71). White[15] anticipates that the next revision of the ICD, which may not be ready until the mid–1990s, will provide this. He envisions a guide to

the classification and counting of people's health problems . . . [which] would recognize the complex mosaic of health factors: genetic and biological, environmental, behavioral, psychological, and social that precipitate health problems, complaints, symptoms, conditions, and diseases . . . (p. iv)

Inasmuch as conceptual evolution is fundamental to scientific enterprise,[16] it should not be surprising that nosologic categories change over time. New categories are formed while some are deleted. Disease groups may be split or coalesced. Disease names are introduced or changed to reflect new or regrouped categories. MacMahon and Pugh[17] describe trends in the bases of disease nomenclature and classification and — most important to this discussion — illustrate the two prime factors underlying these changes, *advancing knowledge* and *practicality*:

There are two primary axes of classification of ill persons: manifestational and causal. *Manifestational* criteria group patients having in common one or more specific manifestations of illness: symptoms, signs, or laboratory determinations. Examples of manifestationally defined illnesses include the common cold, gastric ulcer, and carcinoma of the lung. *Causal* criteria group patients according to some prior experience, judged to be of a causal nature. Examples are tuberculosis, avitaminosis, and suicide. . . .

Originally, disease classification was based primarily on manifestational criteria, and its basis remains predominantly manifestational today. A change to causal criteria is introduced when etiologic factors have been identified as significant and offer promise of major therapeutic or preventive advantage. . . .

Important to keep in mind is the fact that selection of a particular causal component for the purpose of disease classification depends on its usefulness. The supposition that the chosen component has some more essential relationship to disease than other components may be false, for such a supposition leads occasionally to the misconception that the selected factor is *the* cause (e.g., that Mycobacterium tuberculosis is *the* cause of tuberculosis). . . . The desirability of introducing new classifications should be judged by their utility compared to alternate classifications and not on an idea that one classification may be more correct or natural than another. (pp. 13–14, italics in original)*

Feinstein[14] (pp. 72–88) provides a particularly detailed overview of nosologic evolution, paying close attention to the impact of modern technology.

## MEDICAL PLURALISM

The understanding elaborated above — that disease entities are no more than relatively arbitrary and transitory categories or labels applied to groups of sick people — is basic to contemporary epidemiology.[9] This understanding was presented here as "potentially widely acceptable and useful." This does not imply, however, that it *is* widely accepted and widely used. Rather, Fabrega[11] suggests that views of disease, at least within the medical community, are subjective and in states of flux:

*It has no consequence for the discussion at hand, but conceiving only two axes of classification may be unduly restrictive. Feinstein[14] (p. 87) cites a new approach to disease classification that incorporates four separate modalities called *topography*, *morphology*, *etiology*, and *function*.

> It is, of course, not the case that all physicians and students of disease generally hold to the conception that disease represents a time-bound, person-centered discontinuity. . . . it is simplistic to assume that any one view of disease is shared by all physicians or students of disease. What obtains, instead, are views and perspectives composed of elements that shift and fluctuate according to clinically relevant situations. (p. 212)

The diverse approaches to sick people and to disease entities that coexist in the medical community may be illustrated in a number of ways. In medical conferences and journals, when concern is often focused on a disease entity, some contributors express general points in a fashion that reifies the disease in question while others take care to avoid doing so. In clinical situations, when concern is focused on one sick person, a pluralistic terminology is used. This is reflected by the items physicians enter in hospital records as admitting and discharge diagnoses and also by the causes of death they enter on death certificates. Even though two physicians may have just confronted very similar clinical situations and may have dealt with them using very similar interventions, one physician might sum up his or her patient's difficulty in manifestational terms — choosing either a specific category like "acute pulmonary edema" or "alcoholic hallucinosis" or a more general category like "congestive heart failure" or "alcohol withdrawal state" — while another physician might use a term that emphasizes the underlying problem such as "rheumatic heart disease" or "chronic alcoholism."

The facts that nosologic activity periodically generates an ordered list of preferred terms and that these lists attain worldwide distribution do not necessarily mean that these lists are regularly used in medical practice. Actually, special training and a complicated hierarchical rule system are required to enable nosologists to translate many of the causes of death written on death certificates into the standardized categories of the ICD. Medical practitioners, however, generally do succeed in communicating with one another and a physician who employs other than standardized terms is not necessarily lax or in error. As implied previously, each edition of the ICD has its own limitations. "A clinician's primary job is to discover what ails the patient, not merely to diagnose disease"[14] (p. 92).

When clinicians—including those who logically pursue the steps of differential diagnosis described earlier—commit themselves and their patients to particular diagnoses, they generally do so without using standardized *diagnostic criteria*. This situation is developed more fully in the following subsection. The lack of standardized diagnostic criteria, and the lack of their use in those instances where authoritative standards exist, contribute to the pluralism of concepts and terms in medicine.

## Diagnostic Criteria

The precise attributes by which a given sick person is judged to belong in a disease group are called diagnostic criteria. There is seldom, if ever, unanimity in the medical community concerning diagnostic criteria for any disease. This poses a particular problem to those who wish to compare or to aggregate the results of clinical research studies done by separate investigators. Investigators interested in the same disease may or may not agree on the diagnostic criteria that define the group or groups of people attracting their concern. However, when they report the results of their studies, if each investigator characterizes the patients studied by describing the diagnostic criteria used, there is at least some hope of linking one study with another. Unfortunately, many clinical studies describe patients only in terms of diagnosis and are therefore not particularly useful unless readers are willing to extrapolate results based on guesses about the authors' diagnostic criteria.

There is increasing recognition of this problem and how it hinders the expansion of medical knowledge. Groups with specialized interests, like the American College of Chest Physicians and the National Council on Alcoholism, have sought to improve matters within their own fields by proposing criteria for the diagnosis of a few specific diseases such as chronic bronchitis and alcoholism. The situation, then, has begun to improve since Feinstein[14] observed:

> With the rare exceptions already cited . . . , no standardized rigorous criteria exist today for any of the classifications and inferences that convert various combinations of . . . evidence into diagnostic designations. . . .
>
> No other branch of natural science is so imprecise in defining the material exposed to experiment. Although all the diagnoses are made differently, although no uniform standards have been ratified and disseminated, it is commonly believed that rigorous criteria are invariably present. The clinician's capacity for intellectual self-deception is illustrated by the widespread acceptance of this illusion. For most of the "established" diagnoses of modern "disease," standardized criteria do not exist . . . (pp. 98 and 101)

Movement toward consistent explicit use of standardized criteria seems likely to continue in both clinical research and patient care. One day, established diagnostic criteria may be compiled into a companion volume to the ICD. The *Diagnostic and Statistical Manual* of the American Psychiatric Association successfully melds nosologic categories and diagnostic criteria for mental illnesses and it may prove a valuable model for more encompassing efforts.

## THE STUFF OF CONFUSION

So far, this chapter has discussed a general notion of disease. The following will relate this understanding to excerpts from the alcoholism literature. First, however, it may be helpful to describe the writer's frame of reference.

### A Newcomer's View

The writer's exposure to the alcoholism literature has for

the most part taken place over only the last five to six years. This is brief in comparison to that of the contributors to this literature whose publications span periods of twenty years and more.

In early 1973, the writer's first in-depth reading on alcoholism came when preparing, as a medical resident, a seminar presentation on alcohol withdrawal states. In 1974 and thereafter, while reviewing literature relevant to this study and to alcoholism treatment in general, the writer fully encountered the taxonomic controversy in alcoholism. Well before these experiences with the alcoholism literature the writer had internalized the above understanding of disease and of the evolution of disease nomenclature.

The writer's formal introduction to clinical medicine was in the spring of 1968 during a course for second-year medical students called Clinical Examination. The course was taught by Alvan R. Feinstein, the same mathematician-turned-physician whose writings [14, 18–20] and teaching continue to champion better logic and more precise description in medicine. The theme of one lecture was set by the line: *"Il n'y a pas de maladies; il n'y a que de malades."* ("There are no diseases; there are only sick people.") This statement is attributed to Trousseau in the nineteenth century and is a warning against the fallacy of reification. Clark[12] feels this insight "has been emphasized many times" (see block quotation on page 35) and perhaps it has been in epidemiologic circles. Yet misunderstandings and controversy arising from the reification of diseases remain so common that the point clearly needs wider exposure. The writer is grateful he was forearmed by Dr. Feinstein at an early stage of training.

Another educational sequence important to the outlook incorporated in this chapter was a year of graduate study in epidemiology and public health undertaken in 1969–70. This curriculum provided more detailed experience with epidemiologic concepts and methods and also increased the writer's familiarity with the role of the International Classification of Diseases in the preparation of vital statistics and health services utilization reports.*

Upon reading segments of the alcoholism literature, it seemed to the writer that many students of alcoholism could benefit from a clear discussion of the taxonomic controversy in alcoholism in the light of epidemiologic concepts.** This chapter and the following one attempt to provide such a discussion. Very little here is new, even to the alcoholism literature. Seeley,[21] for example, presents much the same notion of disease as that developed here. His understanding of disease is obscured, however, by the multiple themes and difficult language of his paper.

## "Alcoholism is a Disease"

In seemingly endless cycles, the assertion that alcoholism is a disease appears and reappears in the alcoholism literature. In one place it is a carefully supported intellectual conclusion; in another, the subject of reasoned objection. Here it is accepted with fervor befitting religious doctrine; there, rejected with frustration and occasionally contempt. These cycles generate much, if not most, of the written substance of the taxonomic controversy in alcoholism. This is the stuff of confusion.

Many of the debates, when regarded from a relatively detached epidemiologic viewpoint, seem to deal with what might

---

*Given this background knowledge of applications of the ICD, the writer experienced a surprise, at a later stage of training, relevant to medical pluralism as discussed above. During 1971–74 the writer served as an intern and resident at a major teaching hospital where copies of the ICD were readily available, generally positioned in areas where physicians dictate discharge summaries. During this three-year period, on only *one* or perhaps *two* occasions did the writer observe a fellow house officer or attending physician even open a volume of the ICD.

**Epidemiologic *methods* appear widely in the alcoholism literature as illustrated by essays by Edwards[22] and Keller.[23] However, as the discussion of evaluative research in Chapter 7 emphasizes, such methods have often been applied inadequately.

be termed non-issues — non-issues because participants on at least one side of these arguments make assumptions or statements so far removed from the realities perceived from an epidemiological frame of reference that their positions are simply untenable. Pointing out these untenable positions may help students of alcoholism disengage from debates that ultimately can have no practical consequences and thereby free them to address real issues in terms of questions that may be answered empirically.

The specific assumptions or statements regarded here as untenable relate to biologic variability, to reified notions of disease, and to the mistaken idea that there is unified thinking within the medical community. Examples will follow. One important area of contention — the causation of alcoholism — is absent, perhaps conspicuously, from the discussion in this chapter. This topic may also be clarified by viewing it from an epidemiological perspective, but most effectively only after arriving at some simple conclusions about alcoholism as/as not a disease. Therefore, to the extent possible, consideration of the causation of alcoholism is deferred until Chapter 3.

DISSENTERS.   The authors whose positions most clearly illustrate the above "non-issues" seem to be those against alcoholism as a disease. The following quotations represent such dissenters, describing what they oppose:

> Most theories about the conditions associated with the excessive use of alcohol involve an assumption that there is a unitary syndrome of alcoholism. The assumption is that the alcoholics are of one type, possessing a set of behaviors which pertain to the same thing.[24] (p. 99)

> If alcoholism really is a disease, then the direction to be taken in theorizing and experimenting in this area would be to search for the unique set of events — cause, symptoms, course, and sequelae — which, when found, would define it . . . whether the cause

has been sought from genetic, biochemical, dietary, or psychiatric sources, no disease entity has been isolated, . . . [25] (p. 659)

The concept of alcoholism as a single disease, a unitary clinical entity based on a medical model, believed to progress along a known or predictable continuum, and measurable in terms of a single common symptom may be an oversimplified representation . . . [26] (p. 15)

These authors seem to reject alcoholism as a disease because they find variability among alcoholics, and variability, for them, seems incompatible with disease. These passages treat diseases as rigid, perhaps enduring, and seemingly as things. It is difficult to ascertain whether these authors reflect reification of alcoholism as a disease in the thinking of those who accept it as a disease, or whether they themselves tend to think of diseases as independent things rather than as abstract categories. It is perhaps most likely that there are degrees of such thinking on both sides of the controversy. The epidemiologic insight on this particular aspect of the debate is simply that there is no legitimate issue to argue since the notion of disease in question here is a fallacious one.

JELLINEK AND KELLER.    E. Morton Jellinek and Mark Keller are recognized as chief exponents of alcoholism as a disease. [27] Dissenters frequently cite their works.

In *The Disease Concept of Alcoholism*, [4] Jellinek avoids commitment to any particular notion of disease.

One finds difficulties arising out of the fact that alcoholism has too many definitions and disease has practically none.

Medical dictionaries . . . give the following definition: "Disease, an illness, a sickness." And that is about all. In the "Queries and Minor Notes" of the *Journal of the American Medical Association* . . . in answer to an inquiry concerning the grounds for "considering alcoholism as a medical illness," the following definition was given: "A disease is defined as follows: In general, any deviation from a state of health; an illness or sickness; more specifically, a definite marked process having a characteristic train of symptoms. It may affect the whole body or any of its parts, and its etiology, pathology, and prognosis may be known or unknown.''

This is a private definition which adds to the dictionary definition only the marked process having a train of symptoms . . . .

As some students of the problems of alcohol propose to call ''alcoholism'' an illness rather than a disease, it is of interest to note that the two terms are given as synonyms, not as shadings or degrees of a *phenomenon* . . . .

It comes to this, that *a disease is what the medical profession recognizes as such.* (pp. 11–12, italics in original except phenomenon not italicized in original)

Jellinek's readers, and Jellinek himself, have paid considerable attention to a train of symptoms of alcoholics. When diagramming the progressive experiences of alcohol addicts, however, Jellinek acknowledged variability among his more than two thousand subjects: ''Not all symptoms shown in the diagram occur necessarily in all alcohol addicts, nor do they occur in every addict in the same sequence''[28] (p. 676). It seems to be the critics of alcoholism as a disease who have introduced the term ''unitary'' and portrayed alcoholism-as-a-disease as not accommodating the variability that is readily observed among people with alcohol problems.

*Jellinek and Philosophy.*    The theory of knowledge of Immanuel Kant (1724–1804) provides the philosophical foundation of science from the nineteenth century to the present.[29–32]* Jellinek links his own thinking to that of Kant when discussing ''definitions'' prior to stating the definition of alcoholism he uses in *The Disease Concept of Alcoholism*:

The most essential desiderata of definition are given by Kant (*Critique of Pure Reason*): ''A formal definition is one which not

*The statement of Trousseau discussed earlier is consistent with, and may well have been influenced by, Kant's view.

only clarifies a concept but at the same time establishes its objective reality." He also states that neither empirical nor a priori concepts can be truly defined, but can only be expounded. In a true sense only an arbitrary concept can be defined. Furthermore a concept ex hypothesi is not definable but explainable. It may be said here that alcoholism practically belongs in the latter category.[4] (pp. 34–35)

The writer has been unable to securely explicate this passage. If Jellinek's concept of alcoholism is indeed consistent with Kantian theory, there at least would be no question of reification:

Every science operates with concepts. But concepts are products of the human mind, of thought, which do not exist in reality.[31] (pp. 86–87)

But the writer harbors a suspicion that Jellinek's use of Kant* may be fully out of the context of Kant's theory of knowledge and that Jellinek may conceive alcoholism-as-a-disease to have "objective reality."** It can be fairly said, however,

---

*Uncharacteristically, Jellinek does not cite a specific source for the material from Kant. The statement in quotes in the paragraph by Jellinek presented above seems derived from a footnote that appeared only in the first of Kant's two editions of his *Critique of Pure Reason* (see p. 197 in the translation by Muller,[33] p. 261 in that by Smith[34]). The remainder of the comments seem related to a short section on definitions later in the treatise (see pp. 584–588 in the translation by Muller,[33] pp. 586–589 in that by Smith,[34] and pp. 215–217 in that by Meiklejohn[35]).

**Jellinek's use of "phenomenon" in the passage quoted on pp. 46–47 contributes to this suspicion because the usage may not be philosophically appropriate. When discussed in the singular as they are in that passage, it might be said that one encounters or experiences *an* illness or *a* disease (i.e., a sick person) in the same manner that one experiences a rock, a plant, or an animal. One might come to know each of these as a phenomenon. If Jellinek's meaning was this narrow, there would be no philosophical difficulty. However, the relationship of "an illness" and "a disease" to "'alcoholism'" in Jellinek's sentence, wherein alcoholism is apparently used as a category rather than a singular condition, suggests a broader meaning—a meaning that would make the term phenomenon inappropriate.[32]

that any indications of such thinking present in his writing are more subtle than those found in writings that reject alcoholism as a disease.

*Keller: History and Conviction.*   Author and editor, Mark Keller is a prominent figure among contributors to the alcoholism literature. His historical perspective draws upon his own experiences in alcohol studies that extend from the 1930s to the present and from masses of literature reviewed in his early (1939) collaboration with Jellinek and in his work at the Center of Alcohol Studies.[36] Keller[36] has collected instances of people with alcohol problems being thought of as sick or diseased that extend from ancient to modern times.

His belief that alcoholism is a disease is repeatedly expressed—and justified and defended—in Keller's writings. Describing the preparation of a volume of lectures on alcohol, science, and society published in 1945, Keller states:

> We knew that there were many forms and degrees of misbehaviors associated with alcohol, and we spoke of inebriety, later problem drinking. Within this rubric we included something we called alcoholism, and we were sure there was such a phenomenon, and we were sure it was a disease.[36] (p. 23)

Keller tolerates views conflicting with his own. As editor of the *Quarterly Journal of Studies on Alcohol* (which became the *Journal of Studies on Alcohol* in 1975) he has published many of them.[37] He respects the motives of those who refute alcoholism as a disease— "I am as sure that they mean well as that they are wrong"[38] (p. 1712)—and shows occasional sympathy when reviewing the positions of numerous dissenting authors.[38] His own conviction, however, remains unshaken: "So I shall not settle for less than—alcoholism is a disease"[38] (p. 1714).

Diseases, and equally alcoholism as a disease, seem very real to Keller. "Popular slogans may reflect a medical truth: there is such a disease as alcoholism"[39] (p. 126). "I think of alcoholism as a biological phenomenon . . . ''[38] (p. 1713). In spite of repeated use of the words "concept" and "conception," in Keller's writings diseases appear as something discovered and observed in nature. They are not depicted as categories conceived in the human mind.

REIFICATION INCAPACITATES SCIENCE.   The disease reification recognized here on both sides of the alcoholism as/as not a disease controversy is not a trivial matter. Scientific knowledge with its concepts, theories, and laws organizes or integrates experience and, when applied, enables us to cope more adequately with nature. This knowledge merely approximates nature, however, and it is in part revision of scientific ideas over time that permits scientific progress. To regard a scientific concept as real and essentially permanent, yet continuing to interact as though within the domain of science, is to invite untoward consequences.* The inhibited scholarly communication and impeded advance of understanding in alcohol studies testify to this, though these problems do not derive solely from reification of alcoholism as a disease.

THE MYTH OF THE MEDICAL MODEL.   Analogous to notions of disease, understandings of "medical model" are pluralistic. These understandings often differ dramatically from one another, yet authors frequently refer to the medical model as if their own sense were widely accepted.

Whybrow[40] offers a definition of medical model that is

*Remarks from a speech delivered by Louis Pasteur to the French Academy of Medicine on 18 July 1876 are relevant:

Preconceived ideas are like searchlights which illume the path of the experimentor and serve him as a guide to interrogate nature. They become a danger only if he transforms them into fixed ideas—this is why I should like to see these profound words inscribed on the threshold of all the temples of science: "The greatest derangement of the mind is to believe in something because one wishes it to be so." (Translation by René J. Dubos.)

general enough to interrelate disparate understandings from the literature. He begins by noting a close relationship between "medical model" and what physicians do. This leads to *caring for the diseased individual* as a central conceptual theme. Within this framework, Whybrow develops his own emphasis (which is much the same as that of Straus[41] in comments more specifically addressing alcohol problems) by concentrating on the social implications of "caring." To Whybrow, application of a medical model fixes the "responsibility for the care of persons with compromised adaptive function" with "a defined professional group (principally, but not solely the medical profession)"[40] (pp. 334–335). Medical models of other authors emphasize "the diseased individual" or simply disease, rather than those who care for the diseased.

Dissenters from the view that alcoholism is a disease frequently describe a restricted notion of "medical model" and then attack its inadequacies with respect to alcoholism. Glatt[42] objects to their approach:

> The critics of the "medical model" seem to see . . . a rather traditional medical model, rather than the model of the social psychiatrist, or the physician in community medicine; and the conventionally trained medical practitioner rather than the modern, broadening concepts of medicine with doctors actively interested in psychosocial as well as in physical aspects. Many of the arguments regarding the alleged "medical model" strike one as examples of a "man-of-straw" set up in order to give the critic a chance to knock it down. Surely there can be few doctors—if any—who would ever have dreamt of claiming that a purely medical (defined by such critics in purely physical and organic terms) model·was sufficient to explain alcoholism. (p. 126)

The more encompassing medical model implied here is succinctly stated by van Dijk:[43]

> The medical model is a multidimensional construct . . . it takes into account the psychological and social, as well as the physical aspects of the afflicted person. (p. 138)

PHYSICIAN CONTRIBUTORS: SEIXAS AND GITLOW.   This chapter addresses misconceptions that are prevalent in the alcoholism as/as not a disease controversy. Frank A. Seixas and Stanley E. Gitlow, both taking the side of alcoholism as a disease, have sought to clarify some of the same points. These two authors both have backgrounds in internal medicine and between them have over 40 years' professional experience with alcohol problems.

The title of Jacobson's book, *The Alcoholisms*,[26] embodies that author's difficulty reconciling variability among alcoholics with a single disease category. Responding to Jacobson's work, Seixas[44] states:

> We need not postulate a new disease every time we take a different strategy in alcoholic rehabilitation. There is no disease in which all rehabilitative moves are the same for every patient. . . . Even more pertinent, just because there are different manifestations more prominent in different patients with alcoholism (i.e., withdrawal in one, car accidents in another, pancreatitis in a third), there is no more reason to abandon a single disease concept for alcoholism than there is in tuberculosis which may exhibit itself with pulmonary, central nervous system or kidney pathology, with a totally different series of symptoms in each. (p. 412)

Seixas's point here, that variability is rather usual within accepted disease categories, is similar to that developed in a more fundamental way earlier in this chapter. While there has long been a need in the taxonomic controversy for explicit emphasis of this point, the emphasis must be tempered by continued recognition that there are *similarities* as well as differences among members of a disease category.

Gitlow[45] acknowledges "some diversity . . . on the basis of individual variability" (p. 2) but pays particular attention to the factors that people with serious alcohol problems tend to have in common.

> The history, symptoms, and signs associated with alcoholism are largely those related to chronic or recurrent physical dependence

upon any sedative drug: character disorganization, diminished ability to achieve potential, decreased attention span, diminished ability to concentrate, tremulousness, insomnia, recurrent somatic symptoms (especially headache, bowel dysfunction, muscle spasm, fatigue, palpitations, and exaggerated subjective response to minor local pathology), diminished seizure threshold, and eventually elevated tolerance, amnestic episodes, hallucinations, and delirium. The most critical aspect of the patient's history is that revealing recurrent use of the sedative agent despite evidence that the drug adversely affects some facet of his life (health, work, interpersonal relations, marriage, etc.). The progressive nature of this deterioration, usually obscured with an elaborate and powerful denial system, is an almost universal concomitant. Recurrent episodes of increased psychomotor activity, necessitating continued use of some sedative agent in a vain attempt to control the agitation resulting from previous sedation . . . are regularly noted in and almost limited to the alcoholic population. (p. 3)

Gitlow also states why he finds it practical to consider alcoholism a disease:

The ultimate reason for the designation of any individual as sick or diseased is for the singular purpose of separating him from the larger (normal) group in order to channel special resources to him. Whether the patient has a broken bone or is addicted, the "disease" label assists him in obtaining that special care which society reserves for its ill. This is the one term accepted by the public as adequate reason to offer treatment to the alcoholic.[45] (p. 7)

This passage raises the issue of practicality in the classification of ill persons. This issue will be examined more closely after clarifying some conclusions about alcoholism-as-a-disease that are justified at this point.

## SOME SIMPLE ANSWERS

Q:   Is alcoholism a disease?
A:   That's a tricky question and to answer it we'd have to carefully explore how you understand "disease" and

''alcoholism.'' To avoid confusion, all I will say now is that in one sense there are no diseases, there are only sick people. Try to rephrase your question.*

Q:  Okay. Can people with alcohol problems be thought of as sick, as having a disease?

A:  Sure. Apparently this has been done for centuries and many people continue to do so today. The basic requirements for taking such a position are to be consistent with the state of knowledge in the health sciences and to be able to put the conceptual formulation to practical use.

Q:  Hold on. That ''state of knowledge'' requirement confuses me a bit. I know lots of people with alcohol problems have been shown to have various types of organ damage, in the digestive system and nervous system for example. But I think there are many other people with alcohol problems in whom there is no knowledge of organ damage. Does this mean some may be considered diseased and some may not?

A:  No. Useful definitions of disease specify that an organism have a disturbance in structure *or* function. In fact, since the fundamental notion of disease seems to be some sort of adaptational setback, some measure the presence of disease *only* in terms of how an organism functions in relation to its environment.

Q:  Do you mean disturbances of *organ* function?

A:  Yes, but not only that. Disturbances of function could also be assessed in terms of molecules, in terms of an entire organism, or in terms of any level of organization in between.

---

*Throughout, this discussion is scientific. The writer should not be construed as questioning the assertion that ''alcoholism is a disease'' as it is used within the self-help group of Alcoholics Anonymous. As Pattison[8] points out, ''The self-help group should not be *professionalized* nor *scientificized* . . .'' (p. 620, italics in original)

Q:   That sounds pretty broad. Don't lots of trivial prob-
     lems qualify as diseases?

A:   Well, they might if every conceivable difficulty with
     the environment were thought of as a disease. How-
     ever, remember that there is generally a clear relation-
     ship to the health sciences and that practicality is
     generally involved in conceiving disease categories.

Q:   Can you explain that a bit?

A:   All right. If an adaptational setback is minor, and the
     organism or let's now say person involved does not
     need outside help to manage the situation, there would
     not be much of a tendency to think in terms of disease.
     A lightly stubbed toe might be a good example. How-
     ever, if a person's toe struck something quite force-
     fully and the resulting pain and swelling were severe,
     then the injured person might seek medical attention.
     An X-ray might reveal a fracture and medical advice
     and/or treatment might be useful to relieve discomfort
     and promote healing. In this case, health care technol-
     ogy and personnel make a practical contribution and it
     is reasonable to think in terms of disease.

Q:   I think I follow you. But if I extend your toe example
     to alcohol problems I have to conclude that there are
     minor and major difficulties in that area also. Are
     there any guidelines for deciding which alcohol prob-
     lems are serious enough to be thought of in terms of
     disease?

A:   You're right, you do have the idea. Yes, various guide-
     lines have been formulated. Keller, for example, views
     alcoholism as a chronic disease. He suggests this in-
     clude any person who repeatedly drinks alcoholic
     beverages in a manner — characterized perhaps in
     terms of quantity, frequency, associated behavior,
     and circumstances — that appears suspiciously dif-
     ferent from how most people drink *and* whose drink-
     ing causes injury to the person's health or to his or her

social or economic functioning. More precise guidelines have been issued by a committee of the National Council on Alcoholism (NCA) in the form of criteria for the diagnosis of alcoholism.*

If one accepts the widely held belief that there are treatment approaches grounded in the health sciences that are capable of helping at least a portion of those individuals with alcohol problems, then this dialogue obviously implies that *a disease category called alcoholism may be legitimately contructed*. This conclusion, now that "non-issues" have been laid aside, prepares us to examine what is perhaps the most important real issue in the alcoholism as/as not a disease controversy. Is there a conceptual approach to people with alcohol problems that is preferable to the disease approach because it is *more useful*? As Seeley has concluded, "we may call alcoholism a disease if we so desire, the issue is whether we *should*"[5] (p. 10, italics in original).

## PROBLEM DRINKING VS. ALCOHOLISM

This subheading echoes the title of the first chapter of Cahalan's book, *Problem Drinkers*.[5] Cahalan acknowledges limited benefits derived from the "current rather popular conception of alcoholism as a 'disease' " and then presents a justification for "a new or supplementary approach to drinking problems" (p. 2). He favors use of the concepts "problem drinking" and "drinking problems"—or, more precisely, "problems associated with the use of alcohol" and "problem-related drinking" (p. 12)—over alcoholism.

Some of Cahalan's objections to alcoholism as a disease would be met if some of the misconceptions identified above were eliminated and if an epidemiologic view of disease as

*Keller's paper[39] has already been cited. The NCA criteria are described and a reference is provided in Chapter 6.

developed here were to become widely accepted. There would then no longer be a confusing emphasis on "the concept of alcoholism as a physical disease entity"[5] (p. 5). Acceptance of the idea of clinical subgroups within a disease category of alcoholism and the emergence of clinical and population-based studies of operationally defined subgroups would break down the stereotype "of alcoholism as constituting an either-or, all-or-nothing, disease entity"[5] (p. 3). Chronic diseases are frequently analyzed in terms of risk factors that influence, or predict, disease occurrences. The epidemiologic spectrum of a disease is a construct relating identified and unidentified instances of disease.[10, 19] Spontaneous and induced remissions of chronic disease are important clinical and research topics. Wider use of such epidemiologic approaches by students of alcohol problems could help eliminate "the adverse effects of . . . the 'once an alcoholic, always an alcoholic' dictum . . ."[5] (p. 6).

## The Sick Role and Responsibility

Cahalan reviews comments by several authors who hesitate to accept alcoholism as a disease because this formulation has the social consequence of relieving the affected person of responsibility. Their assumption is that "when one is labeled sick . . . one is typically seen in a state of *diminished responsibility*"[8] (p. 593, italics in original).

> To summarize, it would appear that the concept of alcoholism as a disease may have had the undesirable consequences of driving a wedge between the alcoholic and society, of providing the problem drinker with an alibi for failure to change his behavior, and of creating an atmosphere in which alcoholism becomes a stubborn disease to cure because it is perceived as possessing only the derelict or semiderelict or the incompetent who is incapable of control over his own behavior.[5] (p. 10)

Perhaps the main reason Cahalan believes "the concept of problem drinking — always to be accompanied by a statement of what kind of problem — is much to be preferred to that of alcoholism"[5] (p. 11) is that this shift of usage "can help pin the responsibility on both the problem drinker and society to bring about some solution to problems related to excessive drinking at an early stage, rather than after the sufferer hits bottom"[5] (p. 12).

This desirable distribution of responsibility can be achieved in another way, however, that would not require rejecting alcoholism as a disease. Pattison[8] has proposed a more useful view of deviant behavior than the traditional views of the deviant person as sinful (the community has no responsibility) or sick (the individual has diminished responsibility):

1. Human behavior is both chosen and determined.
2. Blame and punishment are not remedial.
3. Therefore, we will not seek to impute blame.
4. However, each person and each community must share responsibility.
5. The community must be responsible and responsive to deviant problems.
6. The socially deviant person must be responsible and responsive to his community. (p. 594)

Wide acceptance of this scheme as a model of illness would enhance the continued viability of alcoholism as a disease. Incidentally, as a general approach to health-related issues, Pattison's model has much to offer a society trying to come to grips with self-imposed risks and environmental improvement.[46]

### Toward Resolution

For the present, it seems advisable to explore the practical value of *both* the concept of problem drinking and the concept of alcoholism as a disease—with the stipulation that any understanding of disease be consistent with epidemiologic thinking as presented here. If it proves necessary to specify one approach as preferable to the other—and the writer suspects such a choice may *not* prove necessary—whichever approach has *demonstrated* the greater usefulness should be selected. The way to resolve this real issue in the taxonomic controversy is, then, to first clarify one's concepts and then proceed to carefully design and execute evaluative research that assesses benefits in relation to conceptual approach.

## INTEREST GROUPS

Issues in the taxonomic controversy have sometimes been clouded by subtle influences on the debaters themselves. Participants in the controversy may be described in terms of their own characteristics and affiliations in a fashion that implies what they stand to gain or lose depending upon how issues are resolved. Keller[38] assumes all participants share a basic honesty and sincere desire to help others. However, he also illustrates how their positions in the controversy may be influenced by self-interest:

> There are physicians who still hold that a disease must exhibit a manifest abnormality of anatomic structure.... And there are social scientists who gladly acquiesce in this backward conception because it allows them to insist that, therefore, behavioral disorders should not be classifed as diseases and, therefore, do not belong to medicine.[38] (p. 1703)

> Most physicians discover early that the fewer alcoholics they see the less cephalalgia they experience. If some of those doctors become convinced that alcoholism is not a disease, it is hardly surprising.[38] (p. 1712)

Bruun[47] regards the models of alcoholism presented by Siegler, Osmond, and Newell[7] as "built up around interest groups within society"[47] (p. 547). For example, the professionals who would develop or be attracted to "the family-interaction model"[7] (pp. 579–580) wherein "family therapy is the only treatment" would likely be those experienced in family therapy. A basic confidence in this treatment approach could lead them to advocate this model for humanistic reasons. However, if they happen to be in the business of providing family therapy, they have an obvious practical interest in acceptance of a model which reminds society it "has the duty to provide facilities for family therapy for alcoholics and their families."

Similar reasoning may be applied to the movement during the 1940s to establish broad recognition of alcoholism in terms of a public health or medical model.* "This movement . . . involved voluntary citizens' committees on alcoholism, public agencies, recovered alcoholics, and some educational and research organizations"[41] (p. 277). Their effort is regarded by Straus[41] as one calculated to encourage alcoholics to seek treatment and "to create a more sympathetic public image of alcoholism and develop support for research and treatment resources" (p. 277). At least some movement participants presumably had personal interests also at stake. With success, recovered alcoholics in the movement could gain greater respect from society and greater assurance that treatment would be available should they relapse. Members of educational and research organizations could be viewed as protecting their livelihoods as well as generating help for people with alcohol problems.

In more recent times, Cahalan[48] notes that "the U.S. liquor industry and many of the leaders in the alcoholism treatment movement" (p. 235) constitute a powerful coalition influencing resource allocation in the alcoholism field.

> The liquor industry naturally would like to stave off all attempts to constrain the sale of alcoholic beverages, so they try to focus public attention on the individual-person 'disease' aspects of alcoholism . . . they make common cause with the leaders of the NCA and related associations, who would like to see practically all of the available public funds spent on treatment of the unfortunate crop of present alcoholics . . .[48] (p. 236)

Because of the strength of these economic and political interests, Cahalan is not surprised "that treatment of alcoholics

---

* See Keller[38] for a more detailed historical discussion.

consumes about 80 per cent of the NIAAA budget'' versus the ''probably . . . no more than 1 or 2 per cent'' (p. 236) allotted for prevention. A similar relationship seems to hold for the 10% or so of the NIAAA budget spent on research. The ''lion's share'' goes to ''eminently scientific, long-term, biomedical research on the causes of alcoholism'' rather than to ''research on the political, economic, and other social implications of the association between the consumption of alcohol and the problems related to that consumption'' (p. 237).

These comments on interest groups should include an acknowledgement that humans are apparently incapable of ever assuming fully disinterested points of view. As in any other realm of human activity, interest groups routinely influence science.[16] However, if those in the alcoholism field are to resolve their taxonomic controversy, and if society is to reduce alcohol-related suffering, it appears there will have to be at least greater awareness of competing interests and perhaps even practical recognition of some interest groups in the form of arbitration.

## Chapter 3

# CAUSES OF ALCOHOLISM: AN
# ECOLOGICAL ANALYSIS

In the conceptual controversy surrounding alcoholism, questions of causality intertwine with questions of terminology. Confusion concerning the causes of alcoholism seems in part a result of divergent thinking about disease causation in general. Epidemiologists are among those who view disease causation as a complex multifactorial process influenced by both constitutional and environmental factors.[1] Some scientists, however, focus almost exclusively on cellular and subcellular disease mechanisms[2] and would apparently like to identify a single, specific cause for every disease. For reasons developed below, the writer believes the second of these two outlooks to be an oversimplification that diverts attention from many factors that might be altered with beneficial results. The writer also recognizes, however, that research in pursuit of a "specific cause" might produce knowledge with beneficial applications. A practice that could help unravel present controversy would be for those with narrow views of causation to express them using the general framework of a multifactorial view.

In the health sciences, etiological discussions are generally concerned with the causation of *disease*. But the models to be presented here as guides for etiological thinking may readily be extended to apply to conditions labeled *health problems*. The writer hopes that the following material will be useful even to readers who prefer not to think of alcoholism as a disease. The terms "alcoholism" and "disease" will be used, but specified types of "problem drinking" and "health problem" could reasonably be substituted.

## ORGANIZING KNOWLEDGE

Information relevant to the etiology of alcoholism is usually presented in the context of theories or approaches seen in competition with one another. These competing causal explanations tend to follow lines either of scientific disciplines (psychological explanations vs. sociological explanations, for example) or of schools within a discipline (learning theory explanation vs. psychoanalytic explanation, for example). Reviewers[3-7] have succeeded in imposing some order on this information. Roebuck and Kessler[5] group studies under constitutional, psychological, and sociological approaches. Such groupings do promote understanding of the literature, but a dynamic integration of this knowledge is needed to effectively promote understanding of alcoholism. Keller[8] has observed that alcohol studies have unfortunately proved to be more *multi*disciplinary than *inter*disciplinary.

Epidemiology has contributed to medical and public health advances by clarifying the conceptualization of variables and causal models.[9] The integration needed to more effectively use existing etiological studies of alcoholism and to generate productive new research seems achievable through application of epidemiological thinking.

### Causal Concepts: Environment, Host, and Agent

In the second chapter of *Causal Thinking in the Health Sciences*,[9] Susser summarizes the evolution of the concepts that have become central to an epidemiological understanding of the causation of disease. Susser identifies Hippocratic writings as the first available works on epidemiology. The Hippocratic writer explained disease occurrences through sequences or chains of causally related events. These works

> distinguished the *environment*, as represented by air, water, and place, from the *host*, as represented by the individual constitution. Thus, they separated environment and host as factors that bring about the specific manifestations of disease.[9] (p. 15, italics in original)

Susser traces a line of research between the seventeenth and late nineteenth centuries in which both the concept of environment and a numerical approach in epidemiological thinking became established.

The concept of *agents* of disease also has a long history.

> The concept of contagion probably existed in antiquity, but it certainly existed by the fourteenth century when it found application in the laws of ports that quarantined disease-ridden ships. . . . In the latter half of the nineteenth century the concepts of the germ theory culminated in the work of Pasteur and the next great breakthrough for medicine and public health. Pasteur's work gave new force to two sets of ideas centered on the disease process and its immediate antecedents. These were first the idea that specific microorganisms had specific effects and second the idea of host immunity. . . .
>
> The discovery of microorganisms and their effects thus gave impetus to the search for specific agents that caused specific conditions. This search still continues.[9] (pp. 22–24)

## Causal Models

All three causal concepts of environment, host, and agent are used in the study of infectious diseases and, increasingly, in toxicology and allergy. In these fields microorganisms and chemical or biochemical substances neatly fit the role of agents of disease. Several chronic diseases, particularly degenerative conditions, do not present obvious candidates for the role of agent. To serve simplicity and familiarity, this brief treatment of causal models that interrelate environment, host, and agent will follow Susser's example and focus on infectious disease.

The simplest epidemiologic model is a causal sequence, or cycle, of events. Infectious agent invades host; infected or diseased host releases agent to environment; environment delivers agent to new host. This approach clarified the etiology of some conditions and its success spurred search for specific agents. However,

> from the standpoint of the development of causal models, this great spurt in medical research [with the advent of microbiology] diminished awareness of the rarity of one-to-one relationships and of the complex relationships between causes and effects that exist in the real world. The concept of specific agents as causes of disease enlarged knowledge, but the concept was adequate only up to a point. Like the miasma theory, the germ theory failed to explain many medical observations and had to be rethought before further advance became possible.[9] (p. 24)

One obvious failing of this first epidemiological model—which can be depicted as a *unidirectional* causal sequence following a triangular course from agent to host to environment and back to agent (see first diagram on page 66)—is that it could not accommodate the frequent observation that many potential hosts exposed to a given agent do not become infected or diseased and therefore do not contribute to perpetuation of the cycle. It was necessary to conceive of variation in host susceptibility as an important determinant of etiology. Expanding knowledge of factors such as immunity, nutrition, and genetics, with its ability to explain individual variation, contributed to understanding host capacity to resist disease or ''to shape the manifestations of disorder''[9] (p. 25). Factors in the environment including ''social conditions such as poverty and crowding as well as nonhuman aspects of the environment such as season, climate, and altitude''[1] (p. 3), and even factors related to infectious agents themselves such as the number of organisms encountering a potential host, were also found to moderate occurrences of disease.

Engel[10, 11] summarizes this situation by pointing out that in infectious disease the presence of particular infectious agents are *necessary* conditions for the development of certain diseases but that, of themselves, these agents are not *sufficient* to cause disease. Other factors contribute. Engel relates preoccupation with *the* ''cause'' of disease to the psychological defense mechanism ''of projecting to the outside what is felt or experienced as uncomfortable, painful, or dangerous''[10] (p. 460). Such thinking ''is characteristic of one phase of the psychological development of every child''[10] (p. 460) and was expressed in the demonologic concepts of prescientific medicine. However, '' 'There are few, if any, simple or single causes in biology; there are instead complex situations and environments in which the probability of certain events is increased' ''[10] (p. 474).

Advances in knowledge and more precise thinking therefore changed the simple sequential epidemiological model

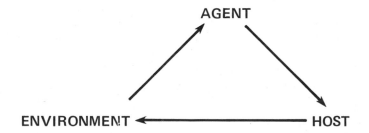

into a more dynamic epidemiological model depicting each

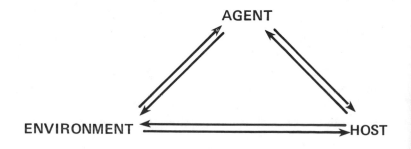

member of the triad in reciprocal interaction with the other two members. Susser has now presented a complex ecological model* as "a still better representation of reality: agent and host are engaged in continuing interactions with an enveloping environment"[9] (p. 30).

# ECOLOGICAL MODEL

The ecological model portrays multiple causal influences and any instance of disease is seen as the result of reciprocal interactions of several factors. The factors themselves — agent, host, and environment or, rather, specific variables associated with each — are perhaps best not viewed as "causes" but as concepts incorporated in *descriptions* of ecological relationships. These descriptions have *predictive* and *representational* value.

Causal relationships are sometimes clarified when several

* Susser explains the name of this model: "The main distinction between epidemiology and ecology is that while epidemiology is centered on the state of health of man, ecology embraces the interrelations of all living things. Epidemiology could be described as human ecology, or that large part of human ecology relating to states of health."[9] (p. 30)

predisposing factors are arranged in the form of a web, network, or configuration. The interrelationships of multiple factors then become more apparent. Webs of causation for particular diseases or for morbid events such as myocardial infarction have been tentatively drawn.[1] However intricate, they are apologetically presented as oversimplifications. The webs include items such as "heredity factors," "social pressures," "industrial society," and "personality and emotional stress," which allow for much variation in the relative importance of each item from one case to the next.* (See Figure 3.1 on p. 77.)

## Unified Thinking

Authors, especially those concerned with the role of psychological factors in the development and progression of illness, are increasingly adopting "a unified concept of health and disease."[10-17] This approach has been elaborated by Dubos,[12] Engel,[10] and Wolff,[13] but debts to general system theory[18] and to Balint[19] have also been acknowledged.[14, 16] This unified thinking incorporates an ecological understanding of etiology as presented above. Further, health and disease are viewed as ranges on an adaptational spectrum with no sharp line separating one from the other.[10] The viewpoint is termed *holistic* because body and personality are regarded "as two integral aspects of a larger whole: *The person*"[16] (p. 4).

> Mind, body, and environment are viewed as elements of a dynamically interacting system. Human health and disease are a continuum of psychobiological states determined to a varying extent by biophysical, psychological, and social variables. These states involve all levels of human organization, from the molecular to the symbolic. This view is equally valid for what, in our dualistic language, we call psychiatric and physical, or mental and organic disorders.[16] (p. 4)

*For the most part efforts dependent upon present knowledge would be crude approximations and there would be little or no practical value to the exercise, but a unique causal web could conceivably be constructed for every person within a disease category.

## Etiological Models in the Alcoholism Literature

The eight models of alcoholism described by Siegler, Osmond, and Newell[20] are not specifically etiological models. These authors collected "theories and points of view . . . regardless of their credibility, source or state of development" and arranged them "along the same set of dimensions"[20] (p. 572). As noted in Chapter 2, this resulted in summaries of the views of alcoholism held by various interest groups. However, etiology is one dimension included in each of these summaries, so Siegler, Osmond, and Newell's paper does review etiological statements or assumptions if not formal etiological models. For example, "The Alcoholics Anonymous Model" posits:

> 2. *Etiology:* Alcoholics are emotionally impaired people who drink to compensate for their inadequacies, and then, because of their body chemistry, become addicted to alcohol, creating a circular process of further inadequacy and further drinking.[20] (p. 577)

"The 'New' Medical Model" states:

> 2. *Etiology:* It appears that alcoholics may have a defect in metabolism, possibly of one of the major amino acids. There are probably also psychological and sociocultural contributing factors.[20] (p. 581)

While Siegler, Osmond, and Newell find "the new medical model" the most promising of the explanations of alcoholism in their review, they do not find it in a form "which can resolve the conflict and enlist the support of most people"[20] (p. 589). The distribution of, and response to, responsibility (see Chapter 2) is one important issue left unresolved. For example, "in the dimension of personnel, the new medical model states that physicians are responsible for the care of alcoholics"[20] (p. 583). Yet "they have been remarkably sluggish about claiming the 5 million or so alcoholic patients in dire need of their services"[20] (p. 588).

EPIDEMIOLOGICAL MODELS.   The use is hardly universal, but the host/agent/environment triad does appear several times in the alcoholism literature. Mendelson[21] describes and diagrams a disease model that assumes

> that the expression of any disease or derangement of function is dependent upon the *interaction* between a host, the agent of the disease, and the environment in which the disease occurs. It is now well known that disease processes can rarely be explained on the basis of any specific factor within each of these three categories, but that the processes of interaction are crucial. (p. 514, italics in original)

Mendelson points out that alcoholism is unlike most other major behavior disorders in that it has, in alcohol, a clearly definable agent of disease.

Goldberg[22] begins a paper on the combined central nervous system effects of alcohol and other drugs with a brief presentation of an epidemiological model. Throughout the paper Goldberg's emphasis is on interaction and the model he presents is the reciprocating triad of agent, host, and environment diagrammed earlier. Elucidation of causal relationships is one reason he gives for assuming this point of view. The etiological factors Goldberg places under agent, host, and environment (Table 3.1) are general and the model is offered as a representation of the emergence of drug abuse and drug dependence rather than specifically of alcoholism.

The importance of interrelationships and interaction in the epidemiological approach is especially evident when the entries in Table 3.1 under agent and host are compared. Some properties of the agent such as physiological or toxic effects cannot be measured in the absence of some living host. Assessing the influence of host metabolism with regard to a particular agent such as alcohol generally means that the agent must be administered. Interrelationships are so important that placement of a factor under one heading or another is somewhat arbitrary. Goldberg lists psychotoxicity under *both* agent and host.

**Table 3.1  Factors of Importance for the Emergence of Drug Abuse and Drug Dependence***

| Agent | Host | Environment |
|---|---|---|
| 1. Chemical structure | 1. Genetic and acquired properties | 1. Infancy |
| 2. Metabolic fate | 2. Metabolism | 2. Home/family relations |
| 3. Physiologic effects | 3. Physiology | 3. Social structure |
| 4. Therapeutic effects | 4. Psychic make-up | 4. Subcultures |
| 5. Toxic effects | 5. Personality structure—neuroticism, deviant personality | 5. Availability of drug—legally, illegally |
| 6. Tolerance phenomena | 6. Age, occupation | 6. Use/abuse |
| 7. Emergence of dependence | 7. Tolerance phenomena | 7. Spread of habit—"contamination" |
| 8. Abuse liability | 8. Dependence liability | 8. Legislation |
| 9. Risk with prolonged use—therapeutic and/or nonmedical | 9. Psychotoxicity | 9. Other social phenomena—alcohol, tobacco, crime |
| 10. Dose | | 10. Risk to public health |
| 11. Mode of Administration | | |
| 12. Type of drug used | | |
| 13. Intervals between doses | | |
| 14. Frequency and duration of administration | | |
| 15. Increase in dose | | |
| 16. Psychotoxicity | | |
| 17. Interactions with other functions and other drugs | | |

* Adapted from Goldberg.[22]

Ewing[23] employs a triangular agent/host/environment construct to illustrate the intervention site and rationale of various treatment modalities. Ewing's emphasis is on the role of the physician in caring for the chronic alcoholic and, apparently to avoid confusing his message, he presents alcoholism simply:

> Alcoholism is a chronic relapsing condition of unknown etiology. This is not a definition but represents a useful concept since it leaves possible causes undiscussed and focuses on the usual course of the illness. (p. 2, first sentence in boldface in original)

In that context, Ewing's epidemiological model is only implicitly etiological.

AN INTEGRATIVE MODEL.    Sytinsky[24] has proposed a diagrammatic working hypothesis related to the etiology of alcoholism. Sociological factors, psychological factors, familial traditions, and a genetic factor (these items are not further developed in the diagram but examples of some specific factors are given in the text of the article) are shown to contribute to alcohol consumption. Alcohol consumption in turn contributes, via a branching and recombining or reinforcing network, to a pattern of specified physiological and biochemical changes in the central nervous system. Gradually these changes lead to physical dependence and a pathological motivation that generates behavior directed to satisfaction of the organism's need for alcohol. Sytinsky relates intermediary central nervous system changes to molecular, cellular, and organ system abnormalities that have been observed in alcohol studies. Ultimately,

> the pathodynamic structure of alcoholism affects appetite and food intake. The decrease in food intake leads to vitamin deficiency and malnutrition of brain cells. Simultaneously, the hormonal controls of various organs are disrupted and the neurological disorders which lead gradually to the degradation of the personality appear.[24] (p. 1144)

Sytinsky concludes by pointing out three sites in the diagram where (presumably hypothetical) drug treatments might prove of benefit to established alcoholics.

An examination of the neurochemical details of Sytinsky's model is outside the scope of this discussion. General comments on his model may be useful, however.

The distinction between *etiology* and *pathogenesis* is sometimes rather artificial, but etiology generally refers to the causation of disease and pathogenesis to the development of disease. That is, pathogenesis represents the evolution of a morbid condition after it is initiated by an etiologic process. Sytinsky's ''schema of the etiology of alcoholism'' might be more accurately identified as a representation of etiology *and* pathogenesis. Material in the model corresponds to what Kissin[25] collects under the heading ''pharmacodynamics of alcoholism'' but then subdivides into discussions related primarily to etiology *or* pathogenesis.

Etiological models are often used to help identify actions that might reduce the occurrence of disease.[1] To isolate opportunities of this sort, Sytinsky's diagram would have to be expanded in the portion that is now essentially its entry level — the consumption of alcohol. It is important to note, however, that the diagram *can* accommodate such expansion. Sytinsky's interest is obviously neurochemistry but he presents his thinking in a format that may be connected with contributions from other disciplines. Fazey[26] observes that Sytinsky's paper in this regard is a rare exception among etiological studies, which tend to cling to discipline-based conceptual frameworks.

AN INTERDISCIPLINARY VIEW.   After recounting his own experiences that exemplify the same disciplinary isolation criticized by Fazey,[26] Keller[8] synthesizes lessons from several disciplines into a descriptive understanding of alcoholism.

> To sum up: This complex hypothesis of the etiology of alcoholism incorporates a genetic or constitutional factor which imposes exceptional susceptibility or immunity; errors of infant

relationship or childhood rearing and resultant psychosexual maldevelopment with a possibly defective, especially hyper-dependent or dependency-conflicted, personality trait; further misfortune in the form of misdirected maturation in the adoles-cent phase, expecially if reinforced by internally well-rewarded drinking experiences; and a subsequent learning or conditioning process, of possibly years-long duration, embedded in culturally and societally determined mores and conditions and directions, with a negative balance of interpersonal relations; and, finally, the pharmacological properties of alcohol assuming a dominant indispensable role in the individual's way of life. (p. 144)

Mendelson, Goldberg, Ewing, Sytinsky, Keller, and Siegler, Osmond, and Newell have helped organize knowledge of al-coholism. A more general, acceptably named model would further these efforts.

## An Ecological Model of Alcoholism

The etiology of alcoholism may be viewed in the conceptual framework of Susser's ecological model. This etiological model may be expanded to a "model of alcoholism" along the 12 dimensions used by Siegler, Osmond, and Newell.

THE ECOLOGICAL MODEL.
1. *Definition*: Alcoholism is a chronic disease characterized by persistent maladaptive use of beverage alcohol. Major diagnostic criteria include, but are not restricted to, evi-dence of physiological or psychological dependency on alcohol. Diagnosis is possible, but may be difficult, when no major criterion is met.
2. *Etiology*: Alcoholism results from interactions over time of multiple factors. Some of these factors relate more closely to the individual or host (such as hereditary and some psychological factors); others to the agent alcohol (such as dose); and others to the environment (such as socioeconomic and some family factors) that envelops both host and agent.
3. *Behavior*: The behavior of an affected individual also has multiple determinants; however, once physiological depen-

dency is established, much behavior is understandable as an effort to control withdrawal symptoms.

4. *Treatment*: Just as factors contributing to the development of alcoholism necessarily vary from one affected person to another, these people also vary in their treatment needs. Several treatment approaches are available and more are needed. The measure of treatment outcome is the patient's adaptive functioning.

5. *Prognosis*: The prognosis varies from one affected person to another. To some extent, those with the best premorbid adaptive functioning seem to also have the best treatment outcomes.*

6. *Function of the hospital*: Early in treatment, hospitals often provide comprehensive medical assessments and detoxification. Before discharging alcoholic patients, hospitals should try to ensure patient participation in continuing alcoholism treatment and in any indicated follow-up medical care.

7. *Personnel*: Any of a variety of treatment personnel may be appropriate depending upon the individual in need of treatment and the treatment approach selected. This implies a spectrum of personnel that would encompass an AA volunteer in a community hall as well as a psychologist in a residential rehabilitation center. Medical personnel help alcoholics with associated illness and often participate in the treatment of their alcoholism. A team approach is common, though often only implicit, among treatment personnel.

8. *Suicide*: Suicide is a risk in alcoholism. Treatment personnel should assess the likelihood of suicide particularly among alcoholics entering treatment and those doing poorly.

9. *Rights and duties of alcoholics*: Alcoholics have the rights to be treated with respect and to have access to appropriate treatment. They have the duties to be responsible and to be responsive to their communities.

10. *Rights and duties of families*: The families of alcoholics have the right to sympathetic support from their communities and, as resources allow, to specific treatment as families.

* See Chapter 7.

Family members have the duties to inform themselves about alcoholism, to not promote drinking by alcoholic family members, and to contribute positively to the treatment of alcoholic family members.

11. *Rights and duties of society*: Society has the right to be spared the dangers and social cost of alcoholism. It has the duties to recognize its own role in the etiology of alcoholism and to eliminate or at least neutralize contributory factors. Society has the duties to be responsible and responsive with regard to those affected by alcoholism.

12. *History of the model*: This model makes explicit some widely held assumptions and current practices in the alcoholism field. The model's assumptions about etiology are drawn from current thinking in the science of epidemiology.

This ecological formulation seems to meet the requirements proposed by Siegler, Osmond, and Newell[20] (pp. 589–590) for a satisfactory model of alcoholism. It is complete in that it provides a framework for raising a diversity of questions about alcoholism and investigating the answers. It is particularly helpful in the dimension of etiology. A tentative web of causation for alcoholism based on this model is presented (Figure 3.1) to illustrate this. Such etiological diagrams help identify targets for intervention programs meant to eliminate or neutralize causal influences, particularly those in the environment.* The causal web given could be expanded to greater detail at any level. It could incorporate the schema of Sytinsky[24] near the bottom of the diagram.

*Prior to undertaking actual program planning, expectations should be clarified. Single interventions, at best, might reduce the occurrence of disease and perhaps also reduce the occurrence of relapses among those under treatment. Feasible single interventions might eliminate an etiologic factor but not eliminate alcoholism since, at least in terms of present knowledge, alcoholism may result from "different constellations of causes"[27] (p. 7). Possible approaches to evaluating the impact of such interventions are discussed in Chapter 8. Prior to use, the causal web should be adapted to the population of interest. "Social gatherings," for example, might imply cocktail parties in suburbia but bottle gangs in the inner city.

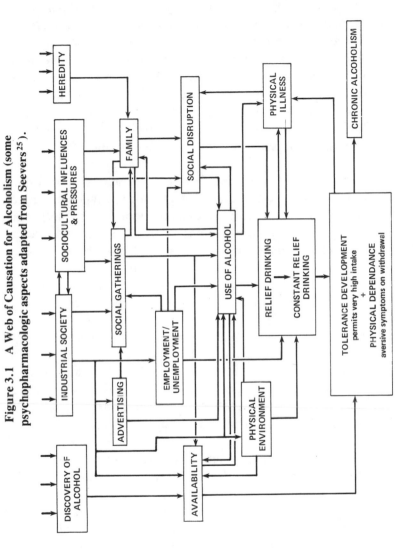

Figure 3.1   A Web of Causation for Alcoholism (some psychopharmacologic aspects adapted from Seevers[25]).

An ecological understanding of alcoholism also seems to satisfy Siegler, Osmond, and Newell's concern that participants in treatment not be required to act contrary to their moral positions:

it accommodates virtually any responsible individual position. Similarly, its acceptance of diversity satisfies their requirement that a model be practical and economical in terms of treatment personnel—yet it accepts readily available personnel like AA members without rejecting the scarce and expensive psychologists and family therapists. Particularly with growing awareness in society of interdependent factors that influence the quality of the environment, which in turn influences human health, an ecological model of alcoholism seems likely to meet the requirements of timeliness and general comprehensibility.

RESISTANCE TO ECOLOGICAL THINKING.    There is an important qualification on the assumption that this model will prove comprehensible "both to professional and lay people"[20] (p. 589). This model retains (though not from necessity, as pointed out at the beginning of this chapter) the designation of alcoholism as a disease. Predictably the term disease, which is quickly associated with medical theory and practice, will be difficult for some to reconcile with thoughts of multiple, potentially changeable environmental causal factors. Their conceptual problem can be related to thinking in terms of "individual medicine," which Terris[28] defines as "the theory and practice of medicine in which the horizon is limited to the relation between the individual patient and the individual physician" (p. 653). This view is in contrast to "social medicine," which "brings to bear on the health of the individual the full medical and non-medical capacities of society" (p. 653).

An example from the alcoholism literature may clarify both the distinction between individual and social medicine and the prediction of some resistance to the latter. In *The Disease Concept of Alcoholism*,[3] Jellinek seems to think in terms of individual medicine. A problem might be "medical, sociological, or economic" or might exist "in all of those three categories" (p. 14) but a system of medicine that perceives social and economic matters as fundamentally relevant to itself is foreign to his outlook. Jellinek quotes from a 1954 paper by Querido[29] * who assumes "that any pattern of behavior shown by man is the result of an interaction of various [individual and social] forces" and that "an extremely complicated network of conditions . . . determine attitude, thought and behavior"[29] (p. 470). Querido's thinking about disease etiology is clearly presented and is quite consistent with the dynamic epidemiological and ecological models depicted above. His view also anticipates other components of a unified theory of health and disease as described earlier. However, while Jellinek respects Querido's position and does not contradict it, he does not seem able to assimilate it into his own thinking as he concludes: "It may not be said that Querido's considerations greatly clarify the idea of 'alcoholism' as an illness, but they facilitate the discussion of the subject"[3] (p. 79). This comment bluntly ends Jellinek's response even though Querido points out— as does this chapter— that "one of the chief needs of the present time is . . . to rearrange knowledge already gathered under new light"[29] (p. 474).

## ETIOLOGICAL STUDIES: CENTRAL THEMES

There are environmental factors associated with inner-city living— which may well exist elsewhere in more subtle forms— which seem to increase the risk of alcoholism in exposed populations. It may be helpful before focusing on those factors to comment on two themes in the literature concerned with the etiology of alcoholism: the characterization of alcoholism as escapism and the competition among theories or "causes" of alcoholism.

### Escapism

Detailed reviews of the many studies related to the etiology

*Querido is identified as Professor of Social Medicine, University of Amsterdam.[29]

of alcoholism are available.[3-7] The intent here is to briefly illustrate the theme of escapism using these reviews and a few other sources.

Euphoria, disinhibition, reduced anxiety and depression, and relief from physical discomfort are psychopharmacologic effects ascribed to beverage alcohol (ethyl alcohol, ethanol).[25] Whether through distraction—feeling high or sociable—or through some direct effect, alcohol consumption can reduce pain, disagreeable feelings, and the perception of unpleasant circumstances. Alcohol therefore offers a type of escape. Repeated use of alcohol as a means of escape is often considered an essential feature of the development of alcoholism.

Jellinek[30] described a prealcoholic phase of alcohol addiction characterized by occasional, then constant, *relief drinking*. For the person developing alcoholism, "the use of heavy drinking to relieve, or as an aid in coping with, one sort of problem will be followed by its use in meeting other problems"[8] (p. 144). Survey respondents who report escape drinking practices, especially if they also drink heavily, are regarded as likely to become problem drinkers.[31-33]

Drinking to escape life situations is characteristic of early alcoholism. A middle stage of alcoholism is characterized by increased drinking, at least partly because heavy drinking frequently leads to social and/or physical problems, and these increase the incentive to escape. Advanced alcoholism is characterized by almost continuous drinking to escape the discomfort and danger of alcohol withdrawal states.[5, 25, 30, 34, 35]

Explaining this pattern, or segments of it, is a basic goal of etiological studies. Researchers taking a *constitutional* approach have emphasized agent-host interaction relatively late in the pattern.

> Constitutionalists explicitly or implicitly maintain that the cause of alcoholism is basically physiological. Many of their theories stipulate the existence of a biochemical predisposition involving some physiological or structural defect which causes the individual to become physically addicted to alcohol. Once a person with such a proclivity begins or continues drinking, he becomes

addicted because of peculiarities of his biochemical makeup. Among physiological causes that have been proposed are genetic propensity, metabolic defects (such as abnormal enzyme levels), disturbed glandular functions, abnormal levels of various body chemicals and allergic reactions.[5] (p. 21)

Roebuck and Kessler[5] examined *psychological* studies representing learning theory, transactional analysis, psychoanalysis, field dependence/independence, and alcoholic personality theories. These studies emphasize the individual or host, with some consideration of agent-host interaction. Psychological approaches to alcoholism depict

the alcoholic as an escapist—alcohol being the means of escape. The type of personality most frequently associated with alcoholism is a passive-dependent one. The combination of these perspectives suggest that the alcoholics are basically dependent personalities who have turned to alcohol as a means of escape from internal or external stress.[5] (pp. 127–128)

Causal relationships described in an early paper by Bales[36] are generally incorporated into *sociological* approaches, which view culture and social organization as important determinants of alcoholism. Emphasis is on environmental factors.

The alcoholic is assumed to be dealing with his problems (perhaps by escaping them) by the use of alcohol. He chooses alcohol as the means of his escape partially because of his attitude about alcohol. These attitudes, in turn, are molded by the groups which impinge upon the drinker's existence.[5] (p. 220)

## A Contest with No Finish, No Prize

Keller[8] and Fazey[26] are among those who find it regrettable that the theorists whose work is summarized in the preceding remarks generally limit their thinking to the range of their own disciplines. The advance of understanding is impeded not only by this disciplinary isolation, but by the tendency of authors to view their contribution not as a complement to other theories but as *the best alternative*. A degree of competitiveness is evident even among the reviewers of these studies. Jellinek[3] pays the most attention to individual-centered factors. Roebuck and Kessler[5] endow the sociological approach to alcoholism with ''current preeminence'' (p. 139).

Statements from an epidemiological viewpoint indicate the pointlessness of this competition. Querido[29] assumes that in the study of a given condition, once biological-clinical, psychological, human interrelational, social, and economic factors have been distinguished,

> the next step is to find out not which of these sets of factors might be the most important as a causative influence—for this is a sterile question without inner meaning—but rather, in which field do the conditions most favoring the changes necessary for achieving the desired results lie. (p. 472)

Friedman[1] seems well aware of a general tendency to follow the path taken by investigators of the etiology of alcoholism, and of the impracticality of that route:

> It is tempting to search for a primary cause, or the most important or most direct of the many causal factors. The benefits of this search are perhaps more philosophical or psychological than practical. In terms of disease prevention it may be most practical to attack a causal web at a spot that seems relatively remote from the disease. To prevent malaria, we do not merely try to destroy the malaria parasite; rather, we drain swamps to control the mosquito population, since this is a practical and effective approach. Similarly, economic development and general improvements in living conditions seem to have done more to reduce mortality from tuberculosis than any chemotherapeutic agent directed specifically at the tubercle bacillus. (p. 5)

The epidemiological/ecological perspective offers investigators a means to lay aside contention and integrate their efforts. It seems to provide the piece that, to Keller, is still missing:

> Frankly, I do not have a clear conception of how the disciplines can be truly integrated in performing the studies required to

verify the . . . [interdisciplinary] etiological perspective, nor exactly
how the professions can be integrated for the first experimental
programs of prevention.[8] (p. 146)

In envisioning an integrated effort to reduce the toll of
alcohol problems, ''prevention'' could imply both the prevention
of new cases and the prevention of relapses among treated cases
of alcoholism. Given the present state of knowledge, environmental factors seem the most vulnerable targets for preventive
efforts. Among environmental factors, those pertaining to the
culture of two particular ethnic groups will be examined in detail
in Chapter 4. The following discussion identifies environmental
etiological factors (separable from cultural ones at least for
purposes of this discussion) contributing to alcoholism that may
prove approachable once placed in perspective with an ecological model.

## THE INNER CITY: A NOXIOUS ENVIRONMENT

> When you ain't got nothing,
> you got nothing to lose.
> — Bob Dylan,
> ''Like a Rolling Stone''

McCord ''maintains that ghetto life magnifies the same
causative factors that lead to alcoholism in the general population ''[5] (p. 204). If McCord's assumption is valid, practical
knowledge gained in the inner city could yield tremendous
benefits. And McCord may be right. A *Time* magazine (5 November 1979) quote from a college student— ''You feel that you can
never get caught up, that you always have something hanging
over you. So you use alcohol to numb your brain so you don't
think about it'' (p. 71)— sounds remarkably like what people
say in the ghetto.

## Deprivation and Disease

An association between deprived living conditions and excessive death and disease has been recognized for a long time[37] and continues to be documented.[38-45] There are theoretical and empirical grounds for assuming that interactions between members of a population and factors in the *social environment*— factors that seem to be exaggerated in the inner city — contribute in a *nonspecific* manner to the population's burden of disease.[46-50] Hinkle and Wolff[47] found clusters of illness at times when people "perceived their life situations to be unsatisfying, threatening, overdemanding, and productive of conflict, and they could make no satisfactory adaptation" (p. 1382). Analysis of environmental factors such as poverty, racial/ethnic discrimination, and social class* has furthered understanding of the unequal distribution of disease.[38-45, 51-53] Anomie and social disorganization/sociocultural disintegration appear relevant,[51, 52, 54-58] as do social positions of domination/subordination,[58] buffers against social disorganization,[58] generalized stress,[57] and urbanization.[53, 59]

Leighton[51] discusses direct and indirect influences of the sociocultural environment in the etiology of "disorders subsumed by the field of psychiatry" (p. 177). He groups relevant factors in a summary of the "main characteristics of the more noxious environments":

> 1. High degree of apparent risk with regard to physical security, sexual satisfaction, expression of hostility, expression of love, securing love, obtaining recognition, expression of spontaneity, orientation in society, membership in a human group, and a sense of belonging to a moral order.
> 2. Sociocultural conditions which permit or foster the formation of those behavior patterns (intrapersonal and interpersonal)

*In popular use, "social class" might be regarded as an individual attribute; however, in etiological thinking an index of a person's position in social strata implies various past and continuing experiences in relationships with *environmental* factors. (See Leighton,[51] pp. 188–225, 290–291.)

which lead to psychiatric disorder rather than to more constructive forms of adaptation.

3. The absence of therapeutic and remedial resources, both
formal and informal. (pp. 177–178)

These characteristics were transformed into operational sets of
disintegration indices for use by Leighton's research team in the
Stirling County Study conducted in rural Nova Scotia. Inner-
city areas such as the South Bronx would be among the environments — acknowledged but considered rare by Leighton — which
demonstrate "all the above features . . . to a really extreme
degree"[51] (p. 178).

## Deprivation and Alcoholism

If people living in deprivation have more disease and alcoholism is considered a disease, one might at least tentatively
expect excessive alcoholism among inner-city residents. There
is also the assumption expressed by Kingham and other learning
theorists (see Roebuck and Kessler,[5] pp. 71–81) and by Farnsworth[60] that a condition characterized by escapism will be more
prevalent among people living under hostile or escape-inviting
conditions. Even Jellinek,[3] whose lack of affinity for environmental explanations of alcoholism has been mentioned, while
considering the lot of "the slum dweller who was driven to
'pubs,' bars or saloons in order to obtain relief from his dreary
home," reluctantly had to "concede . . . that the economic or environmental factors play a prominent role in such cases" (p. 20).

The expectation of more alcohol-related problems among
deprived groups is borne out by mortality and morbidity data.
Bureau of the Census data indicate that nonwhites are a socioeconomically deprived group nationally.[61] In the United States, where
mortality from alcoholic disorders is rising, age-specific death
rates from alcoholic disorders are considerably higher for non-
whites than whites. The rates are also rising much more rapidly
in the nonwhite group.[62] Members of the lowest socioeconomic

classes in the United States have the highest mortality rates from cirrhosis* and cirrhosis deaths show an urban preponderance.[63]

Population or household surveys are regarded as the most accurate source of morbidity data,[67] including alcoholism morbidity.[66] Surveys have found increased alcohol problems and alcoholism associated with lower income, lower education level, and lower occupational status.[68] Studies analyzed in terms of social class indices showed similar associations.[32, 69, 70] Studies have also shown positive associations between alcohol problems or alcoholism and being black,[32, 68, 70] being Latin-American/Caribbean,[70] and living in a city.[32, 70] Some researchers[32, 70] partly explain such findings on the basis of exceptionally stressful environments.

In a cross-cultural community study, Jessor and colleagues[71] tested specific hypotheses relating factors in the social environment to deviant behavior. They found support for the theory that an unequal or discriminatory opportunity structure — which makes socially legitimate means of satisfaction inaccessible — pressures people to adopt deviant means of satisfaction such as heavy alcohol use. Responses to such pressuring seem influenced by sociocultural controls on behavior such as those that encourage or discourage heavy drinking. Reflecting on the work of Jessor's group and that of other authors, Bloom[72] states:

> Cultural variations are not . . . the all important factor in destructive drinking. It is the over-all sociocultural structure in which one group of people shares less of the payoff of society that is more important in the production of large numbers of destructive drinkers. (p. 65)

*A causal relationship between excessive alcohol consumption and many (it appears most) instances of cirrhosis of the liver has been recognized for centuries.[63] Increasing evidence has indicated a rather direct harmful effect of alcohol on the liver,[64] and relatively recently a controlled primate experiment showed that the spectrum of alcoholic liver disease could be produced by alcohol.[65] Edwards[66] and Keller[33] have summarized historical aspects of the use of cirrhosis mortality data as an indicator of alcoholism prevalence.

## A NOTE ON COMPETENCE: IMPLICATIONS FOR THE SPLIT BETWEEN ALCOHOL AND OTHER DRUGS

Christie and Bruun[73] have observed that separation of alcohol problems from problems with other drugs of dependency and abuse goes far beyond distinctions to be found in diagnostic manuals.

> Huge conferences gather to discuss questions of alcohol and alcoholism, while quite different conferences gather to discuss drugs or narcotics. The same split is found in national organizations dealing with alcohol *or* narcotics, laws against alcohol *or* narcotics, institutions for alcoholics *or* people using narcotics, and so on. (p. 65, italics in original)

With practicality serving along with advancing knowledge in the regulation of nosologic disease categories (Chapter 2), this institutionalized separation would seem to prohibit combining drug dependencies into a single category as has sometimes been suggested.

But clarified causal understandings of disease have sometimes more or less forced changes in diagnostic categories. Goldberg's[22] epidemiological model is not drug specific.* Fazey,[26] who also prefers to reconcile etiological theories of drug abuse, pleads for "interdisciplinary research which is not pigeon-holed by type of drug" (p. 90). Farnsworth[60] presents a concept that might prove very helpful to such research. He formulates drug dependence as a "substitute for competence" and finds it more rational to conceive of this as

> a composite of social, cultural, and emotional maladaptations that may result in a wide variety of problems. Numerous life situations that have been frustrating to the individual usually coincide with or precede such disability. (p. 282)

*See also P. C. Whitehead: "An epidemiological description of the development of drug dependence: environmental factors and prevention." *American Journal of Drug and Alcohol Abuse*, 1976, *3*, 323–338.

rather than "as a specific disease in search of a cure" (p. 282). "Maladaptations" in this formulation would include recourse to drug experimentation and drug dependence as substitutes for intrapsychic and interpersonal competence.* Farnsworth's dynamic etiological point of view has obvious implications for treatment and prevention and it happens that approaches directed at improvement of competence in his sense are now being tried. Reality therapy, which helps people acquire the ability to responsibly attain personal fulfillment, is being applied to alcoholism treatment.[74, 75] In substance abuse prevention programs there is a strong trend to reduce the attention given to particular substances of abuse such as alcohol or heroin and to focus on promoting competence.** If these approaches prove especially effective, the present nosologic split between alcoholism and other drug dependencies could become outmoded.

*The text and footnotes in Chapter 7 provide considerably more background on the concept of competence.

**For overviews of this prevention trend see Dohner, V. A., Alternatives to drugs—a new approach to drug education (*Journal of Drug Education*, 1972, *2*, 3–22; reprinted as National Clearinghouse for Drug Abuse Information Publication No. 32); Cohen, A. Y., Alternatives to drug abuse: Steps toward prevention (National Clearinghouse for Drug Abuse Information, DHEW Publication No.[ADM]75-79, 1975); and Smart, R. G., & Fejer, D., *Drug education: Current issues, future directions* (Toronto: Addiction Research Foundation of Ontario, 1974). Resource books that convey the flavor of the trend include Messolonghites, L., ed., *Alternative pursuits for America's 3rd century* (National Institute on Drug Abuse, DHEW Publication No.[ADM]75-242, 1975) and the delightful *Take the Time* (Madison, Wisc.: Substance Abuse Clearinghouse). *National Search: A catalogue of alternatives for young Americans* (National Institute on Drug Abuse, DHEW Publication No.[ADM]76-257, 1976) briefly describes 91 relevant programs around the U.S. Issues in developing such programs are comprehensively examined in *Planning a prevention program: A handbook for the youth worker in an alcohol service agency* (Arlington, Va.: National Center of Alcohol Education, 1976).

*Chapter 4*

# CULTURE AND ALCOHOLISM: BLACKS AND HISPANICS

Worldwide, anthropological studies document an enormous range of variation in terms of the people who drink, the beverages they consume, when and where they drink, their manner of consumption, their apparent motivation for drinking, and so forth.[1] This variation is attributed to multiple factors, particularly "attitudes toward drinking which the culture produces in its members"[2] (p. 482). Further, values and attitudes are identified as major determinants of the direction and persistence of drinking behavior.[3]

In the United States, there has been very little formal study of racial and ethnic differences in attitudes toward alcohol.[4] Available information, however, supports the existence of certain values and attitudes toward alcohol among blacks and Hispanics. In addition, there is information about drinking patterns and alcohol-associated symptoms that illustrates the effect of culture on alcohol consumption and alcohol problems. Some of this material is qualitative—it is based on historical evidence and subjective observations. Other material is quantitative and is based on data such as survey interviews or treatment records.

## AMERICAN BLACKS

No body of literature presents attitudinal tests of black subjects with regard to alcohol. When one prepares to cautiously infer attitudes from descriptions of behavior, it is still necessary to cope with the scantiness of descriptive pieces dealing with blacks and alcohol. Harper and Dawkins[5] report that of the 16,000 alcohol-related studies appearing in scientific journals in the past 30 years, only 77 deal with blacks. These authors classify 27 of the 77 papers under "drinking patterns and behavior." Only nine of the 27 (those subgrouped under "adult blacks" and "blacks and other ethnic groups") seem to deal with populations at all comparable to that presented in Chapter 5.*

Contributors to the small literature on alcohol and blacks are generally aware of the excess of alcohol-related problems among blacks (see Chapter 3) and many convey a sense of urgent need for intervention. For example, King and colleagues[6] term alcohol abuse "a crucial factor in the social problems of Negro men." Bourne[7] comments: "Alcoholism ranks almost certainly as the number one mental health problem if not the most significant of all health problems in black urban communities" (p. 211). Harper[8] writes: "Alcohol abuse is the *number one health problem* and the *number one social problem* in Black America" (p. 1, italics in original).

These three quotations emphasize destructive effects of alcohol consumption on blacks. Black leaders have repeatedly confronted their communities with this extensive human damage.[9, 10] The fact that the problems persist is perhaps testimony to the strength of environmental and cultural factors that support alcohol consumption by blacks in America.

This chapter and Chapter 3 discuss in some detail the factors, or pressures, that contribute to alcohol consumption by blacks. A vivid, poignant account of such factors is offered by

---

*Harper and Dawkins do not provide references for the articles in their tallies, so it is unclear how many of these nine studies are included in this review.

Harper[8] in a poem that lists "some of the positive and negative meanings that alcohol has for Black Americans":

## THE MEANINGS OF ALCOHOL TO BLACK AMERICA

ALCOHOL helps Black Americans to weather the heat of the summer ghetto, the harsh "hawk" of the cruel winter, the perennial bite of the roaming rat, and the endless days of being financially broke.

ALCOHOL is that joy juice which serves as a quasi-suicidal means of tuning out painful realities; it brings courage to the frightened and strength to the weak. It stimulates that mild high so necessary for a cool veneer. It is the social lubricant and overture to a sexual charade.

ALCOHOL helps Blacks to face "The Man"; to rap with the brother on the street and run the line down on the foxy sister; to boogie down and bump to dawn; to "forget" the bad and "remember" the good; to be somebody with high-priced scotch in one hand and a roll of green money in the other.

ALCOHOL to the Black community is that omnipresent catalyst that frees anxiety, jealousy, and anger; that causes one to act out in destroying that he loves or that he hates; that causes one to avenge the self from the lowest depth of insult in the only way he or she knows— by assaulting, by fighting, by destroying.

ALCOHOL is that residue diagnosed in the Black veins and arteries of autopsied victims of homicides, rapes, robberies, accidents, and suicides; that abusive substance that precludes a natural death and facilitates an early funeral.

ALCOHOL is amalgamated into that emotional matrix of the love-hate, happy-sad, up-down seesaw syndrome that keeps Blacks in a quandary of confusion and powerlessness.

ALCOHOL keeps the Black man from going crazy in a castrating and racist world while simultaneously driving his woman up the wall. It prevents mental stress while causing distress. It makes one feel high at night and low at morning; strong like a king on Friday at dusk and weak like a pauper on Monday at dawn.

ALCOHOL takes the man from his home and woman, the father from his family, milk from the baby, and lunch from the school child.

ALCOHOL to many Blacks is so necessary to pump life into a body and community of hopelessness and despair; so necessary for social intercourse, relaxation, partying, and psychological survival; so "good" but yet so "bad." (p. 3)

The following review separates the literature on alcohol and blacks into qualitative and quantitative material.* The qualitative material consists of historical, cultural, and economic accounts and encompasses work designated by Cahalan and Cisin[3] as "anecdotal or anthropological studies." The quantitative studies offer data on such issues as drinking patterns or symptoms of alcoholism.

## Qualitative Studies

Harper[12] offers four hypotheses (Table 4.1) as a theoretical framework for understanding the drinking behavior of black Americans. Harper presents the hypotheses with supportive descriptive material, but their original context does not adequately demonstrate how well the hypotheses synthesize material that

---

*Some pieces, such as that by Vitols,[11] have both qualitative and quantitative information and appear under both headings.

has consistently appeared in the literature. The following sub-sections are organized around Harper's hypotheses and the multiple references demonstrate the consistency between Harper's etiologic thinking and the literature.

**Table 4.1**

*Harper's etiologic hypotheses to explain why blacks drink\**

1.  The historical patterns of alcohol use and nonuse by blacks have played a significant part in influencing their current drinking practices and their current attitudes toward drinking.
2.  Many blacks choose to drink because (1) liquor stores and liquor dealers are readily accessible; and (2) because black peer groups often expect one to drink and at times to drink heavily.
3.  Many blacks, especially men, drink heavily due to the economic frustration of not being able to get a job or not being able to fulfill financial responsibilities.
4.  Numerous emotions and motivations influence heavy drinking among black Americans in their attempt to escape unpleasant feelings or to fulfill psychological needs.

\*From Harper,[12] pp. 31–36.

HISTORY.   The use of alcohol by blacks during the time of slavery in America was regulated by whites. The regulatory practices — one of prohibition and one of indulgence — have both been explained as means taken by whites to maintain social control. Blacks, like Indians, were considered potentially dangerous and unable to use alcohol without increasing the risk of violence and rebellion. Measures were taken by whites, legally and other than legally, to prevent blacks from buying or using alcohol. [7, 9, 10–16] On special occasions, however, such as harvest and Christmas, when slaves had leisure time, alcohol was made available in large quantities and drunkenness was tolerated, if not expected, behavior.[7, 10, 12–15] This promotion of drinking during free time is viewed as a tactic that pacified slaves, distracting and disabling them from possible escape or revolt.

Harper[12] sees "these mixed signals by Whites, some encouraging Blacks to drink . . . and others discouraging Blacks' use of alcohol . . ." as contributing "to a sense of ambivalence and confusion among Blacks in regards to whether or not to drink." So that "often Blacks end up choosing either of two extremes, to drink heavily or not to drink at all" (pp. 31–32). The well-described[7, 9, 10, 12–17] pattern of contemporary blacks drinking heavily on weekends and on paydays Harper sees as connected with the historically established patterns of drinking heavily in free time and drinking as a reward for work.

When slavery ended there was a tendency among American blacks to react against prior prohibition of alcohol by drinking heavily. [7, 9–12, 15, 16] Heavy drinking was especially noted among emancipated young black men who moved to northern cities. [7, 15, 16] Their drinking may also have been in part a response to the stresses of migration and urbanization.

ALCOHOL AVAILABILITY.    Observers have long noted an unusually dense concentration of bars and liquor stores in black neighborhoods, whether the neighborhoods are commercial or residential.[8–10, 12, 15, 16] Some regard this an an example of systematic economic exploitation of blacks. [10, 16] The present number of bars may have a historical connection to the practice during prohibition of locating speakeasies in black communities because "the illegal sale of alcohol and drugs was much simpler and 'safer' [there]"[10] (p. 22). Even today there are bootleg dealers who make alcohol readily available on Sundays[12] or extend credit until payday.[10]

The accessibility of alcohol to blacks is more than just a commercial issue. It relates to a way of life that includes taverns or drinking houses as important social institutions.[14] Opportunities for alcohol-centered socializing are extended temporally by after-hours clubs and spatially by street bottle gangs. [15, 16]

Harper[17] refers to this way of life when he states that blacks tend to be group drinkers and often drink in public.

PEER EXPECTATION.    Harper is not the only writer to develop the theme of group drinking among blacks. [13, 15] Its effect on alcohol availability is not the only reason group drinking is important. Convivial gatherings are an important setting in which cultural pressures promote alcohol consumption. For group participants, drinking represents a means of recreation and enhanced sociability. [7–9, 12, 16, 17] Drinking, particularly with others, is very much a part of celebrations such as birthdays or holidays.[7–9, 13–17] When blacks drink together the type of alcoholic beverage a person consumes is often regarded as a measure or symbol of status. Scotch is a frequent choice.[7–9, 12, 17]

As Harper points out in his second hypothesis, the expectation among blacks is not only that one drink, but also that one sometimes drink heavily.[7, 9, 12, 17] Consistent with that expectation, black groups display a tolerance of drunkenness that incorporates a tolerance of even alcoholic drinking behavior.[7, 8, 10–12, 17] Disapproval of drunkenness as a social control serving to prevent pathological drinking[18] is thus not present, or at least not strong, in the culture of American blacks.

FRUSTRATION.    Alcohol provides relief or escape from the many frustrations of being black in America.[7–10, 12–17, 19] Racism seems the best term for the core problem underlying these frustrations. The role of racism in the development of alcohol problems among blacks is specifically recognized by several authors.[7, 8, 10, 12, 15–17] While the influence of racism on the drinking of blacks living in deprivation is obvious, Davis[16] points out that racism stresses middle- and upper-class blacks as well, often contributing to excessive alcohol consumption among them. Expressions of racism given attention in the alcoholism literature include poverty and urban ghetto living,[7, 8, 10, 12, 15–17] unemployment and underemployment,[12, 16, 17] and the scarcity of alcoholism treatment resources for poor blacks.[17]

## Quantitative Studies

Two types of study contribute quantitative information to what is known about blacks and alcohol. One investigates subjects who *do not* have a known alcohol problem. An example would be a survey designed to estimate the prevalence of alcohol problems among adults in a defined geographic area. The target of such a study is a group of people, some of whom might have alcohol problems, but none of whom are identified as such prior to data collection. Such population-based studies may or may not yield useful information about problem drinkers or alcoholics. Their success would depend upon (1) sample size and whether or not individuals with alcohol problems are present; (2) if they are present, whether or not the survey identifies them; and (3) if they are identified, the type and amount of information collected about them. Information about alcohol problems in blacks and the sociocultural environment in which these problems develop, derived from population-based studies, is reviewed in the first subsection below.

The second type of quantitative study investigates subjects who *do* have a known alcohol problem. These studies are generally descriptions of individuals engaged in alcoholism treatment. As will be evident in the second subsection to follow, the descriptive information contained in such studies is not standardized and is based on limited numbers of subjects.

SUBJECTS WITHOUT KNOWN ALCOHOL PROBLEMS. In *American Drinking Practices*,[20] Cahalan, Cisin, and Crossley present data from interviews of a national probability sample consisting of 2,711 adults. There were 200 blacks in their sample. Table 4.2 summarizes their respondents' drinking behavior. The black men were very similar to their white counterparts in drinking behavior while black women were more likely than white women to either abstain from alcohol or to drink heavily. A subgroup of heavy-escape drinkers "included an above-average percentage of non-Whites" (p. 179). Details about drinking practices such as usual circumstances of drinking were not broken down by race by these authors.

**Table 4.2    Drinking behavior reported by a national probability sample: percentages of respondents in quantity-frequency-variability groups, by race and sex\***

|  | Abstainers | Infrequent Drinkers | Light and Moderate Drinkers | Heavy Drinkers |
|---|---|---|---|---|
| Black men (n=82) | 21% | 13% | 47% | 19% |
| White men (n=1,082) | 23% | 10% | 45% | 22% |
| Black women (n=118) | 51% | 11% | 27% | 11% |
| White Women (n=1,429) | 39% | 19% | 38% | 4% |

*Table adapted from *American Drinking Practices*,[20] p. 48.

Sterne and Pittman's study[14] of ghetto drinking patterns in a St. Louis public housing complex provides some data about "normal drinking" among their black subjects. Drinking respondents expressed a high preference for beer and a low preference for wine in comparison with national samples. The authors discuss possible explanations for these findings such as "subcultural attitudes stigmatizing the use of wine" (p. 227), which might lower wine use, reported use, or both. Friends, followed by relatives and immediate family, were the most popular drinking companions. Solitary drinking was common, with 40% of drinkers drinking alone at times and 21% (26% of the men and

19% of the women) acknowledging that their most frequent drinking situation is when alone. Sterne and Pittman cite other evidence that blacks tend to drink alone. The most frequently reported locales for drinking were the respondents' own homes, taverns, and friends' homes. Only 5% reported drinking outdoors in the project and 4% drinking outdoors elsewhere. In spite of the frequent reports of solitary drinking, the most frequently expressed motivation for drinking was some form of social ritual. Among other possible motivations, "reasons relating to the desire to escape some form of personal distress" (p. 437) were acknowledged as important by 46% of the subjects. The adults in their study population did not demonstrate an unbounded permissiveness toward drinking, but "acceptance of male intoxication is relatively high, with 65 per cent of . . . respondents finding nonhabitual male intoxication acceptable" (p. 642).

Robins, Murphy, and Breckenridge[21] obtained data to support the widespread belief that blacks tend to have first drinking experiences younger than other groups. They also found drinking at an early age associated with subsequent heavy drinking. "Heavy drinking ever" (defined as past or present consumption of at least four drinks daily or one seven-drink occasion per week) occurred over twice as often in their sample of young black men as it has in a similar study of whites. Blacks had 3.5 times the white rate of medical or social problems resulting from drinking. Other social problems not clearly resulting from alcohol were also prevalent among their black subjects.[6]

Additional studies of subjects without known alcohol problems have contributed to knowledge about alcohol and American blacks. Robins and Guze[22] have reported that familial disruption and early school problems may be predictors of future alcohol problems in black males. Maddox[23] found evidence of precocious alcohol use among black male college freshmen. Sterne and Pittman[14] observed that ghetto-resident black youths have a high exposure to alcohol consumption through beverage container litter, numerous and busy alcohol beverage outlets, public drinking, and familial and other role models. Perhaps in part because of this exposure, black youths enter early into adult drinking patterns.

In their survey of Washington Heights in New York City, Bailey, Haberman, and Alksne[24] identified 132 presumed alcoholics. Relative to the population sampled, blacks were over-represented in this group. Independent of race, lack of education was associated with alcoholism. Information about the alcoholic group is not summarized by race, however, so the study does not provide detailed knowledge about its black alcoholic subjects.

SUBJECTS WITH KNOWN ALCOHOL PROBLEMS.    The numbers are comparatively small, but blacks are represented in surveys of problem drinkers. Unfortunately, the major national surveys of problem drinkers[25, 26] do not separate their black respondents in data summaries. The following general statements are provided, however. Blacks and Latin-Americans/Caribbeans showed high rates of untoward social consequences from drinking.[25-27] The same two groups showed the highest rates of very heavy drinking.[26]

Though they can generate only provisional inferences, detailed data about blacks with drinking problems can be obtained from the descriptions of patient characteristics that have been published by some alcoholism treatment programs. The data collection and presentation in these treatment program studies are not standardized. Authors do not consistently specify their criteria for the diagnosis of alcoholism.* Tables 4.3, 4.4, and 4.5 tabulate information from 10 such studies. These sources separate data about black and white segments of the treatment populations by providing breakdowns by race or ethnicity, thus giving some picture of the characteristics of the black subgroup. Papers by German,[33] Zimberg,[35] and Novick, Hudson, and German[36] are included even though they did not subdivide data

* At the present limited level of knowledge this criticism is not of great consequence. The participation of the subjects of these studies in alcoholism treatment is fairly sound presumptive evidence of serious alcohol-related difficulty.

**Table 4.3   Demographic Characteristics of Blacks Engaged in Alcoholism Treatment Programs** (blank boxes indicate data not available)

| Source (Publication date) | Sample | Sex and Age | Residential Status | Marital Status | Education | Occupation | Arrests |
|---|---|---|---|---|---|---|---|
| Strayer[28] (1961) | Outpatients - Bridgeport, Conn. 44 Blacks (B) 1,264 Whites (W) | Men & Women Most 36–45 yrs. Distribution not given | Undomiciled: 4% B 9% W | Married: 50% B 49% W; Single: 11% B 18% W; Separated: 21% B 15% W; Divorced or Widowed: 18% B 17% W | Elementary: 48% B 35% W; Some high school: 28% B 30% W; H.S. Grad.: 17% B 21% W; Some college: 7% B 9% W; Coll. grad.: 5% W | Unskilled: 46% B 17% W; Semi-skilled: 26% B 32% W; Skilled: 5% B 18% W; Service: 20% B 7% W; Clerical, sales, professional, managerial: 20% W | |
| Rosenblatt et al.[29] (1971) | 567 Inpatients - Brooklyn, NYC 60% Black 39% White 1% Puerto Rican | Men Mean age 39.0 yrs. Distribution not given | Age, education, and marital status presented in original by "zones of patient density" | | | | |
| Rimmer et al.[30] (1971) | Inpatients - St. Louis, Mo. (2 hospitals) 63 Blacks (B) 196 Whites (W) | Men & Women Mean age 42 yrs. Mean ages given by sex, race and hospital (B younger than W) | | Given by sex, race & hospital (No racial difference reported) | | | Alcohol-related arrests and auto trouble given by sex, race & hospital (B women more arrests than W women: 50% vs. 17%) |
| Zimberg et al.[31] (1971) | Outpatients - Harlem, NYC 79 Blacks | Men Most 25–44 yrs. Modal range: 35–46 yrs. | | Married: 23% (about half living in "social isolation") | Most patients "socio-economically deprived" (also see Table 4.4) | | See Table 4.4 |

| Study | Sample | Age | Marital Status | Education | Occupation / Social Class | Arrests |
|---|---|---|---|---|---|---|
| Gross et al.[32] (1972) | Inpatients - Brooklyn, NYC 272 Blacks (B) 279 Whites (W) | Men Distributions by race given: Modal B range 20–34 yrs. Modal W range 45–64 yrs. (B younger than W) | Some incidence of disrupted marriages in B & W, but B more separations & W more divorces | Median level 9.5 yrs. (no significant B-W difference) | | |
| German[33] (1973) | Inpatients - Harlem, NYC 101 Blacks 15 Puerto Ricans 6 Whites | Men Distribution given, modal decade 30–39 yrs. | | | | |
| Viamontes & Powell[34] (1974) | Inpatients - St. Louis, Mo. 100 Blacks (B) 100 Whites (W) | Men Mean ages: B 37.0 yrs. W 46.2 yrs. | Twice as many B (28%) as W were single | Mean levels: B 9.3 yrs. W 9.6 yrs. | B and W "if employed were engaged in unskilled or semi-skilled positions" | Alcohol-related arrests: B 55% W 58% |
| Zimberg[35] (1974) | Outpatients - Harlem, NYC 102 Blacks 10 Puerto Ricans 1 White | Men Age range 21–64 yrs. Modal range 35–44 yrs. | Most single or separated: distributions for three treatment groups given | Combining the 3 treatment groups given: Postgrad. 1% College grad. 0% Some college 8% H.S. grad. 19% Some H.S. 26% 7–9 years 29% Under 7 yrs. 17% | Social class distributions given for three treatment groups | Alcohol-related arrests: 65% |
| Novick, Hudson, and German[36] (1974) | Inpatients - Harlem, NYC 66 Blacks 11 Puerto Ricans 4 Whites | Men Mean: 40.3 yrs. Distribution given with modal decade 30–39 yrs. | Marital status known for 74 subjects: Married: 35% Single: 31% Separated: 27% Widowers: 5% Divorced: 1% | H.S. Grad. 27% Some coll. 14% | Work history known for 52 subjects: Unskilled: 75% Skilled: 12% Managerial: 10% Artists: 4% 14 (17%) employed at time of admission | |

**Table 4.4  Drinking Behavior of Blacks Engaged in Alcoholism Treatment Programs***

| Source (Publication date) | Sample | Age of First Drink | Drinking Pattern | | | |
|---|---|---|---|---|---|---|
| | | | Time | Social Setting | Place | Beverage |
| Strayer[28] (1961) | Outpatients— Bridgeport, Ct. 44 Blacks (B) 1,264 Whites (W) | | Daily: 68% B 59% W Weekend: 22% B 15% W Periodic: 10% B 26% W | With others: 58% B 51% W No Preference: 27% B 26% W Alone: 15% B 23% W | | Wine: 30% B 6% W Whiskey: 30% B 9% W Beer: 15% B 40% W |
| Rimmer et al.[30] (1971) | Inpatients - St. Louis, Mo. (two hospitals) 63 Blacks (B) 196 Whites (W) | Given by sex, race, and hospital. For public hospital mean age: B men 14.8 yrs. W men 17.7 yrs. | "Bender" and morning drinking given by sex, race and hospital. Benders: B women 62% W women 39% Morning drinking: B 89% W 67% | | | Higher percentage of Blacks drink over 32 oz. spirits weekly. (Percentages given by sex, race and hospital.) |

**Table 4.4   Drinking Behavior of Blacks Engaged in Alcoholism Treatment Programs (cont.)**

| Source (Publication date) | Sample | Age of First Drink | Drinking Pattern | | | |
|---|---|---|---|---|---|---|
| | | | Time | Social Setting | Place | Beverage |
| Zimberg et al.[31] (1971) | Outpatients - Harlem, NYC 79 Blacks | | Most patients were in the "severe" category on a six-point Scale of Alcohol Abuse, which "uses observable areas of impairment of functioning, such as social and occupational impairment, the number of intoxications, problems with the law related to drinking, health problems related to drinking, and signs of addiction to alcohol." | | | |
| Viamontes and Powell[34] (1974) | Inpatients - St. Louis, Mo. 100 (Blacks) (B) 100 (Whites) (W) | Means: B 15.7 yrs. W 19.0 yrs. | | | | |
| Novick, Hudson and German[36] (1974) | Inpatients - Harlem, NYC 66 Blacks 11 Puerto Ricans 4 Whites | | "Almost all of the 81 men had long drinking histories, consuming large amounts of wine and/or whiskey for most of their adult lives." | | | |

* Blank boxes indicate data not available.

Table 4.5   Symptoms of Alcoholism and Other Problems of Blacks Engaged in Alcoholism Treatment Programs*

| Source (Publication Date) | Sample | Symptoms (or Signs) | | Medical Complications | | Other Drugs | | Suicidal Behavior |
|---|---|---|---|---|---|---|---|---|
| | | Blackouts | Physical Dependence | Liver Disease | Other | Addiction (mainly heroin) | Use | |
| Vitols[11] (1968) | Inpatients - North Carolina 100 Blacks (B) 200 Whites (W) | 20% B 35% W | Anecdotal account of blacks experiencing delirium tremens in early twenties vs. late twenties or older for whites. | | | | | |
| Rimmer et al.[30] (1971) | Inpatients - St. Louis, Mo. (two hospitals) 63 Blacks (B) 196 Whites (W) | 74% males 62% females (Given by sex, race, and hospital— no racial difference.) | Delirium tremens and alcoholic hallucinosis given by sex, race, and hospital. DT's: B 54% W 26% Hallucinosis: B 47% W 16% | B 6% W 20% (Given by sex, race, and hospital.) | Given by sex, race, and hospital when this was the reason for hospital admission. | B 44% W 10% in public hospital (given by sex, race, and hospital.) | Given by sex, race, and hospital. | Given by sex, race, and hospital when this was the reason for hospital admission. |
| Zimberg et al.[31] (1971) | Outpatients - Harlem, NYC 79 Blacks | See summary statement in Table 4.4 | | | | | | |
| Gross et al.[32] (1972) | Inpatients - Brooklyn, NYC 272 Blacks (B) 279 Whites (W) | | Blacks had a "significantly higher incidence of hallucinations, especially visual hallucinations not associated with auditory hallucinations." | Whites had a "significantly higher incidence of medical complications, particularly hepatic disease." | | | | |

**Table 4.5   Symptoms of Alcoholism and Other Problems of Blacks Engaged in Alcoholism Treatment Programs\* (cont.)**

| Source (Publication) Date) | Sample | Symptoms (or Signs) Blackouts | Physical Dependence | Medical Complications Liver Disease | Other | Other Drugs Addiction (mainly heroin) | Use | Suicidal Behavior |
|---|---|---|---|---|---|---|---|---|
| German[33] (1973) | Inpatients - Harlem, NYC 101 Blacks 15 Puerto Ricans 6 Whites | | On admission: 42% in withdrawal 12% with DT's. History of seizures: 23% History of withdrawal seizures: 13% History of DT's 29% | 81% | Majority of patients had some problem. Detailed distribution of conditions given. | 27% | | |
| Viamontes and Powell[34] (1974) | Inpatients - St. Louis, Mo. 100 Blacks (B) 100 Whites (W) | B 82% W 89% | History of seizures: B 16%    W 7% History of hallucinations: B 79%    W 57% History of DT's: B 48%    W 38% | "Medical complications and poor social performance attributable or related to alcoholism characterized the sample." | | | | |
| Novick, Hudson, and German[36] (1974) | Inpatients - Harlem, NYC 66 Blacks (B) 11 Puerto Ricans (PR) 4 Whites (W) | | On admission: 31% in withdrawal 9% with DT's History of seizures: 15% History of withdrawal seizures: 14% | 77% | Majority of patients had some problem. Distribution of conditions given. | 28% Total B   27% PR 45% | | |

\* Blank boxes indicate data not available.

by ethnicity because the composition of black and Puerto Rican male subjects in their studies approximates that of the treatment group represented as "total men" in Chapter 5 of this book. Note that in the tables some subjects may be represented twice because of overlap of subjects in the two articles[33, 36] from the Harlem Model Cities Program.

Table 4.3 presents demographic data. Most of the studies describe men only. The table indicates that blacks engaged in alcoholism treatment tend to be in their late thirties. Rates of marital disruption vary from study to study and baseline community statistics that might help reconcile the differences are not supplied. Few studies present educational or occupational information. Two studies [28, 35] indicate about 80% of their black subjects have not completed high school (vs. 54% of U.S. blacks). Two studies[28, 36] link 75–85% of their black subjects with unskilled or semi-skilled positions. In at least one of these studies[36] the vast majority of subjects were unemployed at the time of data collection.

Tables 4.4 and 4.5 present alcohol-related data. Black men in two studies[30, 34] (Table 4.4) had an average age of first drink of about 15 years, about three years younger than their white counterparts. The columns in Table 4.4 summarizing drinking pattern information are at least useful as a demonstration of lack of standardization and the resulting inability to compare studies. Under "time of drinking," for example, one study[28] reports daily drinking, another[30] morning drinking, and a third[36] offers a summary statement.

Three studies [11, 30, 34] provide data on blackouts. Within each study there are no dramatic black-white differences, though there is a tendency for a higher percentage of whites to report blackouts. The variation between studies is striking, however, with 20% of blacks reporting blackouts in one study[11] and 82% in another.[34]

The sample sizes recorded in Tables 4.3, 4.4, and 4.5 are small — at least for the black segments of the study populations — and thereby emphasize the limitations of available knowledge about blacks with alcohol problems. The data in Chapter 5 add to this slowly expanding body of information.

## HISPANICS

Puerto Ricans* predominate among New York City Hispanics. Cubans and Central and South Americans are also well represented. Mexican-Americans are the largest group of Hispanics in the continental United States, but they are concentrated in the West and Southwest rather than the Northeast. Bullough and Bullough[37] point out that these rapidly growing Hispanic minority groups have distinct traditions, even though they are characterized by a common language and are often grouped together for statistical purposes by their Spanish surnames. It seems appropriate here to review alcohol studies drawn from any of these groups, in part because there are so few studies overall and in part, of course, because these cultures have similarities even though they are not identical. It should be emphasized, however, that specific results obtained from any one of these groups should not be generalized to the others.

Quantitative data, such as that on black Americans summarized in the previous section, is in short supply. Some Puerto Ricans are included with blacks in three study samples cited already, [33, 35, 36] but the quantitative material describes only the total sample — not blacks and Puerto Ricans separately. Jessor and colleagues,[38] in their Tri-Ethnic Community Study, collected suitable detailed information from a Mexican-American group; but their presentation follows the dictates of their social hypothesis testing and they do not present descriptive drinking pattern data. Wanberg and Horn,[39] after administering an alcohol-use questionnaire** to alcoholic inpatients (in Denver, Colorado),

---

*Puerto Rican (or Cuban, etc.) here designates a person with cultural ties to Puerto Rico (or Cuba, etc.), as by birth or ancestry.

**For a discussion of their research instrument see Jacobson, G. R., *The alcoholisms* (New York: Human Sciences Press, 1976), pp. 75–112.

compared the responses of 191 Hispanics, 72 blacks, and 1,622 whites. They analyzed eight symptom-behavior factors.

> The hypothesis that minority ethnic groups would have higher scores on the severity-wine pattern was supported for only the Hispano in the female sample and for both Blacks and Hispanos in the male sample. Male Hispanos also scored higher on the gregarious-beer pattern, meaning that, in comparison to them, Whites and Blacks would tend more toward the solitary drinking pattern (at home and alone). Whites scored higher on the shame, resentment, and fear factor than either Blacks or Hispanos. Hispanos are less apt to seek help for alcoholism than Blacks or Whites. (p. 111)

The remaining literature on Western Hemisphere Hispanics incorporated here clusters around two themes: (1) *machismo* values bear upon Hispanic drinking practices and (2) Puerto Ricans, in comparison to other non-Hispanic or Hispanic minorities, experience extreme deprivation.

## Machismo

The Latin ideal of manliness, or *machismo*, appears consistently in discussions of Hispanic drinking practices. In his 1964 paper on environmental contributors to alcoholism among certain south Texas Mexican-Americans, Madsen[40] views the drinking of beer and liquor as an important way young men assert themselves against parental authority. However, while it is macho to drink gregariously and hold one's liquor, it is also macho to preserve one's dignity and integrity. So while pursuit of the male ideal encourages drinking, drunken excesses may lead to loss of face and self-esteem. While these two influences might be expected to produce ambivalence toward alcohol consumption, Madsen observes that this is not the case. "Despite the realization of the dangers inherent to over-indulgence, Mexican-American society is extremely tolerant of male drinking which does not violate the individual's ideal relations with others" (p. 358). In fact, one of the factors Madsen cites as stressful to Mexican-Americans who attempt cultural transfer to the Anglo-

American way of life is the ambivalence toward drinking that exists in *that* culture.

Similarly, in the context of a discussion of Puerto Rican culture, *machismo*, and alcoholism, Abad and Suarez[41] note a "great tolerance of Puerto Rican culture towards the consumption of alcohol and its behavioral manifestations" (p. 286). With regard to culture, *machismo*, and alcoholism, these authors are much more psychodynamically oriented than Madsen. They cite child-rearing practices "characterized by over-indulgence of male offspring, encouragement of dependence on mothers, and inconsistencies regarding control and expression of basic drives, so that adulthood poses problems of low frustration tolerance" (p. 287). They view discrepancies between practices in the rearing of male children and the expected macho behavior during development as productive of later anxiety, unresolved dependency, and insecurity regarding one's masculinity. Abad and Suarez then explain excessive or negative macho behavior as a defense against unconscious dependency and passivity needs through reaction formation. They take essentially the same aspect of the macho ideal that Madsen viewed as a moderator of drinking behavior— "a macho should be able to control alcohol and ingest large quantities of alcohol without showing drunkenness"[41] (p. 287)— and view it as a factor that heightens anxiety when the ideal is *not* met. Because the anxiety is then treated with more alcohol, the macho ideal becomes a potentiator of drinking rather than a moderator.

Abad and Suarez cite an earlier cross-cultural study that assigned a central role to dependency conflict in the genesis of drinking. Recapitulating the earlier theory, they

> suspect that the Puerto Rican culture fosters high consumption of alcohol in several ways: 1) as a way to alleviate anxiety and tension; 2) because alcohol may be very attractive to individuals with dependency conflicts; and 3) because it allows the indulgence of fantasies of the macho image. In addition to the high degree of tolerance for drinking and aberrant behavior among Puerto Ricans, we hypothesize that public drunkenness will be rare. Two factors are operative here. First, a macho should not

make a fool of himself publicly and expose himself to such embarrassment, and second, his preference for social drinking with friends or relatives insures a protective environment for his drunkenness.[41] (p. 287)

Abad and Suarez cite alcohol consumption data placing Puerto Rico tenth among 21 countries in total ethanol consumption per person, but *first* in the consumption of hard liquor. Since liquor is considered a manly drink, this fits the macho ideal and supports their suspicion that Puerto Rican culture fosters high alcohol consumption. From their second hypothesis, Abad and Suarez predicted that Puerto Ricans should have a lower number of arrests for public intoxication than other ethnic groups. New Haven, Connecticut, statistics for alcohol arrests in 1971 bore this out, with Puerto Ricans having proportionately fewer alcohol arrests than either blacks or whites.

Returning to Mexican-Americans, a paper by Trevino[42] again emphasizes *machismo* as a positive influence—one with potential for controlling drinking behavior. Trevino complains that some researchers pay attention only to exaggerated, stereotyped (negative) macho attributes and accept *machismo* as a cause of drinking problems. Trevino feels other factors such as psychological problems, economic deprivation, and discrimination are of fundamental importance in the production of problem drinking and receive insufficient attention in the literature.

There seems to be agreement, then, that *machismo* values influence drinking practices,[40-42] though some might argue that the influence is a moderating one[40, 42] and others that it is an accelerating influence.[41] Another area of accord is that Hispanics, or at least Puerto Ricans and Mexican-Americans, have strong cultural support for drinking.[40-43] There is acceptance of drunkenness when it is male behavior. Women, however, may be allowed or even encouraged to drink, but drunken behavior is not accepted.[42, 43] A final point, and one carefully emphasized in these papers,[40-43] is that important cultural factors such as *machismo* must be understood and addressed by treatment or prevention programs serving Hispanic groups.

## Extreme Deprivation

Chapter 3 provided a general discussion of how difficult living conditions may contribute to alcohol problems. Puerto Ricans seem to occupy the lowest socioeconomic position in our society, so it might be assumed that they have an exceptionally high risk of developing alcohol problems. Again, Puerto Ricans constitute the largest Hispanic population in New York City and make up 29% of the total population of the Bronx.

There is substantial evidence that mainland Puerto Ricans experience extreme deprivation. Public recognition of this, however, has been very slow to emerge. In 1973, Torres de Gonzalez[43] cited census data and Department of Labor statistics to argue:

> Comparing the Puerto Ricans to the White community and the Black community, Puerto Ricans as a group have the greatest number of young people, the greatest number of those uneducated and miseducated, the greatest number of unemployed and the largest group of the most recent non-English dominant immigrants.
>
> Puerto Ricans are confronted with dilapidated housing, menial jobs, low wages, poor health services and a demeaning educational system in a country where a nice home and a job with good prospects and built-in promotions is the norm. Where how much you make is contingent on how much schooling you've had and how much you make is how much you're worth. Add to this the fact that Puerto Ricans identify along ethnic-cultural-national lines in a society that can only define in terms of Black and White and you can appreciate the many forces that create pressure on the Puerto Ricans. *We are the most victimized minority in the Northeast region of the U.S.* (pp. 4–5, italics added)

Somewhat later, two federal studies reached the same conclusion, first with regard to Puerto Ricans in New York City and then to Puerto Ricans throughout the continental United States. A report issued in early 1976 by the Department of Labor's Bureau of Labor Statistics indicated that "Puerto Ricans are the least well off of all ethnic groups in New York City for which separate data are available.''[44] Editorial comment on this report included:

> The greatest concentration of human misery in this trouble-beset metropolis is among the million-member Puerto Rican community. They represent only about one-eighth of the total population, yet they constitute between a third and a half of New York City's welfare recipients. Thirty per cent live below the poverty line in terms of family income.[45]

A subsequent study by the United States Commission on Civil Rights established that these conditions are not restricted to the 57% of mainland Puerto Ricans who live in New York City.

> The report said that as of March, 1975, while 11.6 per cent of all American families were below the low income level, this was the case for 32.6 per cent of mainland Puerto Ricans. That compared with 24 per cent for Mexican-Americans and 14.3 per cent for Cuban-Americans.
> Thus, it said, the incidence of poverty and unemployment among Puerto Ricans ''is more severe than that of virtually any ethnic group in the United States.''[46]

Moreover, this 32.6% of people at the poverty level represented an increase from 29% in 1970,[46, 47] indicating the situation is worsening.

Since the appearance of the two federal studies, journalistic sources have continued to emphasize the bottom socioeconomic status of Puerto Ricans.[48] In a cover story on Hispanic Americans, *Time* magazine (16 October 1978) reported:

> Puerto Ricans are even more hard pressed than New York's ghetto blacks; 48% earn less than $7,000 a year, compared with 42% among blacks. The proportion of Puerto Ricans on welfare is 34% vs. 32% for blacks. Among Puerto Ricans over 16 years old, only 6% have completed any job training; the rate for blacks is twice as high. With 14% of New York City's population, Puerto Ricans hold only 3.1% of police department jobs and 1.3% of those in the fire department. (pp. 55–58)

The assumption that these extremely deprived living conditions contribute to high levels of problem drinking among Puerto
Ricans remains to be validated. The descriptive data in Chapter
5 are not applicable to this particular question.

## CULTURE AND PROBLEM DRINKING

Cahalan[25] offers the following tentative paradigm as "one
way of explaining the process of becoming a problem drinker":

> First: the culture must permit drinking, and heavy drinking at
> least occasionally, before the individual can get himself into a
> position to become a problem drinker. Second: given that the
> culture is permissive of heavy drinking under at least some
> circumstances, the individual may become a heavy drinker under
> circumstances permitted him in his sex, age, ethnic, social-class,
> and other roles. Third: an individual may find himself suddenly
> to be a problem drinker because of a change in the cultural
> environment; for example, he moves or marries or ages *out* of an
> environment permissive of heavy drinking, but still remains a
> heavy drinker. Fourth: given that the individual may have formed a
> habit of heavy drinking which he discovers to have become
> maladaptive in his environment, he may continue as a heavy
> drinker under one or more of the following circumstances: (a) if
> his social adaptability is hampered by a highly impulsive tendency
> toward resorting to short-term gratifications, he may continue to
> drink heavily even in the face of social disapprobation; (b) if the
> gradient between his usual subjective condition when he is not
> drinking and the way he feels when drinking is a steep one (such
> as might stem from either a highly alienated, neurotic, or depres-
> sive personality, or *living under conditions of high subjective
> deprivation of the worthwhile things in life*), *he may continue to
> drink heavily because of the powerful reinforcements obtained
> from drinking and the lack of rewards for not drinking.* Fifth:
> given that the individual has become a heavy drinker to the point
> where it has occasioned problems for him in his environment, he
> may continue heavy drinking if that environment is modified to
> be more permissive (such as by his becoming separated from
> such significant others as his family, his work associates, and his

cultural peers). (pp. 151–152; "out" italicized in original, remaining italics added)

Cahalan's explanation covers more contingencies than need be developed here. The preceding sections show that the cultures of blacks and Hispanics in America meet Cahalan's basic conditions leading to problem drinking—permissiveness of both drinking and heavy drinking. Blacks and Hispanics also experience the reinforcing conditions of deprivation and alienation.

## Chapter 5

# INNER-CITY CASE STUDY

This study presents characteristics of patients who entered
treatment at the Alcoholism Unit of the Dr. Martin Luther King
Jr. Health Center (MLKHC) from January 1973 through April
1975. Written records of intake interviews are the source of
information. The study was done to formalize and advance
program planning for the Alcoholism Unit and to provide a
foundation for more sophisticated future research. Patient characteristics are presented in detail so that other treatment groups
may be compared with this one. Analysis of results, particularly
regarding ethnic differences, continues in Chapter 6.

Case studies have limited applications. Other studies complement this one in the ensuing chapters, which explore practical
implications of this work.

## METHODS

### Subjects, Interviews, and Sampling

Most patients who come to the MLKHC Alcoholism Unit
present presumptive evidence of a drinking problem, often sub-

stantiated by a referral note or phone call. They may or may not perceive themselves as alcoholic. From March 1971 until June 1976 the format for data collection at patient intake was the Information Sheet, which is reproduced in the Appendix (see Chapter 7 for comments on the subsequent format). An Information Sheet was filled out by an alcoholism counselor during each patient's intake interview. These interviews were held as soon as feasible in the process of caring for each patient. Often interviews were on the day of first contact with a patient but intoxication, an alcohol withdrawal state, or other difficulties on that day sometimes precluded a detailed interview. Missing data were sometimes entered by a counselor during a future visit, but some patients did not recontact the program and were not reached by follow-up efforts. Ease of handling incomplete data sets was an important factor in determining which computerized statistical system to use for this study.

All interviews were conducted at the East 171st Street Alcoholism Unit (a later relocation of the unit is described in Chapter 7). The alcoholism counselors who conducted the interviews and therefore filled out the Information Sheets were all either black or Hispanic. Most of these counselors had personal experience with alcoholism or drug addiction.

Every patient record on file in the Alcoholism Unit was examined and a list was made of all patients who first came to the unit in 1973, 1974, and the first four months of 1975. The Information Sheets for these patients were evaluated for completeness. Those with insufficient information for analysis (e.g., name and address were the only data recorded) were excluded from the sample. Rather than limit the study to a random or systematic sample, the entire group of adequate Information Sheets was used.

## Coding and Data Processing

The content of the Information Sheets was coded and entered in numerial form on code sheets for transfer to Hollerith cards (IBM cards). Punched cards were prepared from the code sheets by the MLKHC Data Processing Department. Basic statistics, frequencies, and various cross-tabulations were obtained using the Data-Text System.* In analysis, probabilities of 0.05 or less have been considered statistically significant.

The Information Sheets did not provide a record of ethnicity. To allow analysis by this variable, each name on the list of patients in the sample was judged either Hispanic or non-Hispanic (coded "other"). The judge was a medical student, bilingual in English and Spanish and of Puerto Rican parentage. His decisions were corroborated by one of the alcoholism counselors with similar linguistic and ethnic qualifications. In data presentation the "other" category has been labelled "black". This substitution is justified because white non-Hispanic patients were virtually nonexistent in this treatment population.

Responses to the question about "D.T.'s" generally were specific descriptions of hallucinatory experiences. Unspecified yeses, visual hallucinations, and auditory hallucinations were coded separately.**

*What* subjects drink was coded as beer, wine, or liquor. *How much* subjects drink was coded in number of pints of beer, wine, or liquor per day. Since subjects frequently reported use of multiple beverages, a variable was defined to represent the number of pints of ethanol consumed per day.

Information about parents and siblings was generally inadequate to establish family histories of alcoholism. Place of education was not recorded often enough to provide a sense of where members of the study group spent their childhood.

---

*Data-Text System, OS/360 Version, Release 3.1x, of the Columbia University Center for Computing Activities. For background and details of Data-Text, see Armor, D. J., & Couch, A. S., *Data-Text primer: An introduction to computerized social data analysis* (New York: Free Press, 1972).

---

**These responses are considered no more than crude indicators of past withdrawal reactions. Delirium tremens, or D.T.'s, means different things to different people — and the literature on alcohol withdrawal proves that medical investigators are no exception. Though frequently used minimal criteria for delirium tremens are tremor, hallucinations, and disorientation, these criteria were *not* explicitly used during completion of the Information Sheets.

## RESULTS

*Administrative and Demographic Data*

The roster of patients who first came to the Alcoholism Unit during the study period included 409 names. Information Sheets on 372 (91%) of these patients were adequate for study. Data collection on these forms tended to be more complete when the interviews took place later in the study period. The tables below identify missing entries either in footnotes or as "not indicated."

SOURCE OF REFERRAL. Forty percent of patients came to the program via health care institutions (MLKHC plus other health institutions; see Table 5.1). A substantial group came via quasi-legal channels (courts, the Addiction Services Agency, etc.). An adverse effect of this referral pattern is discussed in Chapter 7.

In Table 5.1, the 96 patients referred by public institutions or programs include 34 (35%) from the Addiction Services Agency (ASA) Central Referral Unit, 21 (22%) from courts, 14 (15%) from the ASA Mobile Unit, and 12 (13%) from parole officers. A number of the remaining 15 were from the City Department of Social Services. Of the 62 MLKHC referrals, 27 (44%) were from specified team physicians and 10 (16%) from specified family health workers.

### Table 5.1
### Source of Referral

| Source | Number | (Percent) |
|---|---|---|
| Public institutions or programs (courts, Addiction Services Agency, etc.) | 96 | (26%) |
| Health institutions | 85 | (23%) |
| MLKHC | 62 | (17%) |
| Walk-in | 39 | (10%) |
| Alcoholics Anonymous | 19 | ( 5%) |
| Family or friends | 19 | ( 5%) |
| Employer | 7 | ( 2%) |
| Not indicated | 45 | (12%) |

RESIDENTIAL STATUS.   Only 19 (5% of study group) subjects had no residence at the time of interview. They are assumed to have been undomiciled or homeless. The group included 10 (53%) black men, 7 (37%) Hispanic men, 1 (5%) black woman, and 1 (5%) Hispanic woman.

CHIEF COMPLAINT AND LAST DRINK.   Most patients (329 or 98% of the 336 subjects with a chief complaint recorded) specifically mentioned drinking as a reason for coming to the program. Of the entire group of 372 patients, 165 (44%) reported consuming alcohol on the day of the interview and 85 (23%) reported drinking the previous day. Sixty (16%) reported drinking during the preceding week and 50 (13%) reported *not* drinking during the preceding week. (Last drink was not indicated for 12 subjects.)

AGE AND SEX.   Alcoholism Unit patients were generally men near the end of their fourth decade. The age distribution of the study group, by sex, is illustrated in Figure 5.1. The mean age of the 372 subjects was 39.0 years (S.D. 10.2). The 305 (82%) men had a mean age of 39.2 years (S.D. 10.6) and the 67 (18%) women a mean age of 38.0 years (S.D. 7.7).

ETHNICITY.   The study group was predominantly black. It included 273 (73%) blacks and 99 (27%) Hispanics. There were 217 black men (mean age 38.9, S.D. 11.1), 88 Hispanic men (mean age 40.5, S.D. 9.5), 56 black women (mean age 38.1, S.D. 7.6), and 11 Hispanic women (mean age 38.6, S.D. 6.5).

EDUCATION.   Well over half the study group had some high school education and a quarter of the group had completed high school. Table 5.2 presents years of education by sex and ethnicity. Compared to blacks, Hispanics were undereducated (see Chapter 6). The subjects reporting 12 or more years of education include 15 black men and 3 black women with some college or other post-high school formal education.

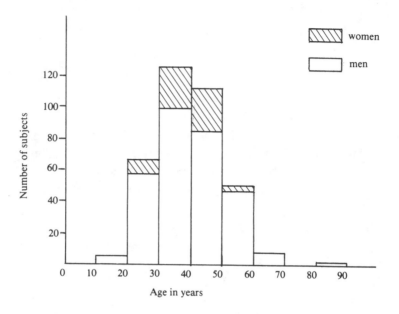

Figure 5.1    Age Distribution of Sample by Sex

MILITARY SERVICE.    Of the 296 men with relevant information recorded, 93 (31%) had served in the military. Seventy-six, or 82%, of those who served were black; 17 (18%) were Hispanic. None of the women in the sample reported military service.

MARITAL STATUS.    Overall, 40% of the subjects were married. Details or marital status by race and ethnicity are presented in Table 5.3. The proportion of married subjects actually living with their spouses at the time of interview could not be determined from the Information Sheets. Drinking habits of the spouses of married or previously married subjects were not recorded often enough to permit comparisons.

**Table 5.2**
**Years of Education by Sex and Ethnicity***

|  | Subjects | Years of Education** | | | |
|---|---|---|---|---|---|
|  |  | Less than 6 | 6 to 9 | 9 to 12 | 12 or more*** |
| MEN | Black men (n=211) | 15 (7%) | 51 (24%) | 79 (37%) | 66 (31%) |
|  | Hispanic men (n=86) | 23 (27%) | 28 (33%) | 24 (28%) | 11 (13%) |
|  | Total men (n=297) | 38 (13%) | 79 (27%) | 103 (35%) | 77 (26%) |
| WOMEN | Black women (n=54) | 1 (2%) | 9 (17%) | 29 (54%) | 15 (28%) |
|  | Hispanic women (n=11) | 2 (18%) | 3 (27%) | 3 (27%) | 3 (27%) |
|  | Total women (n=65) | 3 (5%) | 12 (18%) | 32 (49%) | 18 (28%) |
|  | Total Subjects (N=362) | 41 (11%) | 91 (25%) | 135 (37%) | 95 (26%) |

* Years of education not indicated for 10 subjects.
** Percents are of *row* totals.
*** All subjects in this category reported completing high school.

WORK HISTORY.    Job skills were poor; 75% of patients had no experience beyond the operative and unskilled levels. Past employment by sex and ethnicity appears in Table 5.4.

Employed/unemployed status at the time of interview was recorded for less than half the subjects. Of the 162 subjects with this recorded, 119 (73%) were unemployed. There were 33 black men, 7 Hispanic men, and 3 black women identified as employed.

ARRESTS.    Over half of the subjects in the entire sample (216, or 58%) reported prior arrests. Prior arrests by sex and ethnicity are presented in Table 5.5.

Table 5.3
Marital Status by Sex and Ethnicity*

| Subjects | | Marital Status** | | | |
|---|---|---|---|---|---|
| | | Single | Married | Divorced or Separated | Widowed |
| MEN | Black men (n=199) | 61 (31%) | 78 (39%) | 59 (30%) | 1 (0.5%) |
| | Hispanic men (n=84) | 24 (29%) | 37 (44%) | 20 (24%) | 3 (4%) |
| | Total men (n=283) | 85 (30%) | 115 (41%) | 79 (28%) | 4 (1%) |
| WOMEN | Black women (n=54) | 12 (22%) | 20 (37%) | 19 (35%) | 3 (6%) |
| | Hispanic women (n=10) | 3 (30%) | 5 (50%) | 2 (20%) | |
| | Total women (n=64) | 15 (23%) | 25 (39%) | 21 (33%) | 3 (5%) |
| | Total Subjects (N=347) | 100 (29%) | 140 (40%) | 100 (29%) | 7 (2%) |

* Marital status not indicated for 25 subjects.
** Percents are of *row* totals.

TYPICAL PATIENT.   The typical new patient of the Alcoholism Unit during the study period was a 39-year-old black man referred from a nearby hospital or from MLKHC. He would acknowledge alcohol consumption within the past day or two and that drinking had something to do with his presentation to the unit. He would have at least some high school education but no job skills and no job. He might be married, he would have a place to live, and he would have a history of one or more arrests.

Table 5.4
Past Employment by Sex and Ethnicity*

| Subjects | | Type of job** | | | | | | |
|---|---|---|---|---|---|---|---|---|
| | | Operative | Unskilled | Skilled | Clerical | Managerial | Student | Never Worked |
| MEN | Black men (n=200) | 80 (40%) | 80 (40%) | 29 (14.5%) | 6 (3%) | 1 (0.5%) | 3 (1.5%) | 1 (0.5%) |
| | Hispanic men (n=81) | 35 (43%) | 27 (33%) | 13 (16%) | 5 (6%) | | | 1 (1%) |
| | Total men (n=281) | 115 (41%) | 107 (38%) | 42 (15%) | 11 (4%) | 1 (0.4%) | 3 (1%) | 2 (0.7%) |
| WOMEN | Black women (n=54) | 19 (35%) | 13 (24%) | 8 (15%) | 5 (9%) | 1 (2%) | 1 (2%) | 7 (13%) |
| | Hispanic women (n=11) | | 5 (45%) | 1 (9%) | 1 (9%) | | | 4 (36%) |
| | Total women (n=65) | 19 (29%) | 18 (28%) | 9 (14%) | 6 (9%) | 1 (2%) | 1 (2%) | 11 (17%) |
| | Total Subjects (N=346) | 134 (39%) | 125 (36%) | 51 (15%) | 17 (5%) | 2 (0.6%) | 4 (1%) | 13 (4%) |

* Type of past employment not indicated for 26 subjects.
** Percents are of row totals.

**Table 5.5**
**Prior Arrests by Sex and Ethnicity***

| Subjects | | Prior Arrests** | |
|---|---|---|---|
| | | Yes | No |
| MEN | Black men (n=189) | 141 (75%) | 48 (25%) |
| | Hispanic men (n=78) | 52 (67%) | 26 (33%) |
| | Total men (n=267) | 193 (72%) | 74 (28%) |
| WOMEN | Black women (n=49) | 19 (39%) | 30 (61%) |
| | Hispanic women (n=8) | 4 (50%) | 4 (50%) |
| | Total women (n=57) | 23 (40%) | 34 (60%) |
| | Total subjects (N=324) | 216 (67%) | 108 (33%) |

*Prior arrests not indicated for 48 subjects.
**Percents are of *row* totals.

## Clinical Data

DRUG USE.   About 40% of subjects acknowledged previous non-medical use of drugs besides alcohol. Previous use of heroin, cocaine, marijuana, or other mood-changing drugs was positively or negatively recorded for 328 (88%) subjects. Of these, 132 (40%) acknowledged previous drug use with 14 having been addicted to substances other than alcohol—generally opiates in the form of heroin or methadone. The group with a history of addiction consisted of 6 black men, 2 Hispanic men, 4 black women, and 2 Hispanic women. The previous drug users without a history of addiction consisted of 76 black men, 31 Hispanic men, 9 black women, and 2 Hispanic women. There were 107 black men, 48 Hispanic men, 38 black women, and 3 Hispanic women who denied drug use.

PRIOR HELP.   Positive or negative responses concerning previous psychiatric or alcoholism treatment were recorded for most subjects (360, or 97%). A majority of this group (58%) had not had treatment. The untreated group included 135 (65%) black men, 44 (21%) Hispanic men, 23 (11%) black women, and 5 (2%) Hispanic women.

Among the 153 (43%) subjects reporting prior help, about half (79, or 52%) reported short-term involvement in treatment. This group reported about one week of prior help and included 41 (52%) black men, 24 (30%) Hispanic men, 12 (15%) black women, and 2 (3%) Hispanic women. One month of treatment was reported by 44 (29%) subjects in the treated group, including 23 (52%) black men, 11 (25%) Hispanic men, 7 (16%) black women, and 3 (7%) Hispanic women. Six months of treatment or more was reported by the remaining 30 (20%) subjects in the treated group. This long-term treatment group included 16 (53%) black men, 4 (13%) Hispanic men, and 10 (33%) black women.

Prior alcohol detoxification does not appear explicitly on the form, but this information was recorded for 173 (47%) subjects. Of these, 29 (17%) reported they had been detoxified. This comparatively small group consisted of 22 (76%) black men, 4 (14%) Hispanic men, and 3 (10%) black women.

LONGEST SOBER PERIOD.   Data on the duration of subjects' longest sober period is shown in Table 5.6. Twenty-six (7%) subjects reported sober periods of a year or more, 17 (5%) subjects reported periods of 6 months.

SUICIDE AND TRAUMA.   Histories of suicide attempts were obtained from 1 black man, 2 Hispanic men, 2 black women, and 1 Hispanic woman. Alcohol-related head injuries were reported by 14 black men, 8 Hispanic men, 10 black women, and 3 Hispanic women.

### Table 5.6    Longest Sober Period by Sex and Ethnicity

| Subjects | | Longest Sober Period | | | | | | |
|---|---|---|---|---|---|---|---|---|
| | | None | One Day | One Week | One Month | Six Months | Year or More | Not Indicated |
| MEN | Black Men (n=217) | 33 | 36 | 56 | 18 | 8 | 15 | 51 |
| | Hispanic Men (n=88) | 13 | 12 | 16 | 17 | 7 | 8 | 15 |
| | Total Men (n=305) | 46 | 48 | 72 | 35 | 15 | 23 | 66 |
| WOMEN | Black Women (n=56) | 6 | 12 | 19 | 7 | 2 | 2 | 8 |
| | Hispanic Women (n=11) | 3 | 2 | 4 | 1 | | 1 | |
| | Total Women (n=67) | 9 | 14 | 23 | 8 | 2 | 3 | 8 |
| | Total Subjects (N=372) | 55 | 62 | 95 | 43 | 17 | 26 | 74 |

OTHER SYMPTOMS.    Symptoms related to gastrointestinal bleeding, a common complication of alcohol excess, were reported by several subjects. These symptoms were generally not active at the time of interview. Vomiting blood was reported by 24 (11%*) black men, 6 (7%) Hispanic men, 9 (16%) black women, and 1 (9%) Hispanic women. Rectal bleeding was cited by 12 (6%) black men and 7 (8%) Hispanic men. One black man mentioned internal bleeding.

Difficulty eating — which could be related to either heavy

*Percent figures here refer to ethnic-sex group: 24 is 11% of the black men in the total study group.

drinking or to alcohol withdrawal—was reported by 129 (59%) black men, 55 (63%) Hispanic men, 40 (71%) black women, and 8 (73%) Hispanic women. Difficulty sleeping—a frequent concomitant of alcohol withdrawal—was reported by 129 (59%) black men, 61 (69%) Hispanic men, 39 (70%) black women, and 7 (64%) Hispanic women.

MEDICATION. Use of medication was reported by 74 (34%*) black men, 26 (30%) Hispanic men, 31 (55%) black women, and 5 (45%) Hispanic women. This includes tranquilizer use by 35 (16%) black men, 11 (13%) Hispanic men, 17 (30%) black women, and 2 (18%) Hispanic women. Non-aspirin analgesic use was reported by 8 black men, 1 Hispanic man, and 3 black women. Antidepressant use was reported by 2 black women. Four black men, 1 black woman, and 1 Hispanic woman reported methadone use and 1 black man reported disulfiram (Antabuse) use.

DRINKING HISTORY.

*Age of First Drink.* Subjects tended to report they began drinking in their mid- to late teens, but there was considerable variation around this central tendency. Detailed data on age of first drink appear in Table 5.7.

*Alcohol Consumption.* Data on alcoholic-beverage preference appear in Table 5.8. The beverages favored by each of the two ethnic groups are discussed in Chapter 6.

Estimates of usual daily consumption of each alcoholic beverage were not consistently recorded. Available data provided the following estimates of mean total daily *alcohol*** consumption:

---

*Percent figures here refer to ethnic-sex group: 74 is 34% of the black men in the total study group.

**These figures are based on the assumptions that the alcohol content of beer is 6%; of wine, 13%; and of liquor, 40%.

**Table 5.7    Age of First Drink by Sex and Ethnicity***

| | Subjects | <10 | 10–12 | 13–15 | 16–18 | 19–21 | 22–24 | 25–27 | 28–30 | >30 | Mean Age (S.D.) |
|---|---|---|---|---|---|---|---|---|---|---|---|
| | | | | | | Age in Years** | | | | | |
| MEN | Black Men (n=216) | 15 (7%) | 22 (10%) | 69 (32%) | 51 (24%) | 26 (12%) | 9 (4%) | 9 (4%) | 5 (2%) | 10 (5%) | 16.9 (6.1) |
| | Hispanic Men (n=87) | 4 (5%) | 8 (9%) | 25 (29%) | 23 (26%) | 7 (8%) | 5 (6%) | 5 (6%) | 5 (6%) | 5 (6%) | 18.1 (6.9) |
| | Total Men (n=303) | 19 (6%) | 30 (10%) | 94 (31%) | 74 (24%) | 33 (11%) | 14 (5%) | 14 (5%) | 10 (3%) | 15 (5%) | – |
| WOMEN | Black Women (n=52) | 1 (2%) | 3 (6%) | 12 (23%) | 18 (35%) | 11 (21%) | 2 (4%) | 1 (2%) | 0 | 4 (8%) | 18.2 (5.9) |
| | Hispanic Women (n=11) | 0 | 0 | 3 (27%) | 2 (18%) | 1 (9%) | 0 | 0 | 1 (9%) | 4 (36%) | 24.6 (10.0) |
| | Total Women (n=63) | 1 (2%) | 3 (5%) | 15 (24%) | 20 (32%) | 12 (19%) | 2 (3%) | 1 (2%) | 1 (2%) | 8 (13%) | – |
| | Total Subjects (N=366) | 20 (5%) | 33 (9%) | 109 (30%) | 94 (26%) | 45 (12%) | 16 (4%) | 15 (4%) | 11 (3%) | 23 (6%) | |

* Age of first drink not indicated for six subjects.
** Percents are of *row* totals.

**Table 5.8    Alcoholic Beverage Preference by Sex and Ethnicity\***

|  | Subjects | Beer | Wine | Liquor | Beer & Wine | Beer & Liquor | Wine & Liquor | No Preference |
|---|---|---|---|---|---|---|---|---|
| | | | | | *Preferred Beverage\*\** | | | |
| MEN | Black Men (n=215) | 4 (2%) | 45 (21%) | 24 (11%) | 9 (4%) | 30 (14%) | 36 (17%) | 67 (31%) |
| | Hispanic Men (n=86) | 4 (5%) | 10 (12%) | 5 (6%) | 2 (2%) | 24 (28%) | 10 (12%) | 31 (36%) |
| | Total Men (n=301) | 8 (3%) | 55 (18%) | 29 (10%) | 11 (4%) | 54 (18%) | 46 (15%) | 98 (33%) |
| WOMEN | Black Women (n=54) | 1 (2%) | 3 (6%) | 13 (24%) | 0 | 11 (20%) | 12 (22%) | 14 (26%) |
| | Hispanic Women (n=11) | 1 (9%) | 2 (18%) | 2 (18%) | 1 (9%) | 0 | 3 (27%) | 2 (18%) |
| | Total Women (n=65) | 2 (3%) | 5 (8%) | 15 (23%) | 1 (2%) | 11 (17%) | 15 (23%) | 16 (25%) |
| | Total Subjects (N=366) | 10 (3%) | 60 (16%) | 44 (12%) | 12 (3%) | 65 (18%) | 61 (17%) | 114 (31%) |

\* Beverage preference not indicated for six subjects.

\*\* Percents are of *row* totals.

**Table 5.9**
**Time of Drinking by Sex and Ethnicity***

| Subjects | | Time of Drinking** | | | |
|---|---|---|---|---|---|
| | | Daily: A.M. & P.M. | Daily: P.M. Only | Daily: A.M. Only | Weekends |
| MEN | Black Men (n=214) | 184 (86%) | 19 (9%) | 7 (3%) | 4 (2%) |
| | Hispanic Men (n=83) | 71 (86%) | 5 (6%) | 3 (4%) | 4 (5%) |
| | Total Men (n=297) | 255 (86%) | 24 (8%) | 10 (3%) | 8 (3%) |
| WOMEN | Black Women (n=51) | 40 (78%) | 9 (18%) | 2 (4%) | 0 |
| | Hispanic Women (n=11) | 9 (82%) | 2 (18%) | 0 | 0 |
| | Total Women (n=62) | 49 (79%) | 11 (18%) | 2 (3%) | 0 |
| | Total Subjects (N=359) | 304 (85%) | 35 (10%) | 12 (3%) | 8 (2%) |

*Time of drinking not indicated for 13 subjects.
**Percents are of *row* totals.

| | |
|---|---|
| Black men (n=168) | 0.76 pints (S.D. 0.49) |
| Hispanic men (n=66) | 0.88 pints (S.D. 0.58) |
| Black women (n=41) | 0.71 pints (S.D. 0.38) |
| Hispanic women (n=9) | 0.77 pints (S.D. 0.41) |

*Time of Drinking.* Most subjects (85%) reported drinking in the morning and afternoon every day. Time of drinking is further detailed in Table 5.9. The 10% of subjects reporting a pattern of afternoon-only drinking are discussed in greater detail below.

*Drinking Companions.* Information about with whom subjects drink was not indicated on most Information Sheets. There were comments indicating, however, that 94 individuals drank mainly with friends and 7 individuals drank mainly alone.

*Place of Drinking.*    For over 95% of subjects, a usual place of drinking was recorded. Men seemed to prefer drinking in the street. Women showed a strong preference for drinking at home. Details appear in Table 5.10. The categories in the table are mutually exclusive, but the raw data showed some overlap. The "on the job and elsewhere" category was given precedence so some subjects in it, for example, also drink at home.

*Reason for Drinking.*    Answers to "Why do you drink?" were recorded for 285 (77%) subjects. Responses suggesting the person drinks to forget or to distance him- or herself from problems, including family problems, are grouped under "to escape." Subjects drinking for mood change are under "to get high." "I like it" groups responses such as "it tastes good." "Sociability" covers drinking because of peer pressure and drinking to enhance the subject's own social interaction. Some subjects reported drinking for "courage" or in order to help themselves face some difficult situation. Subjects under "can't stop" indicated drinking because of physical or psychological dependency or both. "Don't know" includes only explicit responses; subjects with this item blank on their Information Sheet were counted as not indicated.

The reasons for drinking in these categories are presented in Table 5.11. Escape drinkers accounted for 45% of the responders. If drinking to get high is considered an escapist distraction, this could be expanded to 57%.

SYMPTOMS OF ALCOHOLISM.

*Blackouts.*    A large proportion of subjects (80%) reported blackouts. Since the counselors who conducted the intake interviews had been trained to understand blackouts as periods of amnesia associated with alcohol consumption, this information is presumably reliable. Responses are summarized in Table 5.12.

*Withdrawal.*    Of 207 black men with responses recorded, 83 (40%) reported "D.T.'s." Visual hallucinations were described

### Table 5.10
### Place of Drinking by Sex and Ethnicity*

| Subjects | Place of Drinking** | | | | |
|---|---|---|---|---|---|
| | Street | Home | Bar | On the Job & Elsewhere | Anywhere |
| **MEN** | | | | | |
| Black Men (n=212) | 100 (47%) | 48 (23%) | 16 (8%) | 13 (6%) | 35 (17%) |
| Hispanic Men (n=79) | 36 (46%) | 19 (24%) | 6 (8%) | 3 (4%) | 15 (19%) |
| Total Men (n=291) | 136 (47%) | 67 (23%) | 22 (8%) | 16 (5%) | 50 (17%) |
| **WOMEN** | | | | | |
| Black Women (n=55) | 7 (13%) | 42 (76%) | 1 (2%) | 2 (4%) | 3 (5%) |
| Hispanic Women (n=11) | 4 (36%) | 7 (64%) | 0 | 0 | 0 |
| Total Women (n=66) | 11 (17%) | 49 (74%) | 1 (2%) | 2 (3%) | 3 (5%) |
| Total Subjects (N=357) | 147 (41%) | 116 (32%) | 23 (6%) | 18 (5%) | 53 (15%) |

* Place of drinking not indicated for 15 subjects.
** Percents are of *row* totals.

**Table 5.11 Reason for Drinking by Sex and Ethnicity***

| | Subjects | Reason for Drinking** | | | | | | |
|---|---|---|---|---|---|---|---|---|
| | | To Escape | To Get High | I Like It | Sociability | Courage | Can't Stop | Don't Know |
| MEN | Black Men (n=167) | 67 (40%) | 19 (11%) | 18 (11%) | 19 (11%) | 5 (3%) | 3 (2%) | 36 (22%) |
| | Hispanic Men (n=70) | 35 (50%) | 10 (14%) | 9 (13%) | 2 (3%) | 1 (1%) | 2 (3%) | 11 (16%) |
| | Total Men (n=237) | 102 (43%) | 29 (12%) | 27 (11%) | 21 (9%) | 6 (3%) | 5 (2%) | 47 (20%) |
| WOMEN | Black Women (n=40) | 22 (55%) | 3 (8%) | 6 (15%) | 1 (3%) | 1 (3%) | 1 (3%) | 6 (15%) |
| | Hispanic Women (n=8) | 3 (38%) | 3 (38%) | 1 (13%) | 0 | 0 | 0 | 1 (13%) |
| | Total Women (n=48) | 25 (52%) | 6 (13%) | 7 (15%) | 1 (2%) | 1 (2%) | 1 (2%) | 7 (15%) |
| | Total Subjects (N=285) | 127 (45%) | 35 (12%) | 34 (12%) | 22 (8%) | 7 (2%) | 6 (2%) | 54 (19%) |

* Reason for drinking not indicated for 87 subjects.
** Percents are of *row* totals.

**Table 5.12**
**Blackouts by Sex and Ethnicity**

| Subjects | | Blackouts* | | | | |
|---|---|---|---|---|---|---|
| | | Yes (Frequency Not Specified) | Yes, Often | Yes, Sometimes | Never | Not Indicated |
| MEN | Black Men (n=217) | 76 (35%) | 53 (24%) | 40 (18%) | 38 (18%) | 10 (5%) |
| | Hispanic men (n=88) | 47 (53%) | 15 (17%) | 11 (13%) | 13 (15%) | 2 (2%) |
| | Total Men (n=305) | 123 (40%) | 68 (22%) | 51 (17%) | 51 (17%) | 12 (4%) |
| WOMEN | Black Women (n=56) | 18 (32%) | 17 (30%) | 10 (18%) | 8 (14%) | 3 (5%) |
| | Hispanic Women (n=11) | 9 (82%) | 1 (9%) | 0 | 0 | 1 (9%) |
| | Total Women (n=67) | 27 (40%) | 18 (27%) | 10 (15%) | 8 (12%) | 4 (6%) |
| | Total Subjects (N=372) | 150 (40%) | 86 (23%) | 61 (16%) | 59 (16%) | 16 (4%) |

* Percents are of *row* totals.

by 60 of these men, and auditory hallucinations by 21. Of 80 Hispanic men, 49 (61%) reported D.T.'s (40 with visual, 13 with auditory hallucinations). Of 54 black women, 23 (43%) reported D.T.'s (19 with visual, 7 with auditory hallucinations). Of 11 Hispanic women, 6 (55%) reported D.T.'s (5 with visual, 2 with auditory hallucinations).

Hispanic subjects reported D.T.'s (hallucinations) more frequently than black subjects (60% vs. 41%). The probability that this difference is due to chance alone is less than 0.005 (chi-square with Yates's correction for continuity). The difference between Hispanic men and black men is significant at the same level. (See Chapter 6.)

## Subgroups

THE HOMELESS.   Subjects undomiciled at the time of interview consisted of 10 black men, 7 Hispanic men, 1 black woman, and 1 Hispanic woman. There was no predominant age group—3 were in their 20's.

In comparison to the rest of the study group, this subgroup reported drinking considerably more wine and somewhat less liquor. They were more often divorced or separated. A greater proportion reported prior detoxifications, prior arrests, and prior drug use.

THE AFTERNOON DRINKERS.   Afternoon-only drinkers included 19 black men, 5 Hispanic men, 9 black women, and 2 Hispanic women. Blacks, women, and somewhat older individuals were overrepresented compared to the rest of the study group.

Several trends appeared in further comparisons between the afternoon-only drinkers and the rest of the study group. The afternoon drinkers were more often employed and more often had done skilled or clerical work. Prior drug use was less frequent. Difficulty eating or sleeping was reported less often. Their total daily alcohol consumption was lower. They reported drinking at home much more often and in the street much less often than other subjects. Afternoon drinkers reported blackouts less often than other subjects. (See Chapter 7.)

OTHER TRENDS.   Other subgroups differed from the rest of the study group in the following ways:

- Those who reported a preference for beer and wine also reported more alcohol withdrawal symptoms.

- The beer and wine drinkers more often reported drug use and street drinking.

- Younger drinkers—those in their teens and 20's—were overrepresented among those reporting the street as their usual drinking place.

- Older drinkers—those in their 50's and 60's—were overrepresented among those reporting home as their usual drinking place.

- Men and younger subjects were overrepresented among subjects reporting drug use.

- Previous drug users more often indicated a preference for wine or wine and liquor.

- Those denying previous drug use more often indicated a preference for liquor or liquor and beer.

- Subjects reporting prior drug use or addiction reported previous arrests much more often than other subjects.

- Women were overrepresented in the group reporting drug addiction.

### EXAMPLE CASES

The following case histories describe the personal and medical background, initial Alcoholism Unit interview, and clinical course of seven inner-city alcoholics. These summaries were prepared from Alcoholism Unit records and MLKHC medical records. They also incorporate some verbal comments of Alcoholism Unit staff members and of the patients themselves. To conceal identities, fictitious names have been used and some specific information has been modified. The six patients who were accessible all gave written consent for the record review and for subsequent case-history publication.

### Walker

A city hospital social worker referred Walker, a 40-year-old black man, to the Alcoholism Unit for follow-up care after his inpatient detoxification from alcohol. Although native to New York City, Walker had few relatives in the area. His father was killed in an accident when Walker was 5 years old (Walker's aunt said of his father: "The man drank too much"). His hypertensive, diabetic mother died from her second stroke when Walker was 38. His two sisters were both well and lived, with their families, in eastern Connecticut.

For several years following graduation from high school, Walker worked in an assortment of semi-skilled jobs. He then established a small extermination and pest control business. Both his work life and his marriage of eighteen years had been stormy, at least in part due to Walker's repeated problems with alcohol and other drugs. He had been addicted to heroin and acknowledged occasional cocaine and marijuana use in the past. At age 35, after his fourth detoxification from heroin in a span of 13 years, he discontinued that drug. His more than 25 arrests and seven convictions were "mostly for drugs." In one drug-related incident, he received an abdominal stab wound, which necessitated emergency surgery. Ten years of heavy drinking also took their toll. Walker developed ulcer disease and had been hospitalized with "pneumonia and an enlarged liver." In the six months prior to his initial Alcoholism Unit interview, his business had deteriorated so badly that he had become effectively unemployed. In the same period, he had also become separated from his wife and five children.

Walker first drank at age six. Before his detoxification he was drinking one quart or more of gin per day. He drank in the morning as well as afternoon and drank both at home and in the street. Walker had blackouts "many times" but denied D.T.'s. After two previous alcohol detoxifications he had not become involved in outpatient treatment. Some time before these detoxifications he had, on his own, stopped drinking for a two-year period.

During his initial interview, this dark, heavy-set man hesitated before responding to each question. His eyes were in almost continuous motion, pausing briefly on the interviewer before each of countless circuits around the room. Physical examination showed slight liver enlargement and blood work showed mild elevation of Walker's liver function tests.

At first the impact of treatment was unclear. Walker's visits to the Alcoholism Unit and his AA attendance were erratic. Sometimes he came in sober, other times he was mildly intoxicated. After about two months, however, Walker's visits became more regular. He had stopped drinking. In two more months he was working part time as a cab driver. Gradually the suspicion and tentativeness that characterized Walker's early contacts with the program gave way to a warm gregariousness and an outspoken commitment to sobriety. Before he was sober a full year Walker had rejoined his family and revived his business. Soon he will be sober four years. He has been discharged from the MLKHC program and remains active in AA.

## Consuela

Consuela, a 50-year-old Puerto Rican woman, was brought to the Alcoholism Unit by her MLKHC family health worker. She readily acknowledged "drinking too much."

Consuela had no family history of alcoholism and had completed the fourth grade in Puerto Rico. "Housewife" was her usual occupation and, though she was long separated from her first husband, most of her 13 years in the Bronx she lived with one man. She had, however, occasionally separated from this common-law husband for periods as long as five months.

Violence had punctuated Consuela's life and she seemed to serve as its agent as often as its object. She reported over 20 arrests in Puerto Rico, "mostly for fighting." She gave no history of illicit drug use. Consuela's health problems included recurrent trauma, asthmatic bronchitis, depression with persistent sleep disturbance, and "attacks" (20-year history of losses of consciousness preceded by an aura and associated with distorted body position, partially responsive to phenytoin).

Consuela began drinking at age 11 and was drinking heavily by age 20. She drank "mostly rum" — about one pint per day. Some days, however, she would consume up to 12 cans of beer, three or four pints of wine, or "anything with alcohol." She drank "all day," usually at home and usually alone. She had blackouts "very frequently" and when questioned about D.T.'s described "voices calling me," seeing "people moving," and experiencing extreme nervousness. She admitted to two suicide attempts: she "cut my veins" at age 16 and intentionally took a pill overdose at age 47. Without assistance (in her initial interview Consuela said she "never heard of AA"), she had stopped drinking for a three-month period at age 48. Consuela had once visited a psychiatrist at the urging of a Social Security Administration worker, but she did not keep her follow-up appointment.

In her initial Alcoholism Unit interview Consuela appeared sober. Her facial expressions remained calm even when recounting experiences in which she narrowly escaped being killed. Physical examination revealed multiple laceration scars — at least 12 longer than six centimeters — on her arms, chest, and face. Consuela's liver was not enlarged, though her liver function tests proved slightly elevated. Her neurologic examination was normal except for the presence of Hoffman's sign on the right. A subsequent electroencephalogram (EEG) was interpreted as "minimally abnormal due to a slight increase in generalized slowing." Skull X-rays were normal.

Consuela readily accepted individual counseling and became active in Spanish AA meetings. Antidepressant medication — particularly doxepin hydrochloride — prescribed by her team physician provided some relief from her sleep disturbance and depressed mood. During her first 10 months of treatment her only alcohol consumption consisted of a single can of beer.

One year from the date of her initial interview, however, Consuela was undergoing inpatient alcohol detoxification. Her attendance at the Alcoholism Unit had lapsed and when she resumed contact with her counselor she had been drinking four quarts of beer per day for at least two weeks. The counselor promptly arranged the detoxification.

A month later, when she was again settled in outpatient treatment, she came to her counselor very upset. Consuela eventually disclosed that her distress derived from a conflict with her common-law husband. Their relationship had always been turbulent, but she was now fearful that she might either cut her own wrists or stab her husband. She also worried that he might throw her from their fourth-floor window. A meeting was hastily arranged to include the patient's alcoholism counselor, her family health worker, the Alcoholism Unit physician, and the patient and her husband. In that setting the two were able to air their differences and, though they did not reach any clear agreement in the meeting, at its close they both indicated that their crisis was eased. The same group met the following week. A third meeting was called off when Consuela declared that her situation was better and that she had no desire for additional sessions. A few months later, however, she did pursue a series of individual discussions with a MLKHC mental health professional who focused on her common-law marital relationship.

Consuela did not drink during her second year of treatment and spent most of nearly every weekday in the Alcoholism Unit day room. In spite of her very limited ability to speak English, her comprehension was fair and she attended English as well as Spanish AA meetings. Midway in her second treatment year she was judged medically capable of full-time work, though no job opportunity materialized.

Early in her third year of treatment Consuela drank for three days after an argument with a relative. She returned to treatment on her own, did not need detoxification, and— with more intensive counseling— entered a 15-month sober period. Subsequently she resumed drinking during a two-month stay in Puerto Rico, returned to New York intoxicated, and continued to drink heavily. When her counselor approached her, Consuela readily agreed to inpatient detoxification and after hospital discharge she returned to daily program participation and abstinence from alcohol.

In spite of the relapses during her more than four years in alcoholism treatment, Consuela regards these years as perhaps the most socially and medically stable of her adulthood. Her overall alcohol consumption is far lower than that of her pre-treatment years and, though the trend is not strong, the length of her sober periods is increasing.

## Gary

Gary, a 29-year-old black man, was referred to the Alcoholism Unit from a city hospital by an Addiction Services Agency counselor. The referral followed his sixth admission to that hospital in 18 months (it was also his tenth hospital admission in three years). Most of these hospitalizations were prompted by grand mal seizures.

A Georgia native, Gary lived in New York City for seven years prior to his initial interview. His deceased mother ''had a drinking problem'' and his father, in spite of ''two strokes and bleeding ulcers,'' was ''still drinking.'' Gary considered one of his two siblings to also have a drinking problem. After graduating from high school Gary did not continue formal education even though he was offered a football scholarship to a state university. He worked in plumbing, carpentry, and welding before being drafted into the Army for two years. Gary fought in Viet Nam and left military service with an honorable discharge and extensive scars on his right leg (minimal functional deficit) from shrapnel wounds.

Following his discharge Gary returned to Georgia and skilled labor. He married and had one child. After hardly more than one year of marriage, he and his wife separated and Gary moved north. In New York he trained as a tractor-trailer operator and, for three years, drove for a medium-size trucking company. This job ended abruptly when Gary had a seizure in the trucking company office. He remained unemployed and had been on welfare for two years when he came to the Alcoholism Unit.

Gary's first seizure occurred at age 26, about five months after neurosurgical repair of a penetrating head injury sustained in an auto accident (the accident was apparently not alcohol related). Gary subsequently experienced single grand mal seizures at irregular intervals, always one to two days after particularly heavy drinking or on days of relatively low alcohol consumption. During one seizure-related hospital admission an EEG revealed asymmetric slowing, which was more prominent on the left, the side of his head injury. Phenytoin and phenobarbital seemed to decrease the frequency of his seizures even though Gary generally failed to take these medications as often as prescribed.

Gary began drinking at age 15. Near the time of his initial Alcoholism Unit interview he had been drinking two quarts of wine per day. He drank "anytime, anywhere." He acknowledged frequent blackouts, denied D.T.'s, admitted to three arrests and one short jail sentence for auto theft, and reported that his illicit drug use had been limited to marijuana and cocaine. He had been detoxified from alcohol as an inpatient once but had not previously been involved in outpatient treatment. He gave "to be social and to get high" as his reasons for drinking and "to stop drinking" as his goal in seeking treatment.

Gary did not resist identifying himself as an alcoholic. With a moderate amount of counseling and heavy use of the day room and AA, he discontinued drinking alcohol. When he had been in treatment four months, efforts to help him resume work were unsuccessful. Six months later, however, he was picking up cleaning jobs several days each week and spending increasing time as a volunteer athletic instructor with a neighborhood youth organization.

It is over five years since Gary's initial interview. He has worked steadily as a security guard for nearly three years and continues his work with the youth group. He abstains from alcohol, takes phenytoin daily, and has not had any seizures at all since he stopped drinking. He has been discharged from the care of the MLKHC Alcoholism Unit but remains active in AA.

## Regina

Regina, a 30-year-old black woman, came to the Alcoholism Unit because she was "drinking too much." She grew up in the Bronx. Both her parents had alcohol problems and Regina began drinking at age 13. Around the time Regina completed high school, her mother died from a complication of alcoholism. Regina was separated from her husband and she and her three children—ages 9 to 13—were living with Regina's maternal aunt.

Drug abuse and heroin addiction had figured prominently in Regina's late adolescence and early adulthood. She had used cocaine, amphetamines, and illicit methadone. She had been addicted to heroin and about three years prior to her initial Alcoholism Unit interview she had required 15 three-dollar bags of heroin per day. She had been enrolled in drug-treatment programs at various times in the past and for one year worked as the assistant director of a drug program.

Regina's heavy alcohol consumption may have been relatively recent. In her initial Alcoholism Unit interview she stated that when she was addicted to heroin she customarily drank two shots of scotch per day and that she was unaware of having any liver problems at that time. For the previous two years, however, she had been rarely using heroin but had been repeatedly going on prolonged alcoholic binges. Her initial interview was in late February and she said that since Christmas she had been drinking about one quart of alcoholic beverages per day—mostly gin but often including wine. Regina drank principally at home at "any time of the day or night." She denied blackouts but acknowledged D.T.'s in the past. She complained of nervousness, morning shakes, and trouble sleeping. There was no history of suicide attempts or of previous alcoholism or psychiatric treatment. Regina denied any particular period of abstinence from alcohol even though about ten months before her initial interview she had developed jaundice and liver and spleen enlargement. A liver biopsy then had revealed cirrhosis. She had not sought any medical attention since her hospitalization for the biopsy, though she was bruising easily and having frequent nosebleeds. She cited nervousness as the reason for her continued drinking. Her goal in seeking treatment was "to become a better person and a better mother to my children."

During Regina's first visit to the Alcoholism Unit, her facial expressions and gestures supported her verbal reports of discomfort and fear. She obviously had once been very attractive, but with her sunken eyes and temples and her thin extremities, Regina's appearance had become an uneasy compromise between youthful beauty and chronic disease. Physical examination revealed vascular signs of advanced liver disease (spider angiomas) on her neck, chest, and arms. Breath sounds were decreased over the right lower chest, consistent with an enlarged liver. A tender mass in her left upper abdomen was consistent with an enlarged spleen and her greatly enlarged liver extended a full eight centimeters below her right ribs. There was no evidence of ascites or hepatic failure.

Regina was taken directly to a hospital emergency room where laboratory tests helped establish that she was medically stable (mild anemia, slightly prolonged prothrombin time, moderately elevated liver function tests, negative stool for occult blood). She was then admitted to an inpatient alcohol detoxification program. Five days later she was transferred to a residential rehabilitation program where she stayed three weeks.

After discharge, Regina visited the Alcoholism Unit and MLKHC two to three times per week for counseling and seeking medications to help her sleep and to relieve persistent symptoms of rhinitis and bronchitis. Within a month she resumed drinking and soon was drinking heavily. Her visits stopped for two weeks, then Regina came to the Alcoholism Unit in some distress. Her daily consumption had climbed to three quarts of gin and wine. Two nights previously she had "heard voices" and she had no recollection at all of the night before. She had gone back to the residential program for help but was refused readmission because of her drug use. (It is not clear whether the program was originally not aware of Regina's past history of heroin addiction or whether they found evidence of an active drug problem.)

The Alcoholism Unit staff arranged admission to a half-way house oriented to patients with drug problems. Regina was initially brought back to the Alcoholism Unit every one to two days so that her withdrawal from alcohol could be medically supervised. She initially disliked the half-way house but acclimated to it during her first six weeks there. She seemed to remain successfully abstinent from alcohol. Summer approached as she ended her second month in the half-way house. On one visit back to the Alcoholism Unit she mentioned she was considering a trip to the South in August, "for a break."

Three weeks later she visited her alcoholism counselor. She was intoxicated and the counselor quickly established that Regina had just been expelled from the half-way house because of persistent drinking in spite of repeated warnings. Regina spent that afternoon on the Alcoholism Unit and agreed to return in the morning. She did not come back. Two days after this last visit, the counselor tried to reach her by phone. Regina's aunt reported that Regina had died in a city hospital that morning.

## Skeet

A friend described the MLKHC alcoholism program to Chauncey, a 55-year-old black man better known as "Skeet." Skeet came to the unit because he had been "drinking too much" and was afraid he had aggravated his diabetes.

Skeet left St. Louis shortly after the breakup of his marriage and had been in New York 12 years. He had no family history of alcoholism. He lived alone in a small South Bronx apartment and was out of touch with his four children. Skeet had a high school equivalency diploma and at various times had worked as a clerk, a truck driver, an elevator operator, a gardener, and a piano player. When he came for treatment he had been unemployed three years and was receiving public assistance.

In addition to 40 years of heavy alcohol use, Skeet reported using heroin regularly for 26 years plus intermittent use of cocaine, marijuana, and "pills." His nine arrests were all drug related. Three years before his initial Alcoholism Unit visit Skeet had discontinued heroin with the help of a methadone program.

Skeet had known about his mild diabetes for two years. Diabetes had been an incidental finding during a hospitalization for emergency ulcer surgery. He had also been told he had cirrhosis but could not recall a liver biopsy. He periodically visited the hospital outpatient department, though his diabetes required no specific treatment. Other than alcoholism, his most active and troublesome medical problem was osteoarthritis — advanced degenerative changes in his left wrist and elbow had resulted from multiple fractures Skeet sustained at age 27 when he was the victim of a homicide attempt.

Skeet began drinking at age 15. In his initial Alcoholism Unit interview he described his usual alcohol consumption as two to three pints of wine per day with frequent inclusion of beer or any liquor available. Skeet usually drank throughout the day at home, in bars, or ''anywhere.'' He had experienced blackouts but never D.T.'s. He had not attempted suicide and had not previously received formal alcoholism therapy. ''I like to get high'' was his reason for drinking and ''peace of mind'' was his goal in seeking treatment.

During his initial interview Skeet did not appear intoxicated though he admitted drinking earlier in the day. A lean man with tan skin and an angular nose and chin, Skeet answered questions with bursts of quick sentences. His movements were sudden, suggesting those of a small mammal. Medical assessment promptly established that Skeet's diabetes, contrary to his fear, was still in good control.

Skeet channeled his considerable energy into the treatment program. His outgoing manner promoted his instant assimilation into day-room activities. Talks with his counselor, in the first few weeks, were frequent and intense. By his third AA meeting, Skeet had begun to participate in the general discussions. Skeet stopped drinking.

During more than three years of treatment Skeet was categorized as ''looking for work but no job available.'' Recently, however, he began working part time in a city public works program. He has been sober more than four years and has been discharged from the MLKHC alcoholism treatment program. He remains active in AA.

## Zenia

Zenia was referred to the Alcoholism Unit by her MLKHC team physician. This 35-year-old black woman was in her pre-school years when she, her parents, and two siblings moved to the Bronx from North Carolina. She has no family history of alcoholism. Zenia graduated from high school and then trained and worked as a practical nurse. Her husband, who "drank a lot," left Zenia three months after the birth of their second child. At the time of her referral, Zenia and her children were living in a project apartment near MLKHC.

Three years prior to her initial Alcoholism Unit interview, Zenia developed such difficulty with an orthopedic condition that she was unable to work. After a year of unsuccessful medication trials, surgical treatment relieved her symptoms. During her year of orthopedic disability, however, emotional problems arose and continued to incapacitate her after she recovered from surgery. Though drinking may have contributed to these problems, Zenia lay some blame on the welfare system. She found it inordinately difficult to maintain herself and her children on her welfare allotment. Her financial problems were further aggravated when several appliances were stolen from her apartment.

During this difficult period, rather than obtaining increased support from her family, Zenia discontinued even seeing her parents and siblings. She complained that they had repeatedly and unfairly criticized her as a parent and cited their outspoken disapproval when she had left her children with a baby-sitter for a weekend. It is possible their disapproval extended to other than parental activities — in a separate context Zenia described her main social outlet at that time as occasionally joining "the party people" for drinking.

Zenia enrolled for care at MLKHC at a stage (about one year prior to her Alcoholism Unit referral) when she felt over-whelmed by her emotional situation. Her MLKHC health care team immediately focused on her symptoms of anxiety and depression. Frequent contact with her family health worker and other team members seemed in itself beneficial. She described some past relief from psychoactive medications (diazepam, meprobamate, chlorpromazine, and amitryptylene) and her team physician prescribed a low dose of amitryptylene. Zenia's symptoms gradually decreased. After about 10 months, her family health worker helped her arrange child care and Zenia returned to nursing. Soon thereafter Zenia told her team physician enough about her alcohol use to reveal its importance in her difficulties.

In her initial Alcoholism Unit interview Zenia described herself as "messed up" but felt she was functioning adequately in her new job. The counselor found her remarkably neat and well-spoken. She had begun drinking at age 27 and was currently drinking "over one-half pint" of Canadian whisky per day, though she sometimes drank wine or beer. Zenia usually drank in the evening, either at "a friend's house" or "in the street" — not at home. She acknowledged "very frequent" blackouts and a few hallucinatory withdrawal experiences (hearing voices, seeing "people with half of a head") in the past. Zenia occasionally had considered suicide when drinking but had not ever attempted to harm herself. She sometimes stopped drinking for "one or two weeks at a time" but had not previously been treated for alcoholism. Her reasons for drinking were "entertainment, to be with friends, and to lift my spirits"; her treatment goal was "to stop drinking."

Zenia's alcoholism recovery proceeded exceptionally smoothly. Without relapse, she discontinued alcohol consumption. She spoke with her counselor regularly and became active in local AA groups. After over four years of these frequent contacts with treatment resources, Zenia gradually decreased her formal treatment participation. Lately such participation has been practically nil but she remains abstinent from alcohol and continues to apply AA principles in her life. Zenia's future is clouded by a new illness — a collagen vascular disease diagnosed two years ago — but she is still in the same job and is enthusiastically looking forward a few months to when she will celebrate the seventh anniversary of her sobriety.

## Santo

Santo, a 55-year-old Puerto Rican man living in the South Bronx for over 10 years, was referred to the Alcoholism Unit from a hospital clinic in another borough. The referral note emphasized need for follow-up of elevated blood pressure readings as well as heavy alcohol consumption.

Santo completed the second grade in Puerto Rico. His mother died from tuberculosis and his father died from alcoholism when Santo was in his twenties. When he left Puerto Rico for New York, Santo separated from his wife. Two of their nine children were already living in New York City at that time. Santo was concerned that one of his sons was drinking excessively. Santo had no formal job training or recognized trade but was experienced at a number of "odd jobs." Six months prior to his initial Alcoholism Unit interview he had been working as a carpenter's helper but lost the job because of drinking. At the time of his interview he was receiving public assistance and living alone in a rooming house.

Santo started to drink when "very young" and had been drinking heavily for over 25 years. During the three or four months before his initial interview he regularly drank two quarts of gin or rum per day. He drank mainly at home, in the morning and in the afternoon. He acknowledged having both blackouts and D.T.'s, gave a vague history of "seizures" 12 years earlier, and reported bleeding from a duodenal ulcer 17 years earlier. Santo described one suicide attempt — he tried to rapidly drink a gallon of liquor but passed out before consuming a lethal amount. He denied previous alcoholism or psychiatric care, arrests, and use of illegal drugs.

Santo, a quiet, portly man, was sober during his initial visit. He attributed his drinking to repeated situational difficulties and gave his counselor the impression he was "not ready to accept he has a problem." Santo, however, became involved in AA and maintained close contact with his counselor. He became a regular in the day room and gradually — through his warm and gently teasing manner — gained the acceptance of black as well as Hispanic patients.

He stopped drinking. His blood pressure, which had been elevated when he first came for treatment, stabilized in the upper-normal range. His liver function tests, which were also initially elevated, became normal. Because of a positive tuberculin test and chest X-ray evidence of inactive tuberculosis, Santo was given isoniazid for one year to protect him against future tuberculosis activation. During medical visits his principal complaints were low-back and left-leg pain. Nonsalicylate anti-inflammatory drugs and exercises provided some relief from these symptoms. He had moderate degenerative arthritis of the lumbar spine on X-ray, but mild depression was assumed to contribute to his pain. When off alcohol three months, Santo developed a depressive syndrome characterized by tearfulness, loss of appetite, and early-morning wakening. He described himself as ''a very bad man.'' These depressive symptoms slowly improved on a moderate dose of amitryptyline and with strong support from members of the Alcoholism Unit staff. When he felt better, Santo became reluctant to either increase or decrease the dose of the antidepressant. When he had been relatively stable for several months, an argument with one of his children led to Santo ingesting assorted pills as a suicide gesture. He recovered quickly from this setback. Four months later, after 15 months on amitryptyline, he agreed to taper the medication. Three months more and he was doing well without it.

Santo has been sober more than four years. He attends at least three AA meetings each week and helps run two Spanish-speaking groups. He has introduced 10 new patients to the MLKHC alcoholism treatment program.

Santo is still unemployed. He doubts his back would tolerate the physically demanding labor he has done in the past. He recognizes that his lack of education and his lack of training severely restrict potential opportunities. Yet he says he would like to work.

*Chapter 6*

# DISCUSSION OF THE
# ALCOHOLISM UNIT STUDY

This chapter (1) reviews data indicating that the study subjects from the MLKHC Alcoholism Unit are indeed alcoholic, (2) relates the results of this study to others in the literature, (3) points out ethnic differences within the MLKHC study group, and (4) discusses hypotheses raised by the cross-cultural findings.

## VALIDATION OF SUBJECTS AS ALCOHOLIC

Chapter 5 describes users of an inner-city alcoholism treatment program. Under "chief complaint," difficulty with alcohol was recorded for 98% of study subjects. Some data items substantiate the assumption that program participants generally meet diagnostic criteria for alcoholism.

A committee of the National Council on Alcoholism (NCA) organized diverse evidence that may indicate serious alcohol problems into a set of diagnostic criteria.[1] The committee established three levels of diagnostic information. The first level includes only characteristics so closely associated with alcoholism that the diagnosis is obligatory if an item is present. Second-level items lend "strong suspicion of alcoholism" and third-level items indicate possible alcoholism. An obligatory or first-level criterion is satisfied if physiological dependency is manifested by either a withdrawal reaction or evidence of tolerance to the effects of alcohol.[1,2]

## Withdrawal

Histories consistent with previous withdrawal reactions were obtained from 161 subjects, 43% of the total MLKHC study group. Both hallucinosis and delirium tremens qualify as obligatory criteria, so it would not matter if some of these subjects misnamed hallucinosis as D.T.'s. Had symptoms of tremor been recorded, the group reporting withdrawal symptoms would likely be much larger. Because these Information Sheet data pertain to moderate-to-severe reactions, a qualifying remark is needed. Individuals who experience moderate-to-severe alcohol withdrawal consisting of hallucinations or delirium tremens and who do so under medical observation often later prove amnesic for the episode. First-person accounts of such states should therefore be regarded with some suspicion.

## Tolerance

The NCA Criteria Committee cited two alternative means of establishing tolerance:

a) A blood alcohol level of more than 150 mg/dl without gross evidence of intoxication.*
b) The consumption of one-fifth of a gallon of whiskey or an equivalent amount of beer or wine daily, for a period of two or more consecutive days, by a 180-lb. individual.[1] (p. 129)

To facilitate use of the second alternative, the committee developed a table (see Appendix) indicating the amounts of various

---

*A blood alcohol concentration of 100 mg/dl represents legal intoxication in most states.

alcoholic beverages that would have to be consumed by drinkers of various body weights to meet this criterion.

Mean total daily alcohol consumptions of MLKHC study subgroups approximate quantities in this table. Black men, Hispanic men, and Hispanic women respectively reported consuming 0.76, 0.88, and 0.77 pints per day of absolute alcohol. These values exceed the 0.74 pints (0.37 quarts) per day of absolute alcohol that represents the tolerance level for a 180-pound person. The 0.71 pints per day of absolute alcohol reported by black women similarly exceeds the 0.66 pints (0.33 quarts) that is the tolerance level for a 160-pound person.

Admittedly, averages of the alcohol consumptions reported in interviews may not accurately depict actual consumption. However, the averages obtained do exceed levels that imply alcoholism even though *under*estimates of consumption are frequently anticipated from people with alcohol problems.

## Other Symptoms

Morning drinking, reported by 88% of the subjects, and blackout periods, reported by 80% of subjects, are both second-level diagnostic criteria. Unemployment, family disruption, and financial problems are third-level criteria that were prevalent in the group.

The Information Sheets analyzed in this study were designed prior to publication of standardized diagnostic criteria for alcoholism. They do, however, provide sufficient evidence to assert that a substantial proportion of subjects meet accepted diagnostic criteria for alcoholism.

## COMPARISONS WITH PREVIOUS STUDIES

## Residential Status

The NCA and other authoritative sources consistently quote 5% as the percentage of alcoholics in the United States sufficiently socially deteriorated to qualify as skid-row alcoholics. If one accepts the premise that the single variable most likely to correlate with skid-row status is lack of a residence, it is somewhat surprising that only 5% of the MLKHC subjects were undomiciled. One might expect, even in a self-selected sample such as this, that the proportion of homeless alcoholics in an inner-city group would exceed the national statistic.

The questions cannot be resolved from the data available here, but this result invites speculation. Do homeless alcoholics not present for treatment? Do homeless alcoholics in the inner city not live as long as homeless alcoholics elsewhere? Could mailing addresses with relatives or friends have been presented or interpreted as residential addresses? Could alcoholics be sufficiently accepted and protected among blacks and possibly Hispanics (see Chapter 4) to offset any tendency to become undomiciled arising from a disadvantaged state?

## Age

The age distribution of the MLKHC subjects (Figure 5.1) is consistent with Cahalan's generalization that individuals younger than 50 years old predominate among problem drinkers.[3] The largest male age group in this study was 30–39 years. This is similar to findings in the three comparable groups in the literature that are summarized in Table 4.3 (see entries for German; Zimberg; and Novick, Hudson, and German).

## Education

Overall, somewhat higher levels of education were attained by men in the MLKHC study than by men in Zimberg's Harlem population or Strayer's Bridgeport group (Table 4.3). This occurred in spite of the inclusion in the MLKHC data of a group of very poorly educated Hispanic men.

## Occupation

Interstudy comparisons of occupation are tenuous because

the occupational categories used in these studies are not standardized. Novick, Hudson, and German's subjects and the black
subgroup described by Strayer (Table 4.3) show greater percentages of unskilled workers than that found for MLKHC men. The
differences, however, could result from the classifications used
rather than from higher occupational skills among the MLKHC
subjects. For example, Novick, Hudson, and German use neither
a semi-skilled nor operative category.

## Arrests

The arrest data on MLKHC subjects are also not directly
comparable to other studies. *Prior arrests* were recorded on the
MLKHC Information Sheets. Percentages of black men and of
black and Hispanic men with *alcohol-related arrests* have been
reported by Viamontes and Powell and by Zimberg, respectively
(Table 4.3). It is not surprising that these percentages are ex-
ceeded by the percentage of MLKHC men acknowledging the
more general characteristic of prior arrest(s).

## Age of First Drink

Kissin[4] reports considerable patient variability around the
mean age of first drink yet found that among "several thousand
alcoholics in New York City . . . whites tended to begin drinking
about the age of 19 or 20 . . . black patients, on the other hand,
tended to have an earlier onset of drinking, often in their early
teens" (p. 23). This result is similar to the black-white comparisons of Rimmer et al. and Viamontes and Powell (Table 4.4),
which were both based on smaller groups.

The reported ages of first drink of MLKHC subjects also
varied widely about the mean value, as indicated by the standard
deviations for subgroups in Table 5.8. This study is not closely
aligned with those just mentioned because the mean age of first
drink for both black men and black women fell in the late teens.
However, 49% of black men and 31% of black women reported
their first drink at age 15 or younger (Table 5.8).

## Drinking Pattern

Strayer (Table 4.4) is the only author in the literature reviewed to quantify the preferred alcoholic beverages of a sample of black alcoholics. The beverage-preference categories used in the MLKHC study are more detailed and are not comparable to those of Strayer. Future studies should employ uniform beverage-preference categories to permit comparing or possibly pooling data. It may also be important to standardize techniques of data collection. For example, some individuals are ambivalent about reporting wine consumption[5] and if an approach emerges that overcomes this, it should be used in all related studies.

Morning drinking was reported by 88% of MLKHC black subjects (Table 5.10), a figure similar to the 89% found by Rimmer et al. (Table 4.4). On the other hand, daily drinking was reported by 98% of MLKHC blacks (Table 5.10), a divergence from the 68% reported by Strayer (Table 4.4). Again, more detailed, standardized information would be helpful. Researchers undertaking prospective studies might be wise to collect sufficient drinking-pattern data to permit comparisons with each of the few formats represented in the literature. Studies such as this one, which are based on existing records, do not have that flexibility.

## ETHNIC DIFFERENCES

Chapter 4 summarized the information published on blacks and Hispanics engaged in alcoholism treatment. Limited cross-cultural perspective on black alcoholics is provided by the studies[6-12] that compare the black and white segments of the same treatment populations. The MLKHC Alcoholism Unit patient population opens a new area of cross-cultural study, inner-city black and Hispanic alcoholics. Because the black and Hispanic patients are self-selected, however, any differences identified can not be extrapolated to black and Hispanic alcoholics in the community.

## Demographic Differences

The MLKHC black and Hispanic groups were similar with regard to residential status, age, marital status, past employment, and arrests. Proportionately, there were nearly twice as many black women as Hispanic women but this finding is of doubtful significance ($0.10 > P > 0.05$).* One prior study,[12] however, indicated that Hispanics are less apt to seek help for alcoholism than blacks or whites. Should it be established that similar proportions of black and Hispanic alcoholics in the community are female, the difference in the MLKHC study might suggest that the greatest reluctance to enter treatment is among Hispanic women.

Of male subjects for whom responses were recorded, 36% of the blacks compared with 20% of the Hispanics had served in the military ($0.02 > P > 0.01$).

The most dramatic demographic discrepancy between black and Hispanic subjects is in level of education. Among Hispanic subjects, 58% had *not* completed 9 years of education, compared to 29% of black subjects. This undereducation of Hispanic subjects compared to black subjects is statistically highly significant** and might have been anticipated from local and national data that reveal low levels of education among Hispanics generally.[13]

## Drinking Pattern

Black and Hispanic subjects were similar with regard to age of first drink, time of drinking, and place of drinking. Rimmer et

---

*Unless otherwise noted, P values have been determined by chi-square tests using Yates's correction for continuity.

**When the data in Table 5.2 are regrouped by ethnicity, chi-square = 35.35 with 3 degrees of freedom and no correction for continuity ($P < 0.001$).

al. (Table 4.4) found a higher percentage of blacks than whites drinking "over 32 ounces of spirits weekly." In the MLKHC study, the mean total daily alcohol consumption of Hispanics was higher than that of blacks, but the difference did not reach statistical significance.

Hispanics did express a preference for beer significantly more often than blacks. Combining the preference categories "beer," "beer and wine," and "beer and liquor" in Table 5.9, 33% of Hispanics were in these beer-preferring categories compared to 20% of blacks ($0.02 > P > 0.01$). It may be relevant that Wanberg and Horn[12] found Hispanics scored higher than blacks on a composite variable that in part reflected beer drinking.

Similar category groupings for wine and liquor revealed no other significant ethnic differences. Wine preference was expressed by 39% of blacks compared to 29% of Hispanics ($0.10 > P > 0.05$). Liquor preference was expressed by 47% of blacks compared to 45% of Hispanics ($P > 0.5$).

Reasons given for drinking were similar in the two ethnic groups. Escape was reported as a motivating factor by 43% of blacks and 49% of Hispanics ($0.5 > P > 0.25$). Blacks more often than Hispanics indicated enhanced sociability as a reason for drinking, but not to a statistically significant degree ($0.10 > P > 0.05$).

## Withdrawal

Hallucinatory experiences were the principal withdrawal symptom recorded on the Information Sheets. As mentioned, while these reports were entered next to the question about delirium tremens, it is not reasonable to assume that these patients actually experienced delirium tremens. It is reasonable, however, to simply relate these reports of hallucinations to other reports of hallucinations in the literature.

Gross et al.[10] give figures that imply that 58% of their black subjects compared to 44% of their white subjects experienced hallucinations during an illness associated with hospital admission for alcohol withdrawal, a statistically significant difference.

Viamontes and Powell[11] reported that 79% of their black subjects acknowledged a past history of one or more hallucinations compared to 57% of whites (P < 0.01). Both groups of authors assumed cultural factors to be major determinants of the differences. As stated in Chapter 5, 60% of MLKHC Hispanic patients reported a history of hallucinations compared to 41% of blacks in the study (P < 0.005). These three studies are based on substantially different populations and methodologic approaches. Direct comparison of percentages would not be appropriate. However, by postulating reasonable behavioral and cultural similarity among the blacks and among the whites across the three studies and by assuming comparability of data *within* each of the studies, these results suggest *a spectrum of susceptibility to hallucinations*. MLKHC Hispanics appear to be the most susceptible, blacks next, and whites least susceptible.

Gross et al.[10] suggest that "a great freedom to hallucinate results from the expectation of a greater tolerance of such behavior by the individual and those around him" (p. 24). In the context of their finding that blacks were more likely to hallucinate than whites, this would imply that black culture restrains hallucinations to a lesser extent than cultural influences on whites. Some characteristics of Puerto Rican culture support the possibility that family and community influences on the largely Puerto Rican MLKHC Hispanic subjects pose even less restraint.

In a general way, the lives of at least the Puerto Rican poor seem uninhibited. Lewis vividly illustrates this in the introduction to *La Vida*:[14]

> The people in this book, like most of the other Puerto Rican slum dwellers I have studied, show a great zest for life . . . Theirs is an expressive style of life. They value acting out more than thinking out, self-expression more than self-constraint . . . Compared with the low-income Mexicans I have studied, they seem less reserved, less depressive, less controlled and less stable.
>
> The Rios family is closer to the expression of an unbridled id than any other people I have studied. They have an almost complete absence of internal conflict and of a sense of guilt . . .
>
> In the Rios family, uncontrolled rage, aggression, violence

and even bloodshed are not uncommon; their extreme impulsiv-
ity affects the whole tenor of their lives. (p. xxvi)

In a specific way, the religious system of spiritualism, which is
integrated into the lives of many Puerto Ricans, may not only
support but actually encourage hallucinatory experiences. In
spiritualistic sessions:

> Persistent hallucinations . . . are not symptoms of a deranged
> mind experiencing things unperceived by others — an interpretation
> which serves to isolate the sick; rather, hallucinations indicate
> the development of psychic faculties that may eventually serve to
> put the lucky person in more permanent contact with the invisible
> world. Relatives, friends, and associates are encouraged to
> cooperate with the sick person so that he will fully develop
> *facultades* [psychic faculties].[15] (pp. 253–254)

While these comments by Rogler and Hollingshead occur in the
context of their detailed study of schizophrenia and are qualified
to refer to ''persistent hallucinations,'' analogous cultural support for the relatively brief hallucinatory experiences of alcohol
withdrawal is plausible particularly because it seems unlikely
that the cultural influences on a potential hallucinator would
selectively distinguish categories of hallucinations.

The extreme underprivilege of Puerto Ricans was discussed
in Chapter 4. Gross et al.[10] wondered if ''an atmosphere of
deprivation is more accepting and accommodating to manifestations of vivid fantasy and imagination'' (p. 24). If deprivation
does promote fantasy and in turn hallucinations, it would hardly be
surprising for the most deprived to have the most hallucinations.

These suggested relationships among whites, blacks, and
Puerto Ricans/Hispanics in a possible spectrum of susceptibility
to hallucinations during alcohol withdrawal may be thought
provoking, but it is important to bear in mind the limitations of
the supportive data. Methodological considerations dictate cau-
tious discussion and nothing more than tentative conclusions.
There are obvious sampling issues: How generally representative
of black and white alcoholics are the groups of patients studied

in Brooklyn[10] and St. Louis?[11] How representative of black and Puerto Rican/Hispanic alcoholics is the MLKHC South Bronx group? Perhaps the Puerto Ricans/Hispanics in the study simply waited longer— until their symptoms were more severe— before seeking help. Also, as mentioned earlier, the frequent association of memory disturbance with states of intoxication and withdrawal leaves the accuracy of any patient reports of past hallucinations open to question. Still further, there is an indication in the MLKHC data that interviewer bias may have influenced at least the results of that study. Cultural or other influences on *interviewers* could conceivably make them more or less likely to elicit and record responses describing hallucinations. In the creation of the records used in the MLKHC study, Hispanic patients were nearly always interviewed by Hispanic counselors. One explanation, then, for the significantly higher proportion of hallucinators among Hispanics compared to blacks would be a greater tendency for the Hispanic counselors to elicit/record hallucinations.

One of the MLKHC Hispanic counselors had interviewed a moderate number of *black* patients, so the proportion of hallucinators the Hispanic counselor found among blacks could be compared to those found among blacks by black counselors. In 54 interviews of black patients, the Hispanic counselor recorded hallucinations for 27 (50%). One of this counselor's black counterparts found 25 hallucinators in 69 interviews (36%) and another found 20 in 52 interviews (38%). A trend is apparent, but chi-square tests comparing the findings of the Hispanic counselor to those of each of the black counselors were not significant ($0.25 > P > 0.10$ and $0.50 > P > 0.25$).

Another issue qualifying conclusions drawn from these studies is whether or not interviews are a reliable data-collection tool when investigating the underprivileged. It is true that the three studies under consideration used records developed from clinical interviews rather than from survey interviews and that, at least for the MLKHC study, the interviewers themselves were more or less members of the community. However, if verbal, structured interchange does not tend to obtain accurate information from the underprivileged, it seems likely that even studies such as these would be affected. From an anthropological perspective, Liebow[16] reviews the comments of several authors and summarizes:

> There is . . . a growing uneasiness about the validity of much of the data already gathered [about lower-class life], especially data gathered by interview and questionnaire. Appeals for data in depth go hand in hand with a widespread suspicion that lower-class persons are less tractable to interview and questionnaire techniques than are persons in the middle and upper strata. (pp. 8–9)*

## SUMMARY

The MLKHC alcoholism treatment program serves a culturally mixed, poor, inner-city patient population. The blacks and Hispanics who comprise this treatment group are largely men, but women are by no means absent. Both the men and women who use the program tend to be in mid-adulthood. Their levels of education vary, but many— especially the Hispanics— are undereducated. The group is predominantly without job skills and out of work. Marital problems, troubles with the law, and potentially serious health problems are common. Most of the patients have homes.

A substantial proportion of this treatment group meets accepted diagnostic criteria for alcoholism even when diagnostic data are not sought in depth. Their average alcohol consumption exceeds the equivalent of one pint of liquor per day, though the afternoon-only drinkers consume less.

The literature (and possibly the proportions of Hispanic and female Hispanic patients in this treatment group) suggests that Hispanic alcoholics may be reluctant to seek alcoholism treatment.

*Liebow used participant observation for data collection in his study of black street-corner men.

A feature that distinguishes the Hispanic from the black alcoholics in this program—a higher percentage of Hispanics reporting hallucinatory experiences—serves as a reminder of the importance of religion in Hispanic culture.

Providing for the needs of these people would not be easy even if resources were unlimited. In the South Bronx this is hardly the case. The following chapter will discuss what are felt to be realistic and useful program additions or changes. Between the early organization of this study and the preparation of this final report, some program changes were made. These completed changes will be described and, to a limited extent, their impact will be assessed.

## Chapter 7

# PROGRAM IMPLICATIONS:
# BETTER TREATMENT

Two sets of program planning cosiderations are discussed be-. low. The first presents relatively simple changes in the MLKHC alcoholism program— several of which have already been implemented— that seem to grow naturally out of the program's immediate past. Some now completed changes may have been catalyzed by the fact that this study was being done, but some would have happened anyway. One change— a change in the location of the Alcoholism Unit— had an unintended beneficial impact on one of the issues raised by the study; reluctance of Hispanic alcoholics to seek treatment.

The second set of planning considerations is more complicated. All along, a goal of the treatment record and library research presented here has been to develop an approach— a realistic, practical approach— which would integrate research methods and the delivery of care in a fashion that would gradually generate both better patient care and a better understanding of alcoholism. This discussion represents a tentative formulation of how this might be accomplished. Another body of literature is explored here for both theoretical background and useful available knowledge. While this material is presently nothing more than a "set of planning considerations," the exercise of using it to formulate a concrete plan was undertaken. The plan is not meant for implementation, but merely to serve as a demonstration that theoretical and practical considerations can be interwoven.

There is, of course, overlap between the two discussions. Both relate intimately to the patients, personnel, and records of the treatment program.

## A PROGRAM IN EVOLUTION

### Patient Intake

REFERRALS.    The MLK Health Center itself referred a relatively small proportion of the patients studied (Table 5.1). The largest group of referrals came from public institutions and these patients, as a group, tended to drop out of the treatment program quickly. Their high attrition rate was understandable for two principal reasons. First, the public-institution referral base was citywide and the residences of many of these patients were distant from the Alcoholism Unit. Second, these patients frequently were not motivated to follow a treatment plan. Many of them did not perceive themselves as having a drinking problem and registered at the Alcoholism Unit because they were coerced by the referring institution to *enter* a treatment program. Continued participation often became voluntary and many stopped coming to the program. Because the Alcoholism Unit staff wanted to apply program resources to individuals likely to obtain longer-lived benefits, routine referrals from these public institutions were discouraged in mid-1975 and thereafter and a concerted effort was made to cultivate referrals from MLKHC's health care teams.

Subsequent referrals from within MLKHC were influenced

both by activities of the Alcoholism Unit staff and by the relocation of the Alcoholism Unit itself. Counselors from the unit
began regularly participating in the weekly meetings of the
health care teams, in order to promote ease of referral and
communication of case details. The approach was also expected
to provide an opportunity for the counselors to interject their
point of view in team discussions of difficult individual and
family problems. It was hoped that exchange facilitated by this
meeting attendance would ultimately lead to closer working
relationships between team members and the unit staff. The
Alcoholism Unit director and physician conducted a series of
interactive educational sessions for three of the professional
groups serving on the health care teams. These experiences
sought to improve the skills of family health workers, nurse
practitioners, and internists in recognizing alcohol problems and
in fostering the desire for treatment in those found to have them.
Some of these sessions were held at the Alcoholism Unit. In
January 1976, the Alcoholism Unit moved from quarters at 507
East 171st Street to 1634 Bathgate Avenue. The new site was
directly across the street from the Bathgate Division of MLKHC,
the location of two of the center's eight health care teams.

The impact of these changes on Alcoholism Unit referrals
can only be fully assessed by another study. One early impression
was that some health team members communicated with counselors more often and in greater detail. Referrals from the six
teams in the main Third Avenue health center seemed to increase
gradually. When the Alcoholism Unit moved, referrals from the
then nearby Bathgate Division teams increased considerably.
These two teams served a predominantly Hispanic patient population and the number and proportion of Hispanics in the program
steadily rose.

FORMS AND OTHER RECORDS.    Considerable data were collected
on the Information Sheets. However, scrutiny of those forms during this study suggested improvements. Had external influences not
made the continued use of locally developed forms unnecessary,

a new intake form would have been an early outgrowth of this project.

From June 1976 onward, the agency funding the Alcoholism Unit, The National Institute on Alcohol Abuse and Alcoholism (NIAAA), required that the program participate in the NIAAA Treatment Monitoring System. This meant collecting and reporting standardized intake and follow-up data. When the regulation went into effect, the Information Sheets were supplanted by NIAAA forms. Overall, the NIAAA forms represented a useful advance in intake data collection. They promoted the recording of greater detail in personal and alcohol-related information. There was a sound format for identifying ethnicity. The drinking history was more explicit. The questions on alcoholic-beverage consumption were confusing but the counselors learned to work with them. Questions capable of helping counselors identify medically unstable new patients were lacking, so these were added as a supplement. The NIAAA package included material for the submission of status reports on the treatment population every six months.

Also in mid-1976, the collection of detailed medical information was expanded to include nearly every patient in the program. MLKHC Administration and the Alcoholism Unit staff formally established the policy that, without regard to insurance coverage or ability to pay, all patients of the Alcoholism Unit could receive comprehensive health care through the unit and the health center. MLKHC health service utilization by Alcoholism Unit patients was not low prior to this, but the formal policy meant that service provision and medical records became more complete. For example, after the policy was in effect, medical records were begun and a physician interview was scheduled for all patients at the time of their Alcoholism Unit registration. A core of medical data was sought even on patients continuing under the primary medical care of an outside physician or clinic. A release of information signed by the patient and a letter from the unit physician were sent to outside primary care providers. The letter reported the patient's participation in the treatment program and requested such information as the results of his or her most recent complete blood count, liver function tests, and tuberculin test. This entire approach not only promoted better patient care, but it also increased the potential breadth and depth of future studies.

INTERVIEWERS.    It was apparent during the extraction of data from the Information Sheets that the counselors completing them differed in their interpretations of at least one question. "Why did you stop?" appears on the Information Sheet after "Prior psychiatric or alcoholism help" with one intervening question. When entered, most responses to "Why did you stop?" indicated patients' reasons for discontinuing any previous treatment. However, one counselor consistently indicated patients' reasons for interrupting their present drinking to come for treatment. This divergent interpretation was trivial to the study as a whole, but nonetheless was undesirable. It was pointed out to the staff as soon as the coding of forms was completed. At the same time, more standardized recording of alcoholic-beverage consumption was suggested for the remaining period the Information Sheets were in use.

## Psychiatric Expertise

Among the 40% of patients who acknowledged prior psychiatric or alcoholism help, the Information Sheet data did not distinguish how many specifically had undergone psychiatric treatment. Past psychiatric hospitalizations were reported by some patients and occasionally nonauthoritative diagnoses of schizophrenia were encountered. In addition to these indications that some patients had active needs for psychiatric attention, both new and old patients often expressed complaints well summarized by the terms nervousness and depression. Those patients with intact families frequently described conflicts at home. The Alcoholism Unit staff recognized that straightforward help to stop drinking was the dominant need of virtually all new patients, but they also recognized that the addition of psychiatric expertise would lead to improved, more individualized patient care.

A staff psychiatrist could participate in the comprehensive evaluation of each new patient directly, by conducting an interview, or indirectly, by training the counselors to refer for interview those patients most in need of psychiatric evaluation. Chafetz,[1] Gross et al.,[2] and Rimmer, Reich, and Winokur[3] are among those authors who have emphasized the widespread need for more adequate psychiatric assessment early in the evaluation of alcohol problems. During treatment, a psychiatrist was envisioned as promoting more effective group therapy and initiating limited family therapy. Regular participants in the program included individuals with chronic mental illnesses and it was assumed a staff psychiatrist could provide their continuing psychiatric care. On the research level, there was the possibility that a better understanding could be reached, for this population, of the relationship between excessive drinking and major psychiatric disease.[4] In late 1977, the Alcoholism Unit director obtained the necessary administrative approvals and initiated a search for a staff psychiatrist.

## Financial Constraints

If a program is to help inner-city alcoholics arrest their alcoholism, it must help them deal with environmental factors contributing to their alcohol consumption. Davis,[5] emphasizing the importance of comprehensive services to poor black alcoholics, states:

> We must realize that ghetto living, destructive for all members of the community, is "special" for the Black alcoholic in that ghetto living is closely related to the desire to escape by whatever means; and because to work, to earn, means independence, usefulness, and the ability to care for and to be cared for in the family and community context. (p. II–19)

Zimberg[6] suggests an approach to "primary socioeconomically deprived population groups" which "should include . . . residential facilities, and provide vocational training, educational and job opportunities" (p. 556).

Seeking a psychiatrist was made the top priority among efforts to provide more comprehensive services within the Alcoholism Unit. Among the alternatives, this choice was the most realistic financially. Other attractive possible additions to the Alcoholism Unit staff included specialists in occupational counseling/rehabilitation and in education. The justifications for adding expertise in these areas were at least as convincing as that for adding a psychiatrist. With about 70% of the patient group lacking job skills (Table 5.4) and perhaps one-half to three-quarters of the group unemployed (see *Work History*, p. 121), there was little question about a general need, at some point, for job training and placement. Nor could there be much doubt as to an educational need, with about 70% of the group not having completed high school and about 35% of the group not having even entered high school (Table 5.2). Any educator joining the program would have to be fluent in both English and Spanish. At a much earlier stage of the MLKHC alcoholism program, when the budget was more ample, a teacher had actually been employed part time to do remedial education.

In program expansion plans, a psychiatrist took precedence over an occupational specialist and an educator simply because funds to pay for a psychiatrist were obtainable. Psychiatric services provided to eligible patients could be reimbursed by Medicare and Medicaid. The unit's federal grant was not sufficient to add a psychiatrist or any type of new resource staff member in the absence of such a payment mechanism. No equivalent reimbursement was available for occupational rehabilitation or educational services. For the near future, counselors would have to continue to direct patients to existing less-than-satisfactory rehabilitation services in the community and would have to remain alert for any potentially applicable

new programs such as those developed for "ex-offenders."
(See Table 5.5 for a summary of the substantial number of
patients reporting arrests; no data on convictions are available.)

## MONITORING TREATMENT OUTCOME:
## BETTER CARE AND BETTER KNOWLEDGE

This study, as is usual with descriptive research, generates
more questions than answers. Chapter 5 offers a detailed look at
participants in an alcoholism treatment program. The data con-
firm that program additions such as occupational rehabilitation
are needed. The data reveal ethnic differences such as the
greater tendency of the Hispanics studied to report hallucinations. However, this study's view of patients is narrow — it is
limited in time to the moment each patient entered the program.
There is no information here about what became of these patients after their entry to the program. The descriptive study is
useful because it answers questions such as "What seems to be
needed?" but it represents only the first of what should become
a series of studies. The next step is to aim to meet patient needs
programmatically and then, by following patients over time,
seek answers to questions such as "What works?" and "What
works best?"

Resources were inadequate to permit developing a longitudinal study while carrying out this more fundamental descriptive
study. But some present program changes may assist such future
research. As described above, procedures were instituted to
collect more complete data at intake. Counselors were encouraged
to increase the frequency and detail of progress notes in Alcoholism Unit patient records. It was hoped, moreover, that
participation in the NIAAA Treatment Monitoring System would
allow future studies to be relatively automated, rather than again
relying upon manual review of local records. The feasibility of
applying biannual NIAAA status reports or some modification

of the Treatment Monitoring System to local research questions remained untested as of the end of 1977, which represents the close of the informal observations incorporated in this discussion.

## Patient Follow-up

Monitoring patients over time is an important clinical activity as well as a research activity. Serious alcohol problems may persist in spite of active treatment or may recur even if treatment succeeds initially. Providers of alcoholism treatment promote continuing treatment success when they periodically reassess each patient's status and modify their treatment efforts as indicated. A new or relapsed patient might require several such reassessments in a single day, whereas the stabilized patient who perhaps regularly participates in the self-help program of Alcoholics Anonymous might be reassessed at monthly or longer intervals.

One of the reasons monitoring promotes successful outcomes is because the reassessments themselves are therapeutic. When the person making contact with the patient serves or has served the patient as a counselor, the reassessment provides an opportunity to strengthen the counselor-patient alliance and renew the patient's own self-help efforts. Such an effect, depending upon the status of the patient, might either help prevent a relapse or facilitate recovery from one. No matter who makes contact with the patient and whether they do so in person or by telephone, follow-up activities at least remind the patient of the continuing concern and the resource availability that the treatment program represents.

MLKHC counselors generally informally followed their patients who were doing well and did some outreach via home visits and phone calls to patients of unknown status or known to be not doing well. The institution of the NIAAA system was an incentive to make these follow-up efforts more formal and more comprehensive— clearly promoting better patient care as well as promoting data collection. The task of doing adequate comprehensive follow-up was more than the counselors could handle, however, without decreasing their attention to those patients in need of relatively intensive care. The need for more staff, perhaps in the specific role of outreach counselors, was apparent but funding for this, as of the end of 1977, remained to be found.

## Clinical Subgroups in Alcoholism Treatment

The MLKHC program developed a range of services or treatment modalities suited to the needs of inner-city alcoholics. For most of its history, at least through 1977, the MLKHC alcoholism treatment program centered in a day-care unit functionally similar to that described by Zimberg, Lipscomb, and Davis[7] at the Harlem Hospital Center. The nondrinking environment of the unit provided the setting for supportive staff-patient and patient-patient interaction. Budget cuts forced decreases in staffing and in hours of operation, but core and ancillary treatment modalities remained essentially unchanged.

The principal means of treatment were individual counseling and Alcoholics Anonymous. Counselors would meet with patients both by appointment and as needed. These encounters might last minutes or hours. AA meetings and patient participation in them were promoted by the program, an indirect service because AA groups mandate that they be independent of institutions. Several AA meetings were held each week either in the unit or in nearby community halls. Ancillary services included limited group counseling, recreational therapy, and work therapy. Treatment of acute medical problems as well as ongoing comprehensive health care were available in the Alcoholism Unit and health center. Selected patients were detoxified from alcohol as outpatients (ambulatory detoxification). When necessary, referrals to resources outside the unit were made for inpatient or in-hospital detoxification, residential alcoholism treatment, and half-way house accommodations.

Working in a context of dwindling financial support, it became increasingly difficult for the Alcoholism Unit staff to continue delivering even this discrete range of services, much less expand to a more comprehensive program. Strategies were needed to overcome the pressing reality of limited resources. One feasible approach discussed earlier was the addition of services, such as those of a psychiatrist, capable of at least supporting themselves and perhaps capable of generating extra funds to assist the overall program. Another possibility would be to apply treatment services more selectively in order to extract the maximum benefit from existing resources. The concluding statement of a systematic discussion of alcoholism treatment by Pattison[8] expresses the general need for greater efficiency in treating alcoholism:

> Although increased support for rehabilitation programs will be welcome, the success of alcoholism rehabilitation lies with making more effective and appropriate use of the resources already available. (p. 648)

Pattison's statement assumes variability among alcoholics and among both treatment methods and treatment facilities. It projects matching "a certain type of patient with a certain type of treatment and facility to yield the most effective results"[8] (p. 591). Pattison emphasizes the need to identify "the various *subpopulations* of alcoholics in the community"[8] (p. 591, italics added). These subpopulations represent clusters of alcoholics with characteristics in common. The subpopulations most helpful to identify are those that respond to particular treatment approaches. Pattison's subpopulations are basically useful subcategories within a disease category and represent the same notion as the term "clinical subgroups" discussed in Chapter 2.

If clinical subgroups of alcoholics could be identified among the patients of the MLKHC Alcoholism Unit and if treatment pathways could be worked out for one or more subgroups that would require, say, less counselor time, the resulting efficiency could free resources for use in other areas, such as patient follow-up. Ultimately, subgroups following treatment pathways determined to be the most appropriate for patients with their particular characteristics should achieve better success rates in treatment than the success rate obtained by the overall group under the present system.* It might be assumed that better success rates would provide a secondary efficiency because there would be fewer relapsed patients consuming dispro- portionate counselor time, but this expectation remains to be verified.

MEASURING SUBGROUPS.    What characteristics can be used to de- fine clinical subgroups? Once identified, what is the best means of establishing subgroup members on the treatment pathway most appropriate for them? These are difficult questions in any setting. The literature suggests starting points and describes some approaches that may be adaptable even to a resource-poor inner-city program.

*Demographic or Sociological Characteristics.*    Some demo- graphic characteristics have demonstrated usefulness in predict- ing how well patients will do in specific treatment settings. Zwerling and Clifford[20] found that married patients persisted in outpatient treatment to a greater degree than other groups. An eight-item prognostic index developed by Mindlin[11] included marital status, present economic resources (e.g., employed or pensioned), usual occupation, and arrest history. These items helped correctly predict the therapeutic outcome in 80% of cases in a validation group of alcoholics treated in a psychiatrically oriented outpatient clinic. Gerard and Saenger,[12] in an analysis of patient intake and follow-up data from eight state-supported alcoholism clinics in the eastern United States, used an index of

---

*The desirability of improving treatment results by matching patients with various types of treatment is a strong theme in Pattison's work[8-10] and in several other relatively recent studies.[11-19] As early as 1942, however, Jellinek wrote: ''Even more criteria of selection among various methods of handling alcohol addicts are desirable, and a more careful choice of treatment in the individual case, based on such criteria, would eliminate many fail- ures.'' (Quoted by Edwards and Guthrie,[13] p. 555.)

social stability "based on whether the patient at intake was (1) married, (2) living with his family, and (3) regularly employed" (p.59). Patients with higher stability maintained better contact with their clinic and showed more improvement with respect to drinking and other outcome measures than did patients with lower stability. It is of interest that two factors generally used in indices of social class—education and occupation—were not helpful predictors of either extent of clinic contact of improvement in Gerard and Saenger's study.

Schmidt, Smart, and Moss[14] present evidence that the social class (derived from residential characteristics, occupational level, and educational achievement) of patients influences the type of therapy recommended and received in a Toronto alcoholism treatment program. However, these authors did not assess treatment outcome and therefore do not further illuminate social class as predictive of treatment response. They did find a significant relationship between social class and the prognosis for individual patients that was expressed by the treatment staff at intake. Class I (highest) patients had a good prognosis the most often and a poor prognosis least often; Class III (lowest) patients had a good prognosis the least often and a poor prognosis the most often; Class II patients were intermediate in both respects[14] (pp. 56–57). This indicates that the prognosis *predicted* by the treatment staff may be influenced by social class, but it hardly establishes that actual prognosis is affected by it. These authors include information on duration of treatment, which is sometimes taken as an indirect indicator of treatment outcome. However, they collapse their data to such an extent (one contact vs. two or more contacts) that any application of it would be exceedingly limited (pp. 66–67).

Schmidt, Smart, and Moss's finding that social class influences assigned treatment pathway could not be duplicated by Lowe and Ziglin[21] in a study of white males in Atlanta, Georgia. The latter study measured social class using the two factors of usual occupation and education. Trice, Roman, and Belasco,[16] in a multiple regression analysis of 81 variables possibly predictive of treatment success in a white-male-patient population that received residential alcoholism treatment at a Maryland state hospital, found 16 variables significant.

> Taking all of the significant demographic variables into account, the patient most likely to adjust successfully subsequent to this treatment has the following pre-treatment history (in order of predictive power):
> 1. Few, or no, arrests previous to hospitalization.
> 2. Low visibility to community referral agencies following treatment . . .
> 3. A skilled, white-collar or professional occupation.
> 4. Few, or no, previous state hospitalizations.
> 5. A first or second generation parent.
> 6. A longer period of alcoholism.
> 7. A first intoxication at a later age.
> 8. A small number of siblings.
> 9. An exposure to alcoholism at a place away from home.[16]
> (pp. 311–312)*

Kissin, Rosenblatt, and Machover[15] compared their own findings to others in the literature and noted:

> certain patterns seem to recur from study to study. Those variables which appear most consistently to act as favorable prognostic indicators are age (over 40–45), marital status, education (some college), occupation (skilled), occupational stability (which appears most significant), number of arrests, and drinking pattern (periodic benders). (p. 26)*

Kissin and colleagues[15, 17] also gained support for the impression that socially intact individuals "do better in either drug treatment or psychotherapy but tend to do less well in an inpatient rehabilitation ward"[17] (p. 22). In an investigation of the efficacy of and the indications for disulfiram (Antabuse) therapy, Baekeland et al.[22] found that "the patient who does best on

---

*The variables in this list that reflect experience(s) with alcohol are not properly "demographic." They fit more appropriately within symptom-history or phenomenological characteristics, which are discussed below.

disulfiram is an older, socially stable person . . . '' (p. 8).

These studies demonstrate the prognostic significance of some demographic variables in some treatment populations and thereby imply that the variables may prove useful in defining clinical subgroups. Whether any of these variables could be successfully applied in this way within the MLKHC program, as is assumed in the plan developed below, would have to be tested by exploratory work.

*Special Subgroups.*    Women and Hispanics are two MLKHC treatment population subgroups identified by demographic characteristics. Special programs to meet their particular needs were either under consideration or already in operation during 1977.

Men and women alcoholics, as classes, have similarities and differences. Increasing attention is being paid to the special needs of the women.[23] In American studies, the sex of patients has not been found to have prognostic significance[11, 12, 20] and it might be argued on that basis that treatment programs do not need to provide separate treatment pathways for men and women. On the other hand, Gomberg[23] cites two British studies of status following alcoholism treatment that show that women fared worse than men.

Regarding black American women, there are suggestions that the frequency and intensity of interpersonal contact during treatment must be high if it is to adequately substitute for what they experience when drinking. Two investigations drawn from separate communities, one a clinical study[24] and the other a survey of drinking patterns,[25] both indicate that black women who are either alcoholic or heavy drinkers have a strong tendency to drink in the company of others. Similarly, anecdotal evidence drawn from the community surrounding the MLKHC program indicated considerable group drinking throughout the day among black women with alcohol problems. To strengthen MLKHC alcoholism treatment services for women by promoting close interpersonal relationships supportive of *non*drinking behavior, the Alcoholism Unit staff prepared to initiate regular group meetings of interested female patients.

Religion is said to permeate Hispanic views of the world[26] and it was suggested earlier that the religious system of spiritualism may influence the manifestations of alcohol withdrawal states in Puerto Ricans/Hispanics. To the limited extent it has been investigated in *non*-Hispanic populations, religious affiliation has not proved a useful predictor of treatment outcome.[11, 15, 17] However, when outcome studies are done on Hispanics, it would be wise to examine not only denominational affiliation but also measures of religious beliefs and/or practices. In the MLKHC program, a counseling group for Hispanics was conducted in Spanish by a Puerto Rican counselor. The counselor structured the alcoholism-oriented discussions around passages from the Bible. This format was stable for over two years and meetings were consistently well attended.

*Psychological Characteristics.*   Their capacity for predicting treatment outcome is inferior to that of demographic characteristics, but the psychological characteristics of alcoholics also have shown prognostic significance. Measurements of intelligence, [11, 13, 15, 16] personality inventories, [10, 13, 16] ratings on Rorschach variables, [11, 15, 17] mood-scale ratings, [16] and indicators of field dependence/independence[8, 15, 27] have all been utilized. Pattison[8] anticipates that indicators of field dependence/independence will prove particularly helpful to clinicians and cites two studies that measure this using the embedded-figures test (EFT). [27, 28]

Assessment of psychological characteristics is not likely to become part of the MLKHC alcoholism program in the near future for two practical reasons. First, measurements of psychological characteristics are generally obtained by clinical psychologists and, as discussed earlier, hiring or even gaining access to specialized personnel poses major financial problems to the program. Once established, a system of assessment might not require the continuous presence of a psychologist — the timing and scoring of EFTs could perhaps be done by a trained nonpsychologist—but psychological expertise would be required to set up and validate such a system. Second, even with adequate staffing, psychological testing places time and effort demands on *patients*, which jeopardize their involvement in the program. Because of the low frustration tolerance, high anxiety, and impulsiveness manifested by many alcoholics, several authors[29-31] have commented on the desirability of avoiding lengthy and tedious diagnostic maneuvers, especially at intake. Test time alone for the short forms of the EFT may range up to 36 minutes.[32, 33]

*Symptom-History or Phenomenological Characteristics\**.    Another way to characterize alcoholics is by the things they say about themselves. Subjective reports of mental experiences such as blackouts, of physical experiences such as tremulousness, of behavior such as alcohol consumption or usual drinking circumstances, and of interpersonal experiences such as marital or legal difficulties are all examples of phenomenological characteristics that might be used to define subgroups among alcoholics. Probably the most familiar existing subgroupings of alcoholics based on such characteristics are those developed by Jellinek[40] and designated by letters of the Greek alphabet. In this typology, for example, an individual reporting withdrawal symptoms and a craving for alcohol along with a sense of not having control

*Symptoms* are the troublesome or unusual experiences a patient reports to a clinician. The patient's full narrative of an illness and his or her responses to problem-oriented and routine questions asked by the clinician are collectively referred to as the patient's *history*. This type of data, which is basically nontechnical and represents the naturally occurring direct experience of an individual, is frequently termed subjective or *phenomenological*. The study of such data of appearances or perceptions, phenomenology, originated as a philosophical movement. It now underlies an important viewpoint and methodologic approach in psychology. Some readers may want to seek out psychological writings for brief, orienting comments on this approach,[34, 35] for discussions of its philosophical roots and expanding influence,[36, 37] or for examples of its clinical application.[38, 39]

over his or her alcohol intake once a drinking episode begins would be classified in the *gamma* subgroup. Jellinek's phenomenological characterizations of alcoholics[40, 41] were based on questionnaire responses from members of Alcoholics Anonymous. Pattison[8] notes that this is a biased sample— AA "members are probably not typical of the [entire] alcoholic population" (p. 598)— and cites studies describing alcoholics who do not fit into Jellinek's framework. However, even though Jellinek's formulations may not have general applicability, it may be that the symptom-histories he describes characterize a clinical subgroup or subgroups that respond well on treatment pathways that emphasize AA. A study reported by Trice and Wahl[42] supports this possibility but can not be considered conclusive.*

The prognostic significance of certain other phenomenological characteristics has been better demonstrated. As indicated earlier, some treatment programs have found more favorable prognosis to be associated with patient reports of exposures to alcoholism at places away from home[16] and with reports of the drinking pattern of periodic benders.[15] Home or job as the principal place of drinking has been more favorable, in some analyses, than drinking in parks, alleys, or bars.[15, 17] Psychiatric diagnoses can be applied to alcoholics based on carefully elicited symptom-histories.[3, 43] Mindlin[11] found that such diagnoses

---

*Two additional studies relate loosely to this issue. G. Edwards (Alcoholism: The analysis of treatment, in *Alcohol and Alcoholism*, Popham, R. E., ed. [Toronto: University of Toronto Press, 1970], pp. 173–178) has compared inpatient and outpatient therapy of gamma alcoholics. Since all patients were in the gamma subgroup and all were exposed to AA, no comparisons to elucidate this question could be made using his data. N. I. Bateman and D. M. Peterson have reported that alcoholism phase (over 90% of subjects were gamma) "did not discriminate between abstinence and drinking" during the six-month period following completion of a treatment regimen that included AA. However, their study (Variables related to outcome of treatment for hospitalized alcoholics, in *International Journal of the Addictions*, 1971, 6, 215–224) has such design limitations (see May and Kuller[63]) that the meaning of this is questionable.

helped correctly predict treatment outcome in a psychiatrically oriented alcoholism treatment clinic.

Analysis of the MLKHC intake information revealed a potentially useful phenomenological variable when the data were grouped by time of drinking. As noted in Chapter 5, the patients who reported drinking only in the afternoon were more likely to be employed and to have done skilled or clerical work. Their average total daily alcohol consumption was lower and they were much more likely to drink at home. Such occupational and alcohol consumption characteristics have had favorable prognostic significance in other studies, but those relationships of course cannot be assumed for the MLKHC treatment group. The afternoon drinkers might have a relatively favorable prognosis, however, and it would be reasonable to look for this in either a prospective study or a retrospective cohort study.* Afternoon drinking might prove to have prognostic significance independent of its association with other drinking characteristics and occupational factors.

*Social Competence.*    For clarity, variables predictive of treatment outcome have been cited singly and under the separate headings of demographic, psychological, and phenomenological characteristics. In practice however, since predictive power is greater when such variables are considered together, it is usual to employ a composite of variables to predict patient response to treatment approaches. [10, 11, 15-17] The most useful prognostic indicators named above are regarded by some authors as measures

---

*The terms prospective and retrospective are used, as suggested by B. MacMahon and T. F. Pugh, in a manner consistent with their everyday meanings. A retrospective study is one based on past data or past events, such as would be found in existing medical records. A prospective study is one planned to observe events that have not yet occurred. (*Epidemiology: Principles and methods* [Boston: Little, Brown and Company, 1970], p. 44.)

of personal development or level of maturity. The authors relate the indicators to developmental notions of social competence[10, 15] or ego competence.[8]*

Social competence as an operational concept was introduced to the literature on alcoholism by Sugerman, Reilly, and Albahary.[46] These authors used the social competence measure of Zigler and Phillips,[47] which is based on the biographical variables of age, intelligence, education, occupation, employment history, and marital status. Zigler and Phillips ordered the possible categories within each variable to represent steps along

*"Mental health" may designate a desirable human state, but the term also sometimes refers to a sphere of activity of the helping professions. In the latter sense, mental health does not have a particularly long history. Early mental health efforts applied Freud's psychoanalytic personality theory to the problems of the mentally ill. Practice focused on exploring or uncovering unconscious repressed drives—particularly the sexual or libidinal drives seen as a general source of energy or motivation—and reducing conflicts with these drives.[44, 45] Mental health thinking about emotional development has reflected the same libidinal preoccupation.[45] From about 1940 on, there has been a growing recognition that the psychoanalytic libido model of motivation—even when modified or translated by neo-Freudians into interpersonal terms—is not adequate to explain all aspects of development. White[45] has reviewed the limitations of the libido and interpersonal models and has strongly argued the need for an additional, complementary model based on *competence*. In White's model, the "competence of an organism means its fitness or ability to carry on those transactions with the environment which result in its maintaining itself, growing, and flourishing"[45] (p. 100).

In formulating this competence model, White both drew upon and gave further expression to the trend in mental health to pay less attention to intrapsychic tensions and more attention to constructive interactions between organism and environment. The continuous expansion of ego psychology implies that this is no less a trend among theorists of psychoanalytic persuasion.[44, 45] Readers wishing to survey contributions to this trend, which might be called ecological, are referred to the National Institute of Mental Health behavioral sciences bibliography *Coping and adaptation* (National Clearinghouse for Mental Health Information, PHS Publication No. 2087, 1969).

a social effectiveness continuum.* The resulting index combines demographic characteristics with the psychological characteristic of intelligence. Sugerman, Reilly, and Albahary point out that this index, in the context of the developmental approach of Zigler and Phillips, has been used to show relationships between social competence and the incidence, form, diagnosis, and prognosis of mental disorder. [47, 50–53]

The study reported by Sugerman, Reilly, and Albahary[46] establishes a relationship between social competence and scores derived from an alcoholism scale that assesses predominantly phenomenological characteristics. The alcoholism scale is the Rudie-McGaughran Essential-Reactive Alcoholism Dimension (ERA scale), a 69-item instrument administered in a structured interview. [18] The items are concerned with past or present experiences and behavioral tendencies in eight areas including economic dependence, age at onset of drinking, drinking habits, types of friendship relations, and history of gastrointestinal symptoms. [18, 54] The ERA scale was designed to distinguish between two classes of alcoholics, essential and reactive, which were described by Knight in 1937. In Knight's psychoanalytic clinical study, essential alcoholics show little evidence of psychosexual development.

> These patients are completely dependent economically and emotionally and have never been able to support themselves financially for more than brief periods. They have never applied themselves persistently to reality tasks, as they lack the personality traits of perseverence, retention, and mastery of the object . . . Drinking starts in the teens and is not related to significant precipitating factors in reality. They will drink anything which

---

*Zigler and Phillips's approach reflects that taken in an earlier measure, the Worcester Scale of Social Attainment, which was designed to apply only to men. [48] That scale, in its turn, had incorporated some items from an Index of Adjustment described by Ruesch. [49] In the future, the categorization of marital status in such scales should perhaps be altered to accommodate homosexual as well as heterosexual relationships.

has the desired pharmacological effect... Their prognosis is poor.[46] (p. 553)

Reactive alcoholics, though portrayed less expressively by Knight, show more evidence of psychosexual development.

between bouts of drinking such patients may be reliable and responsible. They finish schooling and may hold jobs for long periods. Drinking starts later, precipitating factors may be found, and the prognosis is rather better than in the essential group.

... they are older at the time of breakdown ... and may be married.[46] (p. 553)

Some elements in the ERA scale, such as employment history and marital status, are common to Zigler and Phillips's index of social competence. A "moderate but highly significant relationship between social competence and the essential-reactive dimension" was found, with the more severely affected of the two groups, the essential alcoholics, showing less social competence and the reactive alcoholics showing more[46] (pp. 554–555). Additional evidence of mutual consistency between the Phillips-Zigler social competence index and the ERA scale has been reported by Levine and Zigler.[56] These authors emphasize the view that the social competence index and the essential-reactive dimension in alcoholism may both reflect a general development or maturity dimension.

Higher levels of social competence appear related to favorable outcome in the treatment of some mental disorders.[52] There is overlap between the variables included in the social competence index and the demographic and psychological variables discussed above, which have already been shown to have favorable prognostic significance in alcoholism. Therefore it would not be surprising if future studies find that patients with high social competence do well in alcoholism treatment. The logic of such a relationship has been simply stated:

The higher the maturity level attained prior to the onset of illness, the greater the resources for undoing inappropriate (pathological) solutions for social tasks, and the better the prognosis.[57] (p. 165)

There is little or no comment in the studies on social competence cited here about the possible *therapeutic* implications of the positive relationship between social competence and treatment outcome. Can treatment increase a patient's social competence? If so, would this contribute to better treatment outcome? Rosen et al.[57] express the opinion that the best to hope for during treatment is a return to the same level of social competence attained before the onset of illness (premorbid social competence). Other authors, however, have suggested that social competence index (or ERA scale) could be used as one measure of treatment outcome. In this application, a patient's social competence index a year or more after beginning treatment would be compared with that patient's premorbid social competence as a general indicator of treatment response. It is not explicit that the treatment process would be in part *directed* at improving each patient's score on such a scale, but at least the possibility of change is recognized. For many patients— especially in an inner-city setting— at least educational and employment-related characteristics present areas of potential improvement. Specific intervention in these areas would increase social competence scores and might prove very useful in promoting long-term treatment success.

Throughout alcoholism treatment, interventions are already used that could be interpreted as promoting patient maturity and thus as promoting social competence or simply *competence*. An excellent example of a competence-promoting treatment approach is embodied in the notion of *sobriety* that is inculcated by Alcoholics Anonymous. To be sober connotes much more to the successful AA member than leading a life without alcohol. Sobriety implies following a way of growth, taking an approach to life that incorporates an active quest for realistic satisfactions that are adaptive.

The whole point about clinical subgroups is that treatment

programs could work more rationally and likely more effectively by matching their interventions to specifically identified patient needs. If a need for greater development, or competence, in a certain area is identified, the patient's treatment plan would include help in that area. For example, a patient lacking in interpersonal skills might be channelled into family or group therapy; someone lacking a high school education, into a high school equivalency program; and so forth. This process now is usually informal. Formalizing it might not only improve individual patient care but also help mobilize new treatment resources because it would demonstrate how often present resources fail to meet patient needs.

In treatment planning, broad schemes to improve patient "competence" may be preferable to more restrictive plans directed at its subcategory "*social* competence." This would allow attention to *sensory* and *motor* competence as well. Young children generally attain basic levels of sensory and motor competence, but there is no definite ceiling to development in these areas. Through music, art, and exercise adults frequently obtain satisfaction and therapeutic benefits related to sensory and motor growth.* Again relating to an earlier time when the MLKHC program had funds to support innovative activities, a martial-art instructor conducted karate classes in the Alcoholism Unit twice a week. Patient participation was enthusiastic.

In many instances, clinical subgroups as discussed here may overlap. Some patients, for example, might need both family therapy and remedial education. There is no reason they could not receive both, though setting priorities and sequencing the interventions might be desirable. On the other hand, patient or facility characteristics tend to make some subgroups incompatible. A subgroup well suited for treatment in an aversion-

---

*Growth during adulthood is receiving increasing theoretical attention. Erikson[58, 59] has long expressed concern about the problems of growth faced by adults and, as a recent book edited by him illustrates, he is now joined by several others.[60] This work may eventually lead to a better understanding of how to enrich alcoholism treatment programming.

conditioning hospital[8] may not show overlap of practical significance with a subgroup well suited for treatment that emphasizes AA.

MATCHING SUBGROUPS WITH TREATMENT APPROACHES. The preceding discussion envisions that it will one day be usual practice to selectively match clinical subgroups of alcoholics with various treatment approaches. (Within these treatment approaches, an area deserving study is the matching of individual patients and therapists.) The process would be rational and actively undertaken by providers of alcoholism treatment services. Such a situation is widely anticipated in the alcoholism literature.[8-19] However, the matching processes that have so far been described are generally of two sorts (provider-determined and patient-determined), neither of which seems particularly rational.

Schmidt, Smart, and Moss's study of social class and the treatment of alcoholism[14] indicates that, in the program they investigated, "the therapies recommended and administered were affected by patients' class positions" (p. 92).

> For example, there was a tendency to exclude Class III patients [lowest of their three classes] from both uncovering and supportive therapies and instead to recommend protective drugs and also, to a lesser extent, group therapy. The over-all impression gained from this analysis was that recommended treatments *failed to follow established diagnoses but did follow definite social class lines*. (p. 87, italics added)

The authors refer to "inequalities in treatment" (p. 87) and feel "that therapists should be made aware of their tendency to exclude lower class patients from certain treatments" (p. 95). These comments depict treatment personnel establishing differential treatment pathways and the process appears spontaneous — guided more by unconscious influences on the treatment personnel than by explicit, tested criteria.

The treatment-seeking behavior of patients themselves influences the type of treatment they receive. Pattison and colleagues[9, 10] characterized different types of treatment facilities and their patient populations. There were distinct differences among facilities and among patient populations when they compared an aversion-conditioning hospital, an outpatient clinic, a half-way house, and a police work center. [10] They found a "high degree of congruence . . . between the psychodynamic and socio-dynamic needs, defenses, and goals of each population and its respective facility"[10] (p. 200). They have been "struck by the relatively good 'match' found between population needs and perceptions and the philosophies and methods of the facilities to which they go"[10] (p. 225). Because they assume that patients have reasons for seeking care where they do and that the resulting matches may strongly influence the likelihood of treatment success, these authors caution programs not to make changes in their treatment methods without carefully assessing the implications of the changes for *their* treatment population.

Kissin, Platz, and Su[17] found that:

> Both social and psychological factors appear to play a major role in treatment acceptance of outpatient psychotherapy and inpatient rehabilitation. The more socially and psychologically intact alcoholics tend to accept psychotherapy; the less socially and psychologically intact alcoholics tend to accept inpatient rehabilitation. (p. 25)

Their data also suggest "that with a heterogeneous alcoholic population, a greater choice of treatments offered increases the overall success rate" (p. 25).

It cannot be readily judged just how rational patient treatment-seeking decisions are, but results such as these imply that those planning to develop a variety of treatment approaches — whether within one program or within a community under different programs — might be wise to provide for patient participation in the selection of the patient's own treatment pathway. Costello[61] has reviewed additional evidence supporting the utility of such an approach and discusses a possible tendency of alcoholics "to sabotage treatment efforts" (p. 270) when no opportunity for choice is offered.

## Evaluation

This chapter deals with program planning. Evaluative research is the planning tool that tells those responsible for a program, and others, whether or not the program is meeting its objectives. Knowledge of program results permits informed judgments about the program's value and efficiency. When evaluation shows that a program is effective, the program may be continued with a measure of confidence pending future studies. If a program is ineffective or partially effective, the program (or perhaps its objectives) can then be revised. When revision is indicated, frequently the evaluation study assists in determining the most promising new direction. If it is fair to assume that no program is ever perfect, it is apparent that evaluative research must be an ongoing activity and that it must be done if we are to maximize the benefit derived from our finite resources.

Evaluative research is basically a scientific enterprise and its validity depends upon its adherence to scientific methods. Appropriate methods will be detailed here but first it is important to realize that, with few exceptions, *the methods used in published studies that purport to evaluate the treatment of alcoholism have been woefully inadequate*. This point has been emphasized and carefully documented from the current literature by Hill and Blane,[62] May and Kuller,[63] and Baekeland.[64] May and Kuller focus on the methodologic shortcomings of existing studies and conclude that only through valid future studies can it be established whether "what has been believed for years is in fact true, i.e., that alcoholism treatment programs inherently help the alcoholic patient to a successful recovery" (p. 479). Baekeland is no less critical of research methods. But he offers tentative interpretations and constructive suggestions regarding alcoholism treatment drawn from the voluminous literature he reviewed.

ADEQUATE RESEARCH DESIGN.   Hill and Blane[62] summarized basic requirements for a study seeking to evaluate alcoholism treatment:

1. In order to attribute change to a specific treatment, it is necessary to show that the change would not have occurred without the treatment; this requires the use of *a comparison or control condition* (either a non-treated group or a group treated with a form of treatment other than that under investigation).
2. In order to make treatment and control conditions truly comparable, the individual patients in each group must have had an equal chance of being assigned to the treatment or control conditions. This entails the use of a subject-selection procedure that ensures *random assignment* of patients to various treatment conditions.
3. In studying change in behavior it is necessary to select and *define the type of behavior* that is to be evaluated; this selection, however arbitrary, must be either theoretically or empirically relevant to the presumed effects of treatment.
4. It is necessary to establish reliable methods and *instruments for measuring* any change in behavior.
5. If a change in behavior is to be measured, it is necessary to obtain pretreatment *baseline measures* against which later measures, either during or after treatment, can be compared. This means that the same measures must be applied before and after treatment. (p. 77, italics added)

Prominent among the criticisms of existing alcoholism treatment evaluation studies is their lack of control groups. *Un*treated alcoholics sometimes improve.[64] When treated patients improve, unless there is a comparison or control group that shows less improvement during the same period, it is not sound to assume the treated patients got better because of their treatment. Specific patient characteristics are predictive of successful treatment outcome.* It is not yet clear that treatment adds to the tendency of some individuals to improve. Baekeland points out that in the absence of controlled evaluation studies that assign patients randomly, it might well be assumed ''that the nature of the patient is much more important [to treatment

---

*These relationships, incidentally, have generally been demonstrated by comparing subgroups *within* a treatment population. Such intragroup comparisons are valid for establishing associations of predictive value but do not necessarily delineate causal relationships. The findings should not be assumed to apply outside the original treatment group.

outcome] than that of the treatment used on him'' (p. 398).

Measures of treatment outcome have also attracted criticism. Many studies have relied upon patient reports of abstinence from alcohol as the only measure of successful treatment. Pattison[8, 65] especially has addressed the inadequacy of this outcome criterion to deal with the variability that is found among both patients and treatment programs. A trend now seems established to evaluate outcome in terms of demographic and psychological characteristics as well as drinking behavior. Some investigators include other phenomenological characteristics in addition to those related to alcohol consumption.

A number of questionnaires or other instruments that standardize the data collected at intake and follow-up have been devised. Studies that use such instruments have already been cited[9, 10, 54] and other sources might be mentioned.[66–68] Jacobson's compendium of assessment tests[18] is a useful guide to available material. Goal Attainment Scaling (GAS), which measures outcome against individualized treatment goals, represents a potentially powerful evaluation tool. GAS was developed by Kiresuk and Sherman[69] as a general method for evaluating community mental health programs. It has been adapted to the evaluation of alcoholism treatment[70] and its accommodation to individual differences may eventually lead to its widespread use in the alcoholism field. While there was no commitment to future use of GAS in the MLKHC program, the system was described to the Alcoholism Unit staff and they were given literature on it.

Baseline measurements, preferably obtained before treatment even begins, provide a relevant standard with which to compare each patient's outcome measurements. Like control groups, baseline data are missing from many published reports.[62, 63] Still another criticism is that some authors obtained follow-up data too soon. Several reviewers feel that the collection of outcome data should occur no sooner than one year after a patient enters a treatment program. [12, 62, 63, 71]

ADEQUATE RESEARCH REPORTS.    Standards for reporting an evaluative investigation are also provided by Hill and Blane[62] and, like their guidelines for study design, these also highlight deficiencies found in the literature.

1. In order to place the study in perspective, the setting in which it is undertaken should be clearly described.
2. The type of therapeutic technique or program evaluated should be specifically described so that the reader can interpret its relation to the results reported.
3. The population, procedures for selecting patients, and relevant characteristics of the samples must be reported, and when patients are dropped from or lost to study, the reasons and numbers of such omissions should be noted.
4. The nature of the measuring instruments applied, their reliability, and when and how they were applied should be described.
5. Reports of findings and any attendant statistical applications should be stated in sufficient detail to allow the reader to make his own interpretations of the data reported.[62] (p. 78)

The accurate descriptions encouraged in these five points provide a means to at least tentatively relate one study to another. The studies in the literature are generally based on consecutive voluntary admissions to particular treatment programs.[63] Sampling bias* is inescapable in this situation but it can be mitigated by scrupulous attention to observing these guidelines. Interstudy comparisons may prove useful once multiple studies that adhere to these requirements are available. The individual studies should perhaps seek to report data in terms of well-defined clinical subgroups.**

*Detailed discussions of sampling bias are available in the references by Pattison[8] and Baekeland, Lundwall, and Kissin.[71]

**This discussion has assumed that program self-evaluation can be worthwhile and that intramural evaluations of alcoholism treatment programs are likely to outnumber extramural evaluations for some time. See Quinones, M. A., et al., Evaluation of drug abuse rehabilitation efforts: A review, in *American Journal of Public Health*, 1979, 69, 1164–1169, for comments on intramural vs. extramural evaluation.

## A PLAN FOR THE MLKHC PROGRAM

One means of increasing the efficiency of the treatment provided at the MLKHC Alcoholism Unit might be to develop a new treatment pathway for patients presumed to have the best prognosis. Such patients might make satisfactory progress in treatment with less than the usual amount of patient-counselor interaction and the pathway would be planned with that in mind. Patient monitoring would have to be adequate to promptly detect individuals not doing well so that they could be quickly re-routed to more intensive treatment. A portion of the monitoring responsibility, and perhaps even treatment responsibility, might be displaced from the Alcoholism Unit staff to MLKHC health-team members. Particularly the team internists represent potential treatment resources given the success of internists as primary therapists in some alcoholism treatment studies.[12, 15, 17] The new pathway could intensify patient-patient interactions through use of a buddy system or big brother/sister relationships. Patients entering this pathway might be persuaded to use Alcoholics Anonymous and their AA sponsors to a greater extent than usual.

To mobilize this plan without undertaking a preliminary outcome study, it would be necessary to assume that the demographic characteristics that consistently proved good predictors of successful outcome in other populations and programs would also be good predictors for the MLKHC treatment group. The good prognosis subgroup might then be defined in terms of the Phillips-Zigler social competence index modified to exclude the intelligence variable. It is recognized that present evidence is inconclusive and that it may either be reasonable[54] or ill advised[56] to omit intelligence from the index. The deletion, however, would respect resource limitations and would avoid the problem of reconciling intelligence test standards to the ethnic composition of the MLKHC treatment population, an issue that might be troublesome even if Hispanic patients were excluded from initial studies. Defining the subgroup with a social competence index seems preferable to using the ERA scale since the latter has a 30-to-40-minute administration time. A few phenomenological characteristics might supplement the index and could be used as additional selection criteria, particularly if it were necessary to limit the size of the subgroup defined. However, simply raising the cutoff point on the social competence index would also limit subgroup size.

To serve both methodological and patient-care considerations, patients would have to be selected for the new treatment pathway in step-wise fashion. During their intake interviews all new patients meeting the selection criteria could be identified. In those same interviews, when the discussion turns to treatment planning, every eligible patient could be offered the opportunity to participate in the evaluation of the new treatment pathway. Thus, each patient in the defined subgroup would have a choice concerning participation in the program trial. However—and this would have to be explained to each patient before his or her choice was made—the randomization of patients into a treatment group that would start on the new pathway and a control group that would follow the usual pathway would take place *after* their decisions about participation have been made. Therefore, a patient choosing to participate would have about a 50% chance of starting on the new pathway. The random assignment of a patient to the treatment or control group could be made via a sealed envelope opened by the interviewer once an eligible patient has decided to participate. The evaluation study would examine intake and follow-up data on the entire eligible subgroup, including those who declined to participate in the controlled trial and thereby reverted to the usual pathway. Patient choice concerning participation in the randomized trial seems warranted from an ethical point of view and, as mentioned above, an opportunity to make such a choice may of itself have therapeutic value. Randomizing the patients into the two groups after they volunteer to participate helps protect the results from bias. Looking, in the data analysis, at those eligible patients who chose not to participate would help assess any bias resulting from the self-selection step.

The intake and follow-up data already required of the MLKHC treatment program by the NIAAA Treatment Monitoring System would be incorporated into this proposed evaluation study. A sheet to facilitate computation of the social competence index could be used both at intake and at each follow-up assessment. Data collection on each patient in the subgroup could formally take place every six months for, say, a two-year period, though clinical contacts with most patients would probably be more frequent. Outcome would thus be measured in terms of demographic (sociological) characteristics and, among phenomenological characteristics, at least drinking behavior.

In operation, this plan would decrease the program resources applied to a portion of the patients presumed to have good prognoses. It should at least preserve the previous level of care for all other patients regardless of their prognosis. Such an arrangement is actually counter to a common practice among social-service agencies. At least in the relatively recent past, many agencies have withdrawn resources from those most difficult to help and "confined themselves . . . to a clientele with whom they can relate and from whom they can expect some successes"[44] (p. 656). The opening lines of Mindlin's paper on predicting therapeutic outcome candidly portray the outlook of one such agency:

> The staff of the Alcohol Clinic . . . are naturally interested in the problem of predicting the outcome of therapy. Although the doors of the Clinic are open to all applicants with an alcohol problem, the question of whether some of our time and efforts might be spent more wisely with some patients than with others has been raised, at least by our own staff.[11] (p. 604)

It may be argued that the plan described for MLKHC is premature. It assumes prognostic relationships that as yet have no empirical support from this treatment population. It would alter patient care. The Phillips-Zigler social competence index suggested for modified use has previously neither been applied to outpatient alcoholics nor related to the outcome of alcoholism treatment. [54, 56]

An alternative plan — to undertake a retrospective study — would show more regard for these objections. The NIAAA forms provide a reasonable baseline measurement of demographic and some phenomenological variables. Patients who entered the program from June 1976 on would have intake information in this format and follow-up data could be sought from this group. Such a study would not have a control group and could therefore not be used to evaluate the treatment program. Comparisons within the group, however, would help establish the prognostic significance of various intake characteristics and the prognostic value of a modified social competence index could be assessed.

*Chapter 8*

# COMMUNITY IMPLICATIONS:
# TIME FOR PREVENTION

The usual message to society from groups concerned about alcoholism has been that society should recognize and become informed about alcoholism as a disease, should provide specific help for those affected by this disease, and should promote research on alcoholism.[1] It is reasonable that those in the alcohol field take an advocacy role but their message addresses too few of the factors that jointly determine society's burden of alcohol-related problems. Their approach only indirectly supports prevention and is consistent with a conceptual system of individual medicine rather than of social medicine (see Chapter 3). Cahalan[2] has summed up the status quo:

> The alcohol field is peopled with some very strange bedfellows,
> all of whom settle upon the treatment of the problem drinker,
> rather than on policies to prevent alcoholism. (p. 17)

A call to action that is expanded to an ecological view might lead to beneficial changes in etiological factors overlooked or underemphasized in the present approach. People in the alcohol field are aware that their impact to date has been a limited one. Keller, often a spokesman for a segment of those in this field, has asked, ''Why hasn't there been more significant progress?''[3] (p. 24). His own answer to that question — even though he does not seem to know where it will lead — suggests that the time has come for a broader understanding of how society can deal with alcohol problems: ''We haven't made more progress because we haven't learned how to prevent''[3] (p. 25).

If progress consists of initially halting increases in alcohol-related problems and eventually decreasing the overall toll of alcohol abuse and alcoholism, progress can derive from both preventive efforts and treatment efforts. Chapter 7 examined ways to improve treatment efforts. This chapter will outline community approaches to the prevention of alcohol problems. In this discussion the inner city provides material to illustrate points that are relevant to many settings.

Substance abuse prevention programs are sometimes distinguished as either *substance-specific* (would seek to educate participants about one or more particular drugs of abuse) or *nonspecific* (would seek to promote the development of individuals unlikely to use drugs as a coping mechanism). Analogous divisions will be used here, though the latter will be expanded from an individual-centered notion to an ecological one. That is, the heading ''nonspecific'' will cover activities that promote individual competence plus activities that promote an environment that engenders competence and does not itself induce individuals to use drugs as a coping mechanism.

Before discussing particular community prevention approaches, it may be helpful to explore how communities might initiate preventive action and also determine whether their efforts to control alcohol problems are accomplishing anything. Moser[4] tentatively recommends that concerned countries and communities ''should establish suitable mechanisms to keep the situation continually under review, to develop policies and programmes and to promote their implementation'' (p. 139). Any actual suggestions concerning mechanisms that may be suitable for these purposes, however, Moser defers to future communications from an ongoing World Health Organization project. Meanwhile, fruitful discussion or even concrete planning may be stimulated by the following portrayal of one possible mechanism.

## AN EXPERIMENTING SOCIETY

In a discussion of problems — particularly urban problems — that "have multiple and complex sources" and for which a variety of solutions might be proposed, Ashmore and McConahay[5] state:

> We would like to see an experimenting society such as Donald Campbell . . . has proposed: one that seeks solutions to problems, uses the best possible method of evaluating the effects of a given solution and, most importantly, is willing to try a new approach if the first one fails. (p. 5)

The notion of an experimenting society is quite useful here because it combines the assumption that evaluative research is an essential component of planned social change (see Rieker and Suchman[6]) with the assumption that the responsibility for success and for the research rests with the society or community and not, at least in the first analysis, with any narrow group within it.

To evaluate efforts planned to reduce alcohol problems, it would be necessary to measure the occurrence of such problems before and after specific interventions or, perhaps better, to monitor the occurrence of these problems continuously. Some possible monitoring methods are mentioned below. Trist[7] provides a conceptual view relevant to such a broad need:

> If fundamental research is discipline-based, problem-oriented research may be said to be *domain-based*. Domain-based inquiry links a group of sciences to a major sector of social concern. The problems are generic rather than specific. They give rise to meta-problems. They require on-going endeavour leading to

cumulations of findings. . . . These findings contribute simultaneously to the advancement of knowledge and to human better-
ment. The development of a domain is jointly determined by the
social and scientific interests concerned. (pp. 91–92, italics in
original)

Trist's statements imply that evaluative research should be
integral to any societal action to reduce alcohol problems. But
before either action or research can begin, several questions
must be answered. Who will identify targets for intervention?
Who will plan and carry out the interventions? Who will do the
evaluative research?

Society needs a mechanism to organize and distribute these
responsibilities in order to act on them. New institutions may be
needed. One existing U.S. institution — the National Institute
on Alcohol Abuse and Alcoholism (NIAAA) — might be expected to orchestrate community action on alcohol, but so far the
NIAAA has not developed the breadth and depth of participation
and of influence that are requisite for this function.[8]

Two similar, innovative institutional suggestions might be
further developed and then successfully applied to this problem.
Commoner[9] has proposed a biologic field station to study the
city, a laboratory that would develop an integrated research and
teaching approach to the urban environment similar to the
approach the Marine Biological Laboratory in Woods Hole,
Massachusetts, takes to the marine environment. Commoner
assumes that such an institution could "illuminate the need for
action on the stubborn economic, social, and political problems
that are the real source of the degraded state of the city as a place
to live" (p. 111). Kennedy[10] has made a related proposal, but
his vision of "community health observatories" takes an additional step. Kennedy's field stations would have a similar broad
responsibility for research, but they would also have responsibility for changing factors that adversely affect health in their
communities. They would not simply illuminate needs for action,
they would take action. To legitimize such action and promote
successful results, a health observatory would have to be very

much a part of its community. Close health observatory/community interdependence might be the only way to fairly represent and integrate the diverse needs and interests existing within each community.

Ecologically oriented effector and monitoring institutions that are *in* and *of* communities might prove well suited to deal with the multiple interrelationships that contribute to rates of alcohol problems. They could, of course, have global missions with regard to health and need not restrict their activities solely to matters related to alcohol.

How might such institutions — or anyone — monitor alcohol problems in a community?* Pattison[11] calls for "a community epidemiology approach" (p. 640) as a tool for planning alcoholism treatment efforts. He suggests identifying and enumerating all subpopulations or subgroups of alcoholics in a community, cataloguing the helping resources available to each subgroup, and then planning new services directed at unmet needs. These steps are not exhaustive, but if envisioned as reiterated at appropriate time intervals, they convey some sense of the monitoring process needed.

Pattison lightly touches on one method applicable to community epidemiology by commenting that "preliminary community epidemiology can be conducted with minimal resources" (p. 641) and then citing one relatively inexpensive community prevalence *survey*. Manis and Hunt[12] have also reported some success with a community survey. Yet Manis and Hunt and others generally view such surveys as ponderous and expensive means of gathering information. On the other hand, pollsters seem rather efficient as they monitor public opinion and television-viewing practices with survey methods. Streamlined data collection instruments may make routine alcohol problem

---

*The methodologic discussion in the text is confined to monitoring alcohol problems, a practice that would provide an ongoing indication of the results of treatment and prevention efforts. Undiscussed in the text are multiple social, economic, and other possible factors that an institution like a community health observatory might seek to change and would want to monitor directly.

surveys feasible. Short (less than 15 items), self-administered questionnaires that screen for alcohol problems have already been developed for adults[13] and for adolescents.[14]

But even efficient surveys require person-by-person or household-by-household data collection. Alternative approaches to assessing alcohol problems in communities use data already collected for other purposes. Alcohol-related mortality data compiled by bureaus of vital statistics are used to estimate the prevalence of alcoholism.[15–17] These mortality-based prevalence estimates, however, involve considerable extrapolation since the basic data generally represent only advanced drinking problems. Further, some components of the data, such as deaths due to alcoholic cirrhosis, might be slow to respond to community intervention. Partly because of these limitations of the methods that rely on mortality information alone, more sensitive systems have been developed, which may prove reliable for monitoring relatively small populations over relatively short time periods. Westermeyer and Bearman[18] have proposed combining information obtained from multiple social agencies to produce specific rates of events that have a known relationship to alcohol use. Their method incorporates readily available statistics on events such as child abuse, alcohol-related deaths, and alcohol-related hospital admissions. A Canadian group[19] has reported pilot tests of such an approach and Cleary[17] has analyzed data from counties in Wisconsin using a social-indicator method very similar to that of Westermeyer and Bearman. The capabilities of such systems might be extended if, without compromising patient confidentiality, they could also draw upon the often detailed information appearing in outpatient medical records.

## PREVENTION APPROACHES

### Alcohol-Specific Activities

There is a possibility of confusing prevention efforts with treatment efforts particularly because both alcohol-specific prevention approaches and alcoholism treatment approaches pay considerable attention to human interactions with beverage alcohol. It may be helpful to point out how these two classes of activities differ in their goals, the groups they address, and their methods. Prevention promotes avoidance of potential suffering, treatment promotes relief of present suffering and avoidance of recurrences. Alcoholism treatment addresses people with serious drinking problems and generally tries to help them eliminate their use of alcohol.* Alcohol-specific prevention addresses people who do not now have serious drinking problems and tries to help them regulate their use of alcohol such that future problems are minimized. Some treatment methods, such as the approach of Alcoholics Anonymous, are relatively well established. No prevention methods have achieved comparable acceptance. Various prevention methods have been tried and more have been suggested, but, perhaps partly because of society's low priority on prevention and related research,[8] their reliability remains to be established.

Moser[4] uses the causal concepts of host, agent, and environment to help describe programs that seek to prevent alcohol-related problems. Particular programs may attempt "to interrupt the pathological processes between agent, host and environment or to render the host more resistant, the agent and environment less harmful"[4] (p. 136). An example of prevention programs seeking to interrupt dangerous interactions between host-identified factors and agent-identified factors would be programs that help children from alcoholic families avoid repeated use of alcohol-induced escape as a means of coping with problems.[20]

---

*The traditional emphasis on abstinence in alcoholism treatment became a hotly debated issue following the mid-1976 release of the Rand Report (Armor, D. M., Polich, J. M., & Stambul, H. B., *Alcoholism and Treatment* — now in general circulation [New York: John Wiley & Sons, 1978])[2] So far there seems to be insufficient evidence to support widespread departure from the practice of encouraging alcoholics to not drink. However, exploratory studies of selected, closely supervised patients may eventually identify a subgroup of alcoholics who need not pursue lifelong abstinence.

Prevention programs directed primarily at people susceptible to alcohol problems (host) and at alcoholic beverages (agent) are discussed within this subsection on alcohol-specific activities. Programs that alter the environment to limit demand for alcohol are discussed both in this subsection and in the one on non-alcohol-specific activities.

HOST-DIRECTED ACTIVITIES. Host-directed alcohol problem prevention approaches are basically educational; they assume that the large percentage of the population who drink are better able to avoid harm if they are knowledgeable about the effects of alcohol. However, at the same time that the body of knowledge pertinent to safe drinking has been increasing, there has been increasing recognition that knowledge alone is often insufficient to ensure safe drinking behavior.[2,4] Even so, it may still be argued that alcohol-specific knowledge is at least useful and perhaps often necessary if drinkers are to ever sort out reasonable drinking options from unreasonable ones. Three types of potentially valuable alcohol-related information will be distinguished here.

The first will be termed *experiential*, though the same points could also be developed from a more detached, scientific viewpoint. At one time or another, most drinkers experience drowsiness as an effect of alcohol. This is a manifestation of alcohol's sleep-producing or sedative-hypnotic properties. Other manifestations would include impairment of coordination and reaction time. These alcohol effects contribute to accidental deaths and injuries. Prevention programs concerned with highway safety frequently remind people that driving soon after drinking may be dangerous and emphasize that a drinker's physical size, associated food consumption, and previous experience with alcohol are factors that, in addition to dose of alcohol, influence degree of impairment. Exhibitionistic youthful drinkers are too often unaware of another danger arising from alcohol's sedative properties. Rapid consumption of a large amount of liquor can effectively turn off the nerve center that drives breathing so that, without external life support, the suddenly sedated drinker dies from lack of oxygen. Some young people learn of this danger from formal preventive education, but perhaps more learn of it through the experience of either knowing the victim of a fatal alcohol overdose or hearing of such a tragedy from a friend or acquaintance.

A second type of useful knowledge is *alcoholism-related* and sometimes appears as lists of safe drinking practices. The do's and don'ts on these lists in part represent habits recollected by alcoholics that seem to have contributed to the progression of their illness. Examples include the suggestions that drinkers always measure liquor carefully, avoid gulping alcoholic beverages, occasionally find substitutes for alcohol at traditional drinking times, and learn to refuse alcoholic drinks gracefully by quietly selecting juices and other soft drinks. Another suggestion is that people be aware of symptoms that warn of alcoholism* and seek help at the earliest hint of difficulty. One 20-item list of safe drinking pointers that includes these suggestions and others is published by the New York Blue Cross/Blue Shield organization in its booklet *The Alcoholic American*.

*Biomedical* information is a third type of knowledge potentially useful to drinkers. There is no clearly defined level of personal alcohol consumption at which drinking becomes dangerous, but findings of biomedical research that bear on this issue are attracting increasing attention.[21-23] Possible consequences of regular alcohol consumption include liver tissue alterations that may progress to liver disease, most seriously cirrhosis.[24-28] The risk of alcohol-induced liver injury seems to rise with increasing amount and duration of alcohol intake. European and U.S. studies suggest that average-size male drinkers who wish to avoid liver disease would be prudent to keep their regular alcohol intake *below* the equivalent of eight ounces of 86-proof whisky per day,[21, 23, 27, 29] or roughly four to six drinks. Experi-

---

*Lists of warning symptoms are available from both NCA and NIAAA and frequently appear on posters and in popular magazines.

mental data indicate that ''amounts of alcohol consumed by many 'social' drinkers are enough to damage the liver, and one need never have been drunk to sustain alcohol-induced hepatic injury''[29] (p. 869). Other biomedical research strongly suggests that regular consumption of three or more drinks per day increases a drinker's risk of hypertension.[30] The guideline implicit in these findings—that regular alcohol consumption should be limited to two or fewer drinks per day—is harmonious with other findings[31, 32] that alcohol consumption in the same range (two or fewer drinks per day) is associated with lowered risk of coronary heart disease. Of course, *it may be unsafe for persons prone to alcoholism, pregnant, or having elevated serum triglycerides to drink even small amounts of alcohol.*

In varying proportions, experiential, alcoholism-related, and biomedical information are incorporated into host-directed alcohol problem prevention activities. Adult audiences have been approached largely through mass media. Any evaluation of these efforts—and little has been attempted—would be difficult even if a system of community epidemiology were already in place. However, adolescent audiences have generally been approached in school settings, where at least limited program evaluation has been feasible.

Available evaluation studies indicate that the manner in which information is presented to teenagers may be considerably more important than the information itself.[33, 34] Programs that dramatized the hazards of excessive drinking in order to scare youthful drinkers and potential drinkers away from alcohol seemed, if anything

> to make alcohol misuse more attractive as a symbol for those
> young people who are inclined toward risk-taking behavior and
> who engage in deviant acts to test out the limits of the adult
> world.[34] (p. 170)

Less sensational programs that sought simply to transmit information about alcohol effects and alcohol-associated risks perhaps avoided unintentionally increasing alcohol misuse, but they have not clearly had their intended effect of decreasing such misuse. One reason given for the lack of effectiveness of these information-transmission or intellectual approaches is that they do not allow "for an adequate consideration of the affective or noncognitive elements, such as attitudes, values, and developmental needs, that influence alcohol use"[34] (p. 170). Attempts to constructively influence these nonintellectual determinants of drinking behavior have employed techniques that include drama and group discussions among peers. The ability of these values clarification programs to promote responsible alcohol-related behavior will remain unclear pending comprehensive, relatively long-term evaluation studies.

Chapter 3 mentioned the trend in prevention programs away from the alcohol-specific educational approaches just described and toward nonspecific approaches, which, rather than impart knowledge about either alcohol or drinkers, seek to remedy factors believed to predispose young people to maladaptive drinking. These newest programs try to ensure present and future satisfaction for participants by fostering independence, coping skills, and the ability to set realistic objectives and then attain them using available resources.*

In addition to host-directed prevention activities for general adult and adolescent audiences, special programs serve people with special needs. Children of alcoholics, for example, may avoid alcoholism and other difficulties if they receive sensitive counseling coupled with transmission of alcoholism-related knowledge.[20] If a biologic "marker" is discovered that can identify persons especially susceptible to alcoholism[35] or if an efficient means of testing for a "prealcoholic personality" can be developed,[36] these individuals at high risk for alcoholism could also be given prophylactic attention. Language and culture circumscribe the prevention methods and program contents appropriate for some audiences. In the South Bronx, Spanish-

---

*See the footnote near the end of Chapter 3 for several references relevant to non-substance-specific substance abuse prevention programs.

language programs would be necessary to reach a large segment of the population. Harper[37] generated a list of 23 safe drinking suggestions that are culturally relevant for many blacks. Harper's suggestions are based upon recurrent, unfortunate alcohol-associated experiences of American blacks. The list includes:

4. Liquor, guns, and arguments in the same room or setting don't mix. This combination should be avoided. Drinking while gambling is one classic example where resulting arguments have ended in many fights and deaths in the Black community . . . .

6. Liquor and high blood pressure don't mix. Neither do other Black-related diseases that are contrary to regular or heavy drinking. Blacks with such diseases should be discouraged from alcohol use that could cause danger to health and life.[37] (p. 15)

The finding of some studies that blacks who develop alcohol problems begin drinking at an early age suggests that alcohol-specific preventive activities among blacks should extend to very young age groups.

It is worth emphasizing that host-directed preventive activities can seek to prevent a variety of alcohol-related problems, not just alcoholism as a disease. Programs for drinking drivers, for example, aim to prevent highway injuries and deaths.[38] Moser[4] delineates a wide range of alcohol-related problems and cites various rising statistics to highlight need for a diversified augmentation of preventive efforts. One impediment to progress along the broad front of preventive needs may be "a tendency to see prevention only in terms of educational measures"[39] (p. 19). Dekker[39] states that "measures to deal with [alcohol] distribution are equally important" (p. 19).

AGENT-DIRECTED ACTIVITIES.   Approaches to alcohol problem prevention that seek to limit the distribution or availability of alcoholic beverages may be classified as agent-directed. Advocates of these approaches generally cite evidence of a fixed relation between average alcohol consumption and excessive alcohol consumption.[40, 41] They point out that the present rise, in many populations, of alcohol-related problems is associated with a rise in overall alcohol consumption by those populations. To halt the rise in problems, they argue, it is necessary to halt the rise in consumption. Further, an eventual decrease in overall consumption would presumably lead to a decrease in alcohol-related problems.

The agent-directed activities proposed as means of decreasing consumption are basically legislative. Increased taxation to raise the price of alcoholic beverages has been mentioned. Other possible measures include restricting the number or density of alcohol outlets, curtailing hours of alcoholic beverage sales, and putting more stringent limits on conditions of sale, as by raising the legal drinking age.

It is well recognized that abrupt enactment of these legal interventions would have a negative impact on some economic interests. Several authors point out that strong public support would be essential before measures such as these could be effective.[4, 39, 41, 42] Dekker[39] and Kendell[41] both describe steps — largely educational — that might gradually produce enough shift in public opinion to make legislative action on alcohol viable. Some of their steps are reflected in the comments that follow.

A SOCIAL MOVEMENT.   Breslow,[43] exhorting the American medical community to become more prevention oriented, states:

> Habits that are harmful to health arise from both cultivated appetites for, and the ready availability of such things as animal fat, alcohol, cigarettes, and physical inactivity. Developing healthful habits in such a milieu will require attention both to individual choice and *to the circumstances in which such choice is made*. (p. 2094, italics added)

Support for both host-directed and agent-directed preventive approaches can be drawn from this passage. However, a third type of alcohol-specific approach, environment-directed, is implied here also. Consider one person at a social gathering where alcohol is available. Whether and how much that person drinks can often be strongly influenced by the behavior of the other people in the person's immediate social environment. NIAAA posters and television spots remind people that, without caution, they may contribute to alcohol-related harm to others. These educational devices sometimes suggest guidelines for responsible behavior toward others whenever alcohol is available. Such alcohol-specific preventive communications are directed at the social environment of drinkers. In the physical environment, alcoholic-beverage advertising is a possible prevention activity target.

Cahalan[2] displays a guarded optimism when discussing alcohol-specific community interventions. He doubts that mass media educational campaigns, of themselves, are likely to matter much. Rather, he favors interactive schemes as he succinctly integrates host-, agent-, and environment-directed alcohol-specific preventive approaches:

> Given the right kinds of medical advice, public education and small-group discussions of techniques to minimize drinking, society may play a major role in defeating alcoholism. These efforts must be linked with controls over alcohol advertising and marketing, laws restricting hours and condition of sale, and regulations over hosts and bartenders.[2]

These are hardly final suggestions, and Cahalan encourages "experimental programs to test the effectiveness of different approaches"[2] (p. 19).

No few, discrete activities appear adequate to reverse the tide of alcohol-related problems. Even within the alcohol-specific area, launching diversified prevention efforts, evaluating them, and repeatedly improving them represents an enormous task. Cahalan feels "the only program that might minimize alcoholism would be a broad social movement"[2] (p. 19). Perhaps as economic incentives for preventive action become more clear,[44] such a movement can gain momentum.

## Nonspecific Activities: The Competent Community*

In any community, competing interests make coordinated collective action difficult.[45] For such action to take place smoothly requires a very high level of mental health among community members and an effective community itself might be thought of as mature or competent. However, lest this point dissuade some communities from even attempting coordinated efforts, Cottrell[45] points out that simply engaging in collective action can improve the mental health of individuals and in turn that of their communities. It seems important to proceed.

Communities may be conceived at various levels. Some alcohol-specific preventive activities might best be carried out by neighborhoods or municipalities. Yet the non-alcohol-specific factors that contribute to alcohol problems in the inner city — poverty, racism, unemployment and underemployment, and undereducation — cannot be overcome solely by local community action. Undoing these problems requires resources far beyond those that exist within the South Bronx or other inner-city areas.

Ashmore and McConahay[5] emphasize the limitations of poor communities: "lack of economic resources is the heart of the problem of poverty" (p. 52). As Ashmore and McConahay's and similar positions become more widely accepted, constructive change in the South Bronx becomes more likely. Poust and Tumulty,[46] in a suburban New York newspaper, report:

> the root cause of the problems associated with the South Bronx has been identified as the low average income of residents there.
>
> And attacking that root cause would mean providing jobs, and skills, and a reversal of the perception among South Bronx residents — particularly its young — that there is no place for them in the mainstream of society. (p. A9)

*The phrase "the competent community" is adopted from Cottrell,[45] also a source of background on the concept of competence beyond that included in Chapter 7.

Poust and Tumulty caution, however, that "identifying economics as the cause of the problem [of inner-city decay] is not the same as a cure"[46] (p. A9).

Not only resources but effective infusion routes must be found. In late 1978, for example, the federal government was eager to commit substantial funds to improve housing in the South Bronx.[46, 47] A key proposal, however, for a new 732-unit housing project on Charlotte Street, was rejected by the city's Board of Estimate because the plan did not specifically provide for redevelopment of the surrounding area.[46] The Board of Estimate presumably rightly reasoned that in the absence of adequate job opportunities for project residents, any environmental gain from the new buildings would have been short-lived.

In August 1979, the South Bronx Development Office released a comprehensive plan to restore the South Bronx that places the highest priority on economic redevelopment. Though some feel the plan is too modest, it does suggest "a number of specific projects that the city, state, and federal governments can undertake to promote economic development in the Bronx"[46] (p. A9). Through appropriate tax incentives, these same governments might also stimulate private-sector initiative and investment in inner-city projects.

Those formulating justifications for inner-city economic redevelopment might bear in mind that economic factors are important determinants of health and that successful projects can have positive effects on the physical and psychological as well as the fiscal well-being of those affected. Since health problems related to alcohol are so visible and costly in the inner city, it may be useful to single them out as major reasons for improving the economic situation of inner-city residents.

To reverse the escalation of human and architectural waste in the inner city, financial resources must be found and somehow infused. The same holds for human resources. Scientists, like businessmen and -women and many others, have contributions to make. Social scientists seem an especially relevant example. There is evidence that resolution of the entangled problems of poverty and racism can be promoted by attention to the psychological needs of both the dominant socioeconomic group (''perceived racial threat'') and the minority group(s) (''perceived personal power'').[5] Further, scientifically informed interventions can sometimes efficiently bring about desirable changes, such as the reduction of prejudice that followed the introduction of multiethnic readers in schools.[5]

But the alcoholism field as a whole has a recognized problem attracting scientific manpower. Because it combines two causes that traditionally have been less than popular, science involving alcoholism in the inner city would seem to compound this problem. Straus[48] suggests that long-range commitment to confronting alcohol problems with an ecological orientation should stimulate interest among scientists:

> The problems of alcohol are so vast and so interrelated with other health and social problems that only involvement of the mainstream of resources for human well-being can provide an adequate response. In this regard, there is also special need for long-range commitment to planning and long-range support for research and intervention as a part of federal policy. This is essential in order to attract the best thinkers in the sciences and professions to invest their careers in a national effort that must be categorical in commitment, longitudinal in perspective, multidisciplinary in orientation, and comprehensive in organization.

Recognition that inner cities are areas of great need and areas where some causal interrelationships may be relatively easy to study should enhance their appeal to scientific personnel.

Society's present widespread concern about alcohol problems may generate this needed commitment. Community health observatories might be an effective means of translating that commitment into action. If the observatories were established to deal with a number of complex health problems including alcohol problems, any residual reluctance of scientists to become involved might disappear. The above quote from Straus serves as a reminder that the fiscal support and commitment needed to deal with alcohol problems may have to be national. The idea of community health observatories serves as a reminder that the intervention and evaluation needed to deal with alcohol problems may have to be local. A final ecological point is that the success of community health observatories in inner-city areas would be judged in part by how well they promote satisfactory employment *throughout* their communities—the satisfactory employment of scientists would not be enough.

## CONCLUSION

Ecological thinking clarifies the conceptual confusion and controversy that has long impeded action to reduce alcohol problems. The literature reviewed and the data presented in this report underline the importance of socioeconomic environmental factors as determinants of alcohol problems among inner-city blacks and Hispanics. With special reference to these two minority groups, this book has explored in detail possible improvements in alcoholism treatment, prevention, and evaluative research. Inner-city programs seeking to assist both blacks and Hispanics must take into account their cultural and socioeconomic differences as well as their similarities.

People in the inner city continue to suffer and die because of their use of alcohol. Environmental factors are important determinants of this process. The situation will change. It can change for the better. For the process that will determine that outcome, we are all responsible.

# APPENDIX

INFORMATION SHEET

*Dr. Martin Luther King Jr. Health Center*
*3674 Third Third Avenue, Bronx, New York 10456*

*Alcoholism Unit*

Date:
Name:                    D/O/B
Address:                 Telephone#          Apt.#
Referred by:
Chief complaints:


Drinking history:
Age started:

217

Last drink:

Pattern of drinking (a.m., eve.):

Blackouts:

D.T.'s (describe):

What do you drink:

How much?

Period of sobriety:

Where do you drink? (home, bar):

Nightmares:

Prior psychiatric or alcoholism help:

How long?

Why did you stop?

Have you ever been arrested?

Did you ever use drugs?

Appearance:

Work history:

Education:

Where:

Military:

Hospitalization:

    a. Mother

    b. Father

Siblings:

    a. Bros.

    b. Sis.

Spouse:

Children:

Health — Sleeping:

Eating:

Medication:

Legs:

Bleedings:

Head injuries:

Being treated anywhere for anything? Which hospital?

Responsible friend or relative:

Address:

Why do you drink?

What do you wish to accomplish?

Impression:

Plans:

---

**Approximate Alcohol Equivalents of Whisky, Wines, and Beer,
in Proportion to Weight of Drinker**

Equivalents are based on:
(1 quart = 32 ounces = 0.946 liter; one-fifth U.S. gallon = 0.8 quart)
Whisky contains 45 percent ethyl alcohol
Fortified wine contains 20 percent ethyl alcohol
Table wine contains 12 percent ethyl alcohol
Beer contains 4.5 percent ethyl alcohol

| Person's Weight (pounds) | Whisky or Distilled Spirits (quarts) | Fortified Wine (quarts) | Table Wine (quarts) | Beer | | Absolute Alcohol (quarts) |
|---|---|---|---|---|---|---|
| | | | | (quarts) | (12-oz. container) | |
| 220 | 1.00 | 2.25 | 3.75 | 10.0 | 26.7 | 0.45 |
| 200 | 0.91 | 2.05 | 3.41 | 9.1 | 24.3 | 0.41 |
| 180 | 0.82 | 1.85 | 3.08 | 8.2 | 21.9 | 0.37 |
| 160 | 0.73 | 1.64 | 2.74 | 7.3 | 19.5 | 0.33 |
| 140 | 0.64 | 1.44 | 2.40 | 6.4 | 17.1 | 0.29 |
| 120 | 0.55 | 1.24 | 2.06 | 5.5 | 14.7 | 0.25 |

Prepared under the guidance of Mr. Mark Keller, Editor, *Quarterly Journal of Studies on Alcohol*

# REFERENCES

## Chapter 1

1. Martin, F. M. Social and psychological aspects of alcoholism. *Health Bulletin*, 1973, *31*, 320–323.

2. Kaufman, E. Polydrug abuse or multidrug misuse: It's here to stay. *British Journal of Addiction*, 1977, *72*, 339–347.

3. Going back to the booze. *Time*, 5 November 1979, *114*, 71.

4. Keller, M. Multidisciplinary perspectives on alcoholism and the need for integration. *Journal of Studies on Alcohol*, 1975, *36*, 133–147.

5. Fazey, C. On the need to reconcile the aetiologies of drug abuse. In *Alcoholism and drug dependence: A multidisciplinary approach.* Madden, J. S., Walker, R., & Kenyon, W. H., eds., New York: Plenum Press, 1977, 85–93.

6. Kendell, R. E. Alcoholism: A medical or a political problem? *British Medical Journal*, 1979, *1 (6160)*, 367–371.

7. Hyman, M. M. The Ledermann curve: Comments on a symposium. *Journal of Studies on Alcohol*, 1979, *40*, 339–347.

8. Edwards, G. Epidemiology applied to alcoholism: A review and an examination of purposes. *Quarterly Journal of Studies on Alcohol*, 1973, *34*, 28–56.

9. Susser, M. *Causal thinking in the health sciences: Concepts and strategies of epidemiology.* New York: Oxford University Press, 1973.

10. Friedman, G. *Primer of epidemiology.* New York: McGraw-Hill Book Company, 1974.

11. Lester, D. Etiology of alcoholism. In *Proceedings of the Fourth Annual Alcoholism Conference of the National Institute on Alcohol Abuse and Alcoholism*, Chafetz, M. E., ed., Rockville, Md.: The Institute, 1975, 205–208.

12. Westermeyer, J. Alcoholism from the cross cultural perspective: A review and critique of clinical studies. *American Journal of Drug and Alcohol Abuse*, 1974, *1*, 89–105.

## Chapter 2

1. Christie, N., & Bruun, K. Alcohol problems: The conceptual framework. In *Proceedings of the 28th International Congress on Alcohol and Alcoholism*, Vol. 2. Keller, M., & Coffey, T. G., eds., Highland Park, N.J.: Hillhouse Press, 1969, 65–73.

2. Bacon, S. D. Concepts. In *Alcohol and alcohol problems: New thinking and new directions*. Filstead, W. J., Rossi, J. J., & Keller, M., eds., Cambridge, Mass.: Ballinger, 1976, 57–134.

3. Mann, M. *New primer on alcoholism*. New York: Holt, Rinehart and Winston, 1958.

4. Jellinek, E. M. *The disease concept of alcoholism*. New Haven: College and University Press, 1960.

5. Cahalan, D. *Problem drinkers*. San Francisco: Jossey-Bass, 1970.

6. Larkin, E. J. *The treatment of alcoholism: Theory, practice, and evaluation*. Toronto: Addiction Research Foundation of Ontario, 1974.

7. Siegler, M., Osmond, H., & Newell, S. Models of alcoholism. *Quarterly Journal of Studies on Alcohol*, 1968, *29*, 571–591.

8. Pattison, E. M. Rehabilitation of the chronic alcoholic. In *The Biology of Alcoholism*, Vol. 3. Kissin, B., & Begleiter, H., eds., New York: Plenum Press, 1974, 587–657.

9. Friedman, G. *Primer of epidemiology*. New York: McGraw-Hill Book Company, 1974.

10. Lilienfield, A. M. *Foundations of epidemiology*. New York: Oxford University Press, 1976.

11. Fabrega, H. *Disease and social behavior: An interdisciplinary perspective*. Cambridge: MIT Press, 1974.

12. Clark, D. W. A vocabulary for preventive medicine. In *Preventive medicine*. Clark, D. W., & MacMahon, B., eds., Boston: Little, Brown and Company, 1967, 1–9.

13. Price, R. B., & Vlahcevic, Z. R. Logical principles in differential diagnosis. *Annals of Internal Medicine*, 1971, *75*, 89–95.

14. Feinstein, A. R. *Clinical judgement*. Baltimore: Williams and Wilkins Company, 1967.

15. White, K. L. Foreword. In *The International classification of diseases, 9th revision, Clinical modification*, Vol. 1. Ann Arbor: Edward Brothers, 1978, iii–v.

16. Kuhn, T. S. *The structure of scientific revolutions*. Chicago: University of Chicago Press, 1970.

17. MacMahon, B., & Pugh, T. F. Causes and entities of disease. In *Preventive medicine*. Clark, D. W., & MacMahon, B., eds., Boston: Little, Brown and Company, 1967, 11–18.

18. Feinstein, A. R. Clinical epidemiology: I. The populational experiments of nature and of man in human illness. *Annals of Internal Medicine*, 1968, *69*, 807–820.

19. Feinstein, A. R. Clinical epidemiology: II. The identification rates of disease. *Annals of Internal Medicine*, 1968, *69*, 1037–1061.

20. Feinstein, A. R. Clinical epidemiology: III. The clinical design of statistics in therapy. *Annals of Internal Medicine*, 1968, *69*, 1287–1312.

21. Seeley, J. R. Alcoholism is a disease: Implications for social policy. In *Society, culture, and drinking patterns*. Pittman, D. J., & Snyder, C. R., eds., New York: John Wiley & Sons, 1962, 586–593.

22. Edwards, G. Epidemiology applied to alcoholism: A review and an examination of purposes. *Quarterly Journal of Studies on Alcohol*, 1973, *34*, 28–56.

23. Keller, M. Problems of epidemiology in alcohol problems. *Journal of Studies on Alcohol*, 1975, *36*, 1442–1451.

24. Wanberg, K. W., & Horn, J. L. Alcoholism syndromes related to sociological classifications. *International Journal of the Addictions*, 1973, *8*, 99–120.

25. Rudie, R. R., & McGaughran, L. S.: Differences in developmental experience, defensiveness, and personality organization between two classes of problem drinkers. *Journal of Abnormal and Social Psychology*, 1961, *62*, 659–665.

26. Jacobson, G. R. *The Alcoholisms: Detection, diagnosis and assessment*. New York: Human Sciences Press, 1976.

27. Roebuck, J. B., & Kessler, R. G. *The etiology of alcoholism: Constitutional, psychological and sociological approaches*. Springfield, Ill.: Charles C. Thomas, 1972.

28. Jellinek, E. M. Phases of alcohol addiction. *Quarterly Journal of Studies on Alcohol*, 1952, *13*, 673–684.

29. Weldon, T. D. *Kant's critique of pure reason*. Oxford: Oxford University Press, 1958.

30. Northrop, F. S. C. Natural science and the critical philosophy of Kant. In *The Heritage of Kant*. Whitney, G. T., & Bowers, D. F., eds., New York: Russell & Russell, 1962, 39–62.

31. Klinke, W. *Kant for Everyman*, Bullock, M., trans. New York: Collier Books, 1962.

32. Heidegger, M. *What is a thing?* Barton, W. B., & Deutsch, V., trans. Chicago: Gateway, 1970.

33. Kant, I. *Critique of pure reason*, Muller, F. M., trans. New York: Macmillan, 1896.

34. Kant, I. *Critique of pure reason*, Smith, N. K., trans. New York: St. Martin's Press, 1968 (first edition, 1929).

35. Kant, I. *The critique of pure reason*, Meiklejohn, J. M. D., trans. In *Great Books of the Western World*, Vol. 42, Chicago: Encyclopedia Britannica, 1952, 1–250.

36. Keller, M. Problems with alcohol: An historical perspective. In *Alcohol and alcohol problems: New thinking and new directions*. Filstead, W. J., Rossi, J. J., & Keller, M., eds., Cambridge, Mass.: Ballinger, 1976.

37. Keller, M. Multidisciplinary perspectives on alcoholism and the need for integration: An historical and perspective note. *Journal of Studies on Alcohol*, 1975, *36*, 133–147.

38. Keller, M. The disease concept of alcoholism revisited. *Journal of Studies on Alcohol*, 1976, *37*, 1694–1717.

39. Keller, M. Definition of alcoholism. *Quarterly Journal of Studies on Alcohol*, 1960, *21*, 125–134.

40. Whybrow, P. C. The use and abuse of the "medical model" as a conceptual frame in psychiatry. *Psychiatry in Medicine*, 1972, *3*, 333–342.

41. Straus, R. Alcohol. In *Contemporary social problems*. Merton, R. K., & Nisbet, R. A., eds., New York: Harcourt, Brace & World, 1966, 236–280.

42. Glatt, M. M. Loss of control: Extensive interdisciplinary borderland, not a sharp pharmacological borderline. In *Alcoholism: A medical profile*. Proceedings of the First International Medical Conference on Alcoholism, London, 10–14 Sept. 1973. Kessel, N., Hawker, A., & Chalke, H., eds., London: B. Edsall, 1974, 122–132.

43. van Dijk, W. K. Problems concerning the application of the medical model in alcoholism. In *Alcoholism: A medical profile*. Proceedings of the First International Medical Conference on Alcoholism, London, 10–14 Sept. 1973. Kessel, N., Hawker, A., & Chalke, H., eds., London: B. Edsall, 1974, 133–142.

44. Seixas, F. A. Afterword. In *The alcoholisms: Detection, diagnosis and assessment*. Jacobson, G. R., author, New York: Human Sciences Press, 1976, 407–413.

45. Gitlow, S. E. Alcoholism: A disease. In *Alcoholism: Progress in research and treatment*, Bourne, P. G., & Fox, R., eds., New York: Academic Press, 1973, 1–9.

46. White, L. S. How to improve the public's health. *New England Journal of Medicine*, 1975, *293*, 773–774.

47. Bruun, K. Finland: The non-medical approach. In *29th International Congress on Alcoholism and Drug Dependence*. Kiloh, L. G., & Bell, D. S., eds., Sydney: Butterworths, 1971, 545–559.

48. Cahalan, D. Why does the alcoholism field act like a ship of fools? *British Journal of Addiction*, 1979, *74*: 235–238.

## Chapter 3

1. Friedman, G. *Primer of epidemiology*. New York: McGraw-Hill Book Company, 1974.

2. Thomas, L. *The lives of a cell: Notes of a biology watcher*. New York: Viking Press, 1974.

3. Jellinek, E. M. *The disease concept of alcoholism*. New Haven: College and University Press, 1960.

4. Wallgren, H., & Barry, H. *Actions of Alcohol*, Vol. 2. Amsterdam: Elsevier, 1970.

5. Roebuck, J. B., & Kessler, R. G. *The etiology of alcoholism: Constitutional, psychological and sociological approaches*. Springfield, Ill.: Charles C. Thomas, 1972.

6. Report from the Secretary of Health, Education and Welfare: *Alcohol and health*. New York: Charles Scribner's Sons, 1973.

7. Mellor, C. S. Aetiology in alcoholism. In *Alcoholism: A medical profile*. Proceedings of the First International Medical Conference on Alcoholism, London, 10–14 Sept. 1973. Kessel, N., Hawker, A., & Chalke, H., eds., London: B. Edsall, 1974, 30–42.

8. Keller, M. Multidisciplinary perspectives on alcoholism and the need for integration. *Journal of Studies on Alcohol*, 1975, *36*, 133–147.

9. Susser, M. *Causal thinking in the health sciences: Concepts and strategies of epidemiology*. New York: Oxford University Press, 1973.

10. Engel, G. L. A unified concept of health and disease. *Perspectives in Biology and Medicine*, 1960, *3*, 459–485.

11. Engel, G. L. *Psychological development in health and disease*. Philadelphia: W. B. Saunders, 1962.

12. Dubos, R. J. *Man, medicine, and environment*. New York: Praeger, 1968.

13. Wolff, H. G. A concept of disease in man. *Psychosomatic Medicine*, 1962, *24*, 25–30.

14. Whybrow, P. C. The use and abuse of the "medical model" as a conceptual frame in psychiatry. *Psychiatry in Medicine*, 1972, *3*, 333–342.

15. Fabrega, H. *Disease and social behavior: An interdisciplinary perspective*. Cambridge: MIT Press, 1974.

16. Lipowski, Z. J. Physical illness, the patient and his environment. In *American handbook of psychiatry*, Vol. 4. Reiser, M. F., ed., New York: Basic Books, 1975, 3–42.

17. Beiser, M., & Leighton, A. H. Personality assets and mental health. In *Further explorations in social psychiatry*. Kaplan, B. H., Wilson, R. N., & Leighton, A. H., eds., New York: Basic Books, 1976, 178–192.

18. Von Bertalanffy, L. *General system theory*. New York: Braziller, 1968.

19. Balint, M. *The doctor, his patient, and the illness*. New York: International Universities Press, 1957.

20. Siegler, M., Osmond, H., & Newell, S. Models of alcoholism. *Quarterly Journal of Studies on Alcohol*, 1968, *29*, 571–591.

21. Mendelson, J. H. Biochemical mechanisms of alcohol addiction. In *The biology of alcoholism*, Vol 1. Kissin, B., & Begleiter, H., eds., New York: Plenum Press, 1971, 513–544.

22. Goldberg, L. The interaction of alcohol and other CNS-acting drugs in man and animal. In *Alcoholism: Modern concepts of cause and theory*. Saffron, M. H., ed., Bloomfield, N.J.: *Transactions of the Academy of Medicine of New Jersey*, 1972, 6–46.

23. Ewing, J. A. How to help the chronic alcoholic. Center for Alcohol Studies, University of North Carolina, Chapel Hill, N.C. Undated pamphlet.

24. Sytinsky, I. A. A schema of the etiology of alcoholism as a pathological motivation: A working hypothesis involving the interplay of sociological, psychological and physiobiochemical factors on molecular, cellular and organosystemic levels. *Quarterly Journal of Studies on Alcohol*, 1973, *34*, 1140–1145.

25. Kissin, B. The pharmacodynamics and natural history of alcoholism. In *The biology of alcoholism*, Vol. 3. Kissin, B., & Begleiter, H., eds., New York: Plenum Press, 1974, 1–36.

26. Fazey, C. On the need to reconcile the aetiologies of drug abuse. In *Alcoholism and drug dependence: A multidisciplinary approach*. Madden, J. S., Walker, R., & Kenyon, W. H., eds., New York: Plenum Press, 1977, 85–93.

27. MacMahon, B. Introduction: Concepts of multiple factors. In *Multiple factors in the causation of environmentally induced disease*. Lee, D. H. K., & Kotin, P., eds., New York: Academic Press, 1972, 1–12.

28. Terris, M. On the distinction between individual and social medicine. *Lancet*, 1964, *2*, 653–655.

29. Querido, A. Alcoholism as a public health problem. *Quarterly Journal of Studies on Alcohol*, 1954, *15*, 469–476.

30. Jellinek, E. M. Phases of alcohol addiction. *Quarterly Journal of Studies on Alcohol*, 1952, *13*, 673–684.

31. Cahalan, D., Cisin, I. H., & Crossley, H. M. *American drinking practices: A national study of drinking behavior and attitudes*. New Brunswick, N.J.: Rutgers Center of Alcohol Studies, 1969.

32. Cahalan, D. *Problem drinkers*. San Francisco: Jossey-Bass, 1970.

33. Keller, M. Problems of epidemiology in alcohol problems. *Journal of Studies on Alcohol*, 1975, *36*, 1442–1451.

34. Graham, J. D. P. Recent theories on the pharmacological basis of tolerance and dependence. *British Journal of Addiction*, 1972, *67*, 83–87.

35. Rodgers, D. A. A psychological interpretation of alcoholism. *Annals of the New York Academy of Sciences*, 1972, *197*, 222–225.

36. Bales, R. F. Cultural differences in rates of alcoholism. *Quarterly Journal of Studies on Alcohol*, 1946, *6*, 480–499.

37. Rosen, G. The evolution of social medicine. In *Handbook of medical sociology*. Freeman, H. E., Levine, S., & Reeder, L. G., eds., Englewood Cliffs, N.J.: Prentice-Hall, 1972, 30–60.

38. Hollingshead, A. B. & Redlich, F. C. *Social class and mental illness: A community study*. New York: John Wiley & Sons, 1958.

39. Antonovsky, A. Social class, life expectancy and overall mortality. *Millbank Memorial Fund Quarterly*, April 1967, Part 1, *45*, 31–73.

40. Frazer, A. B., et al. *Social forces and the nation's health: A task force report*. USDHEW Health Services and Mental Health Administration, Bureau of Health Services, 1968.

41. Susser, M. W., & Watson, W. Social class and disorders of health. In *Sociology in medicine*. London: Oxford University Press, 1971, 128–176.

42. Graham, S., & Reeder, L. G. Social factors in the chronic diseases. In *Handbook of medical sociology*. Englewood Cliffs, N.J.: Prentice-Hall, 1972, 63–107.

43. Kitagawa, E. M., & Hauser, P. M. *Differential mortality in the United States: A study in socioeconomic epidemiology*. Cambridge: Harvard University Press, 1973.

44. National Center for Health Sciences Research. *Health: United States 1975*. DHEW Publication No. (HRA) 76–1232.

45. Jenkins, C. D., Tuthill, R. W., Tannenbaum, S. I., & Kirby, C. R. Zones of excess mortality in Massachusetts. *New England Journal of Medicine*, 1977, *296*, 1354–1356.

46. Hinkle, L. E., & Wolff, H. G. Health and the social environment: Experimental investigations. In *Explorations in Social Psychiatry*. Leighton, A. H., Clausen, J. A., & Wilson, R. N., eds., New York: Basic Books, 1957.

47. Hinkle, L. E., & Wolff, H. G. Ecologic investigations of the relationship between illness, life experiences and the social environment. *Annals of Internal Medicine*, 1958, *49*, 1373–1388.

48. Hinkle, L. E. Ecological observations of the relation of physical illness, mental illness, and the social environment. *Psychosomatic Medicine*, 1961, *23*, 289–297.

49. Wolff, H. G. A concept of disease in man. *Psychosomatic Medicine*, 1962, *24*, 25–30.

50. Levi, L., ed. *Society, Stress and Disease*, Vol. 1. London: Oxford University Press, 1971.

51. Leighton, A. H. *My name is legion: Foundations for a theory of man in relation to culture, The Stirling County study of psychiatric disorder & sociocultural environment*, Vol. 1. New York: Basic Books, 1959.

52. Kark, S. L. *Epidemiology and community medicine*. New York: Appleton-Century-Crofts, 1974.

53. Ashmore, R. D., & McConahay, J. B. *Psychology and America's urban dilemmas*. New York: McGraw-Hill Book Company, 1975.

54. Durkheim, E. *Suicide: A study in sociology*, Spaulding, J. A., & Simpson, G., trans. Glencoe, Illinois: Free Press, 1951.

55. Merton, R. K. *Social theory and social structure*. Glencoe, Ill.: Free Press, 1957.

56. Leighton, D. C., Harding, J. S., Macklin, D. B., Macmillan, A. M., & Leighton, A. H. *The character of danger: Psychiatric symptoms in selected communities, The Stirling County study of psychiatric disorder & sociocultural environment*, Vol. 3. New York: Basic Books, 1963.

57. Neser, W. B., Tyroler, H. A., & Cassel, J. C. Social disorganization and stroke mortality in the black population of North Carolina. *American Journal of Epidemiology*, 1971, *93*, 166–175.

58. Cassel, J. An epidemiological perspective of psychosocial factors in disease etiology. *American Journal of Public Health*, 1974, *64*, 1040–1043.

59. Syme, S. L. Behavioral factors associated with the etiology of physical disease: A social epidemiological approach. *American Journal of Public Health*, 1974, *64*, 1043–1045.

60. Farnsworth, D. L. Substitute for competence: Drug dependence and its amelioration. In *Further explorations in social psychiatry*. Kaplan, B. H., Wilson, R. N., & Leighton, A. H., eds., New York: Basic Books, 1976, 273–285.

61. Herbers, J. Urban poor worse off than ever. *New York Times*, 24 July 1977.

62. Metropolitan Life. Statistical bulletin. July 1974, 2.

63. Chalmers, T. C. Potential contributions of multiple risk factors to the etiology of cirrhosis. In *Multiple factors in the causation of environmentally induced disease*. Lee, D. H. K., & Kotin, P., eds., New York: Academic Press, 1972, 29–42.

64. Feinman, L., & Lieber, C. S. Liver disease in alcoholism. In *The biology of alcoholism*, Vol. 3. Kissin, B., & Begleiter, H., eds., New York: Plenum Press, 1974, 303–338.

65. Rubin, E., & Lieber, C. S. Fatty liver, alcoholic hepatitis and cirrhosis produced by alcohol in primates. *New England Journal of Medicine*, 1974, *290*, 128–135.

66. Edwards, G. Epidemiology applied to alcoholism: A review and an examination of purposes. *Quarterly Journal of Studies on Alcohol*. 1973, *34*, 28–56.

67. Siegel, M. Indices of community health. In *Preventive medicine*. Clark, D. W., & MacMahon, B., eds., Boston: Little, Brown and Company, 1967, 67–79.

68. Bailey, M. B., Haberman, P. W., & Alksne, H. The epidemiology of alcoholism in an urban residential area. *Quarterly Journal of Studies on Alcohol*, 1965, *26*, 19–40.

69. Knupfer, G. Epidemiologic studies and control programs in alcoholism: V. The epidemiology of problem drinking. *American Journal of Public Health*, 1967, *57*, 973–986.

70. Cahalan, D., & Room, R. *Problem drinking among American men*. New Brunswick, N.J.: Rutgers Center of Alcohol Studies, 1974.

71. Jessor, R., Graves, T. D., Hanson, R. C., & Jessor, S. L. *Society, personality, and deviant behavior: A study of a tri-ethnic community*. Huntington, NY: Robert E. Krieger, 1975 (original edition 1968).

72. Bloom, J. D. Sociocultural aspects of alcoholism. *Alaska Medicine*, September 1970, 65–67.

73. Christie, N., & Bruun, K. Alcohol problems: The conceptual framework. In *Proceedings of the 28th International Congress on Alcohol and Alcoholism*, Vol. 2. Keller, M., & Coffey, T. G., eds., Highland Park, N.J.: Hillhouse Press, 1969, 65–73.

74. Glasser, W. *Reality therapy*. New York: Harper and Row, 1965.

75. Brattner, T. E. Reality therapy: A group psychotherapeutic approach with adolescent alcoholics. *Annals of the New York Academy of Sciences*, 1974, *233*, 104–114.

## Chapter 4

1. Heath, D. B. Anthropological perspectives on the social biology of alcohol: An introduction to the literature. In *The biology of alcoholism*, Vol. 4. Kissin, B., & Begleiter, H., eds., New York: Plenum Press, 1976, 37–75.

2. Bales, R. F. Cultural differences in rates of alcoholism. *Quarterly Journal of Studies on Alcohol*, 1946, *6*, 480–499.

3. Cahalan, D., & Cisin, I. H. Drinking behavior and drinking problems in the United States. In *The biology of alcoholism*, Vol. 4. Kissin, B., & Begleiter, H., eds., New York: Plenum Press, 1976, 77–115.

4. Kinder, B. N. Attitudes toward alcohol and drug use and abuse: I. Demographic and correlational data. *International Journal of the Addictions*, 1975, *10*, 737–760.

5. Harper, F. D., & Dawkins, M. P. Alcohol and blacks: Survey of the periodical literature. *British Journal of Addiction*, 1976, *71*, 327–334.

6. King, L. J., Murphy, G. E., Robins, L. N., & Darvish, H. Alcohol abuse: A crucial factor in the social problems of Negro men. *American Journal of Psychiatry*, 1969, *125*, 1682–1690.

7. Bourne, P. G. Alcoholism in the urban Negro population. In *Alcoholism: Progress in research and treatment*. Bourne, P. G., & Fox, R., eds., New York: Academic Press, 1973, 211–226.

8. Harper, F. D. Overview: Alcohol and blacks. In *Alcohol abuse and black America*. Harper, F. D., ed., Alexandria, Va.: Douglass Publishers, 1976, 1–12.

9. Larkins, J. R. *Alcohol and the Negro: Explosive issues*. Zebulon, N.C.: Record Publishing, 1965.

10. Larkins, J. R. Historical background. In *Alcohol abuse and black America*. Harper, F. D., ed., Alexandria, Va.: Douglass Publishers, 1976, 13–25.

11. Vitols, M. M. Culture patterns of drinking in Negro and white alcoholics. *Diseases of the Nervous System*, 1968, *29*, 391–394.

12. Harper, F. D. Etiology: Why do blacks drink? In *Alcohol abuse and black America*. Harper, F. D., ed., Alexandria, Va.: Douglass Publishers, 1976, 27–37.

13. Sterne, M. W. Drinking patterns and alcoholism among American Negroes. In *Alcoholism*. Pittman, D. J., ed., New York: Harper & Row, 1967, 66–99.

14. Sterne, M. W., & Pittman, D. J. *Drinking patterns in the ghetto*. St. Louis, Mo.: Social Science Institute of Washington University, 1972. Two-volume mimeograph.

15. Davis, F. T. Alcoholism among American blacks. Presented at the 1973 annual meeting, Alcohol and Drug Problems of North America. (Copies distributed by the National Council on Alcoholism.)

16. Davis, F. T. Effective delivery of services to black alcoholics. Undated mimeograph distributed by Roy Littlejohn Associates, Washington, D.C.

17. Harper, F. D. *Alcohol and blacks: An overview*. Alexandria, Va.: Douglass Publishers, 1976.

18. Barry, H. Sociocultural aspects of alcohol addiction. *Research Publications of the Association for Research in Nervous and Mental Disease*, 1968, *46*, 455–471.

19. Roebuck, J. B., & Kessler, R. G. *The etiology of alcoholism: Constitutional, psychological and sociological approaches*. Springfield, Ill.: Charles C. Thomas, 1972.

20. Cahalan, D., Cisin, I. H., & Crossley, H. M. *American drinking practices: A national study of drinking behavior and attitudes*. New Brunswick, N.J.: Rutgers Center of Alcohol Studies, 1969.

21. Robins, L. N., Murphy, G. E., & Breckenridge, M. B. Drinking behavior of young urban Negro men. *Quarterly Journal of Studies on Alcohol*, 1968, *29*, 657–684.

22. Robins, L. N., & Guze, S. B. Drinking practices and problems in urban ghetto populations. In *Recent Advances in Studies of Alcoholism*. Mello, N. K, & Mendelson, J. H., eds., National Institute of Mental Health, 1971, 825–842.

23. Maddox, G. L. Drinking among Negroes: Inferences from the drinking patterns of selected Negro male collegians. *Journal of Health and Social Behavior*, 1968, *9*, 114–120.

24. Bailey, M. B., Haberman, P. W., & Alksne, H. The epidemiology of alcoholism in an urban residential area. *Quarterly Journal of Studies on Alcohol*, 1965, *26*, 19–40.

25. Cahalan, D. *Problem drinkers*. San Francisco: Jossey-Bass, 1970.

26. Cahalan, D., & Room, R. *Problem drinking among American men*. New Brunswick, N.J.: Rutgers Center of Alcohol Studies, 1974.

27. Cahalan, D., & Room, R. Problem drinking among American men aged 21-59. *American Journal of Public Health*, 1972, *62*, 1473–1482.

28. Strayer, R. A study of the Negro alcoholic. *Quarterly Journal of Studies on Alcohol*, 1961, *22*, 111–123.

29. Rosenblatt, S. M., Gross, M. M., Broman, M., Lewis, E., & Malenowski, B. Patients admitted for treatment of alcohol withdrawal syndromes: An epidemiological study. *Quarterly Journal of Studies on Alcohol*, 1971, *32*, 104–115.

30. Rimmer, J., Pitts, F. N., Reich, T., & Winokur, G. Alcoholism: II. Sex, socioeconomic status, and race in two hospitalized samples. *Quarterly Journal of Studies on Alcohol*, 1971, *32*, 942–952.

31. Zimberg, S., Lipscomb, H., & Davis, E. B. Sociopsychiatric treatment of alcoholism in an urban ghetto. *American Journal of Psychiatry*, 1971, *127*, 1670–1674.

32. Gross, M. M., Rosenblatt, S. M., Lewis, E., Chartoff, S., & Malenowski, B. Acute alcoholic psychoses and related syndromes: Psychosocial and clinical characteristics and their implications. *British Journal of Addiction*, 1972, *67*, 15–31.

33. German, E. Medical problems in chronic alcoholic men. *Journal of Chronic Diseases*, 1973, *26*, 661–668.

34. Viamontes, J. A., & Powell, B. J. Demographic characteristics of black and white male alcoholics. *International Journal of the Addictions*, 1974, *9*, 489–494.

35. Zimberg, S. Evaluation of alcoholism treatment in Harlem. *Quarterly Journal of Studies on Alcohol*, 1974, *35*, 550–557.

36. Novick, L. F., Hudson, H., & German, E. In-hospital detoxification and rehabilitation of alcoholics in an inner city area. *American Journal of Public Health*, 1974, *64*, 1089–1094.

37. Bullough, B., & Bullough, V. L. *Poverty, ethnic identity, and health care*. New York: Appleton-Century-Crofts, 1972.

38. Jessor, R., Graves, T. D., Hanson, R. C., & Jessor, S. L. *Society, personality, and deviant behavior: A study of a tri-ethnic community*. Huntington, N.Y.: Robert E. Krieger, 1975 (original edition 1968).

39. Wanberg, K. W., & Horn, J. L. Alcoholism syndromes related to sociological classifications. *International Journal of the Addictions*, 1973, *8*, 99–120.

40. Madsen, W. The alcoholic agringado. *American Anthropologist*, 1964, *66*, 355–361.

41. Abad, V., & Suarez, J. Cross-cultural aspects of alcoholism among Puerto Ricans. In *Proceedings of the fourth annual alcoholism conference of the National Institute on Alcohol Abuse and Alcoholism* (1974). Chafetz, M. E., ed., Rockville, Md.: The Institute, 1975, 282–294.

42. Trevino, E. M. Machismo alcoholism: Mexican-American machismo drinking. In *Proceedings of the Fourth Annual Alcoholism Conference of the National Institute on Alcohol Abuse and Alcoholism* (1974). Chafetz, M. E., ed., Rockville, Md.: The Institute, 1975, 295–302.

43. Torres de Gonzalez, B. Treating the inner city young Spanish speaking alcohol abuser. Paper presented on behalf of the East Harlem Tenants Council (2193 Third Avenue, New York, N.Y. 10035) and the Puerto Rican Inter-Agency Council, 5 December 1973.

44. Vidal, D. City Puerto Ricans lag in income gains. *The New York Times*, 20 January 1976, 35.

45. Editorial. *The New York Times*, 30 January 1976, 28.

46. Vidal, D. Puerto Rican plight in U.S. is deplored. *The New York Times*, 14 October 1976, 18.

47. Leebaw, M., & Heyman, H. Puerto Ricans and economics. *The New York Times*, 17 October 1976, Section 4, 5.

48. Vidal D: Dream still eludes mainland Puerto Ricans. *The New York Times*, 11 September 1977, Section 4, 6.

## Chapter 6

1. Criteria Committee, National Council on Alcoholism. Criteria for the diagnosis of alcoholism. *American Journal of Psychiatry*, 1972, *129*, 127–135.

2. Kane, G. P. Helping the alcoholic into treatment. *Hospital Physician*, 1979, *15*, 55–66.

3. Cahalan, D. *Problem Drinkers*. San Francisco: Jossey-Bass, 1970.

4. Kissin, B. The pharmacodynamics and natural history of alcoholism. In *The biology of alcoholism*, Vol. 3. Kissin, B., & Begleiter, H., eds., New York: Plenum Press, 1974, 1–36.

5. Sterne, M. W. Drinking patterns and alcoholism among American Negroes. In *Alcoholism*. Pittman, D. J., ed., New York: Harper & Row, 1967, 66–99.

6. Strayer, R. A study of the Negro alcoholic. *Quarterly Journal of Studies on Alcohol*, 1961, *22*, 111–123.

7. Vitols, M. M. Culture patterns of drinking in Negro and white alcoholics. *Diseases of the Nervous System*, 1968, *29*, 391–394.

8. Rosenblatt, S. M., Gross, M. M., Broman, M., Lewis, E., & Malenowski, B. Patients admitted for treatment of alcohol withdrawal syndromes: An epidemiological study. *Quarterly Journal of Studies on Alcohol*, 1971, *32*, 104–115.

9. Rimmer, J., Pitts, F. N., Reich, T., & Winokur, G. Alcoholism: II. Sex, socioeconomic status, and race in two hospitalized samples. *Quarterly Journal of Studies on Alcohol*, 1971, *32*, 942–952.

10. Gross, M. M., Rosenblatt, S. M., Lewis, E., Chartoff, S., & Malenowski, B. Acute alcoholic psychoses and related syndromes: Psychosocial and clinical characteristics and their implications. *British Journal of Addiction*, 1972, *67*, 15–31.

11. Viamontes, J. A, & Powell, B. J. Demographic characteristics of black and white male alcoholics. *International Journal of the Addictions*, 1974, *9*, 489–494.

12. Wanberg, K. W., & Horn, J. L. Alcoholism syndromes related to sociological classifications. *International Journal of the Addictions*, 1973, *8*, 99–120.

13. Russell, G., & Satterwhite, B. It's your turn in the sun. *Time*, 16 October 1978, *112*, 48–61.

14. Lewis, O. *La Vida*. New York: Random House, 1965.

15. Rogler, L. H., & Hollingshead, A. B. *Trapped: Families and schizophrenia*. New York: John Wiley & Sons, 1965.

16. Liebow, E. *Tally's corner*. Boston: Little, Brown and Company, 1967.

## Chapter 7

1. Chafetz, M. E. Clinical syndromes of liquor drinkers. In *Frontiers of alcoholism*. Chafetz, M. E., Blane, H. T., & Hill, M. J., eds., New York: Science House, 1970, 309–319.

2. Gross, M. M., Rosenblatt, S. M., Lewis, E., Chartoff, S., & Malenowski, B. Acute alcoholic psychoses and related syndromes: Psychosocial and clinical characteristics and their implications. *British Journal of Addiction*, 1972, *67*, 15–31.

3. Rimmer, J., Reich, T., & Winokur, G. Alcoholism: V. Diagnosis and clinical variation among alcoholics. *Quarterly Journal of Studies on Alcohol*, 1972, *33*, 658–666.

4. Roa, A. Alcoholism and endogenous psychosis. In *Alcohol & alcoholism*. Popham, R. E., ed., Toronto: University of Toronto Press, 1970, 121–125.

5. Davis, F. T. Effective delivery of services to black alcoholics. Undated mimeograph distributed by Roy Littlejohn Associates, Washington, D.C.

6. Zimberg, S. Evaluation of alcoholism treatment in Harlem. *Quarterly Journal of Studies on Alcohol*, 1974, *35*, 550–557.

7. Zimberg, S., Lipscomb, H., & Davis, E. B. Sociopsychiatric treatment of alcoholism in an urban ghetto. *American Journal of Psychiatry*, 1971, *127*, 1670–1674.

8. Pattison, E. M. Rehabilitation of the chronic alcoholic. In *The biology of alcoholism*, Vol. 3. Kissin, B., & Begleiter, H., eds., New York: Plenum Press, 1974, 587–658.

9. Pattison, E. M., Coe, R., & Rhodes, R. J. Evaluation of alcoholism treatment: A comparison of three facilities. *Archives of General Psychiatry*, 1969, *20*, 478–488.

10. Pattison, E. M., Coe, R., & Doerr, H. O. Population variation among alcoholism treatment facilities. *International Journal of the Addictions*, 1973, *8*, 199–229.

11. Mindlin, D. F. The characteristics of alcoholics as related to prediction of therapeutic outcome. *Quarterly Journal of Studies on Alcohol*, 1959, *20*, 604–619.

12. Gerard, D. L., & Saenger, G. *Out-patient treatment of alcoholism*. Toronto: University of Toronto Press, 1966.

13. Edwards, G., & Guthrie, S. A controlled trial of inpatient and outpatient treatment of alcohol dependency. *Lancet*, 1967, *1*, 555–559.

14. Schmidt, W., Smart, R. G., & Moss, M. K. *Social class and the treatment of alcoholism*. Toronto: University of Toronto Press, 1968.

15. Kissin, B., Rosenblatt, S. M., & Machover, S. Prognostic factors in alcoholism. American Psychiatric Association, *Psychiatric Research Report*, 1968, *24*, 22–43.

16. Trice, H. M., Roman, P. M., & Belasco, J. A. Selection for treatment: A predictive evaluation of an alcoholism treatment regimen. *International Journal of the Addictions*, 1969, *4*, 303–317.

17. Kissin, B., Platz, A., & Su, W. S. Social and psychological factors in the treatment of chronic alcoholism. *Journal of Psychiatric Research*, 1970, *8*, 13–27.

18. Jacobson, G. R. *The alcoholisms: Detection, assessment, and diagnosis*. New York: Human Sciences Press, 1976.

19. Martin, F. M. Social and psychological aspects of alcohol and alcoholism. *Health Bulletin*, 1973, *31*, 320–323.

20. Zwerling, I., & Clifford, B. J. Administrative and population considerations in outpatient clinics for the treatment of chronic alcoholism. *New York State Journal of Medicine*, 1957, *57*, 3869–3875.

21. Lowe, G. D., & Ziglin, A. L. Social class and the treatment of alcoholic patients. *Quarterly Journal of Studies on Alcohol*, 1973, *34*, 173–184.

22. Baekeland, F., Lundwall, L., Kissin, B., & Shanahan, T. Correlates of outcome in disulfiram treatment of alcoholism. *Journal of Nervous and Mental Disease*, 1971, *153*, 1–9.

23. Gomberg, E. S. Alcoholism in women. In *The biology of alcoholism*, Vol. 4. Kissin, B., & Begleiter, H., eds., New York: Plenum Press, 1976, 117–166.

24. Strayer, R. A study of the Negro alcoholic. *Quarterly Journal of Studies on Alcohol*, 1961, *22*, 111–123.

25. Sterne, M. W., & Pittman, D. J. *Drinking patterns in the ghetto* (two-volume mimeograph). St. Louis, Mo.: Social Science Institute of Washington University, 1972.

26. Gregory, D. D. Transcultural medicine: Treating Hispanic patients. *Behavioral Medicine*, 1978, *5*, 22–29.

27. Karp, S. A., Kissin, B., & Hustmyer, F. E. Field dependence as a predictor of alcoholic therapy dropouts. *Journal of Nervous and Mental Disease*, 1970, *150*, 77–83.

28. Reilly, D. H., & Sugerman, A. A. Conceptual complexity and psychological differentiation in alcoholics. *Journal of Nervous and Mental Disease*, 1967, *144*, 14–17.

29. Vogel, S. An interpretation of medical and psychiatric approaches in the treatment of alcoholism. *Quarterly Journal of Studies on Alcohol*, 1953, *14*, 620–631.

30. Kerner, O. J. B. Initiating psychotherapy with alcoholic patients. *Quarterly Journal of Studies on Alcohol*, 1956, *17*, 479–484.

31. Sterne, M. W., & Pittman, D. J. The concept of motivation: A source of institutional and professional blockage in the treatment of alcoholics. *Quarterly Journal of Studies on Alcohol*, 1965, *26*, 41–57.

32. Jackson, D. N. A short form of Witkin's Embedded-Figures Test. *Journal of Abnormal and Social Psychology*, 1956, *53*, 254–255.

33. Witkin, H. A., Dyk, R. B., Faterson, H. F., Goodenough, D. R., & Karp, S. A. *Psychological differentiation*. New York: John Wiley and Sons, 1962.

34. Chaplin, J. P., & Krawiec, T. S. *Systems and theories of psychology.* New York: Holt, Rinehart and Winston, 1974.

35. Bem, D. J. Social psychology. In *Introduction to psychology.* Hilgard, E. R., Atkinson, R. C., & Atkinson, R. L., eds., New York: Harcourt Brace Jovanovich, 1975, 525–561.

36. Watson, R. I. *The great psychologists.* Philadelphia: J. B. Lippincott, 1971.

37. Wilson, C. *New pathways in psychology.* London: Victor Gollancz, 1972.

38. Glasser, W. *Reality therapy.* New York: Harper & Row, 1965.

39. McCall, R. J. *The varieties of abnormality.* Springfield, Ill.: Charles C. Thomas, 1975.

40. Jellinek, E. M. *The disease concept of alcoholism.* New Haven: Hillhouse Press, 1960.

41. Jellinek, E. M. Phases of alcohol addiction. *Quarterly Journal of Studies on Alcohol,* 1952, *13*, 673–684.

42. Trice, H. M., & Wahl, J. R. A rank order analysis of the symptoms of alcoholism. In *Society, culture, and drinking patterns.* Pittman, D. J., & Snyder, C. R., eds., New York: John Wiley & Sons, 1962.

43. Schuckit, M. A. Alcoholism and sociopathy—diagnostic confusion. *Quarterly Journal of Studies on Alcohol,* 1973, *34*, 157–164.

44. Rae-Grant, Q. A. F., Gladwin, T., & Bower, E. M. Mental health, social competence and the war on poverty. *American Journal of Orthopsychiatry,* 1966, *36*, 652–664.

45. White, R. W. Competence and the psychosexual stages of development. In *Nebraska symposium on motivation 1960.* Jones, M. R., ed., Lincoln, Neb.: University of Nebraska Press, 1960, 97–141.

46. Sugerman, A. A., Reilly, D., & Albahary, R. S. Social competence and essential-reactive distinction in alcoholism. *Archives of General Psychiatry,* 1965, *12*, 552–556.

47. Zigler, E., & Phillips, L. Social effectiveness and symptomatic behaviors. *Journal of Abnormal and Social Psychology,* 1960, *61*, 231–238.

48. Phillips, L., & Cowitz, B. Social attainment and reactions to stress. *Journal of Personality,* 1953, *22*, 270–283.

49. Ruesch, J. *Chronic disease and psychological invalidism.* Berkeley: University of California Press, 1951 (original edition, 1946).

50. Zigler, E., & Phillips, L. Case history data and psychiatric diagnosis. *Journal of Consulting Psychology,* 1961, *25*, 458.

51.  Phillips, L., & Zigler, E. Social competence: The action-thought parameter and vicariousness in normal and pathological behaviors. *Journal of Abnormal and Social Psychology*, 1961, *63*, 137–146.

52.  Zigler, E., & Phillips, L. Social competence and outcome in psychiatric disorder. *Journal of Abnormal and Social Psychology*, 1961, *63*, 264–271.

53.  Zigler, E., & Phillips, L. Social competence and the process-reactive distinction in psychopathology. *Journal of Abnormal and Social Psychology*, 1962, *65*, 215–222.

54.  Rudie, R. R., & McGaughran, L. S. Differences in developmental experience, defensiveness, and personality organization between two classes of problem drinkers. *Journal of Abnormal and Social Psychology*, 1961, *62*, 659–665.

55.  Knight, R. P. The dynamics and treatment of chronic alcohol addiction. *Bulletin of the Menninger Clinic*, 1937, *1*, 233–250.

56.  Levine, J., & Zigler, E. The essential-reactive distinction in alcoholism: A developmental approach. *Journal of Abnormal and Social Psychology*, 1973, *81*, 242–249.

57.  Rosen, B., Klein, D. F., Levenstein, S., & Shanian, S. P. Social competence and posthospital outcome. *Archives of General Psychiatry*, 1968, *19*, 165–170.

58.  Erikson, E. H. *Childhood and society*. New York: W. W. Norton, 1963 (first edition, 1950).

59.  Erikson, E. H. Identity and the life cycle: Selected papers. *Psychological Issues*, Monograph 1, 1959.

60.  Erikson, E. H., ed. *Adulthood*. New York: W. W. Norton, 1978.

61.  Costello, R. M. Alcoholism treatment and evaluation: In search of methods. *International Journal of the Addictions*, 1975, *10*, 251–275.

62.  Hill, M. J., & Blane, H. T. Evaluation of psychotherapy with alcoholics: A critical review. *Quarterly Journal of Studies on Alcohol*, 1967, *28*, 76–104.

63.  May, S. J., & Kuller, L. H. Methodological approaches in the evaluation of alcoholism treatment: A critical review. *Preventive Medicine*, 1975, *4*, 464–481.

64.  Baekeland, F. Evaluation of treatment methods in chronic alcoholism. In *The biology of alcoholism*, Vol. 5. Kissin, B., & Begleiter, H., eds., New York: Plenum Press, 1977, 385–440.

65.  Pattison, E. M. A critique of alcoholism treatment concepts with special reference to abstinence. *Quarterly Journal of Studies on Alcohol*, 1966, *27*, 49–71.

66. Wanberg, K. W., & Horn, J. L. Alcoholism syndromes related to sociological classifications. *International Journal of the Addictions*, 1973, *8*, 99–120.

67. Pattison, E. M., Headley, E. B., Gleser, G. C., & Gottschalk, L. A. Abstinence and normal drinking: An assessment of changes in drinking practices in alcoholics after treatment. *Quarterly Journal of Studies on Alcohol*, 1968, *29*, 610–633.

68. Willems, P. J. A., Letemendia, F. J. J., & Arroyave, F. A categorization for the assessment of prognosis and outcome in the treatment of alcoholism. *British Journal of Psychiatry*, 1973, *122*, 649–654.

69. Kiresuk, T. J., & Sherman, R. E. Goal Attainment Scaling: A general method for evaluating comprehensive community mental health programs. *Community Mental Health Journal*, 1968, *4*, 443–453.

70. Lang, A. R. The use of Goal Attainment Scaling in the evaluation of alcohol abuse services. Unpublished mimeograph, Wisconsin Division of Mental Hygiene.

71. Baekeland, F., Lundwall, L., & Kissin, B. Methods for the treatment of chronic alcoholism: A critical appraisal. In *Research advances in alcohol and drug problems*, Vol. 2. Gibbins, R. J., et al., eds., New York: John Wiley & Sons, 1975, 247–327.

## Chapter 8

1. Siegler, M., Osmond, H., & Newell, S. Models of alcoholism. *Quarterly Journal of Studies on Alcohol*, 1968, *29*, 571–591.

2. Cahalan, D. Can alcoholism be defeated? *The Sciences*, 1977, *17 (2)*, 16–19.

3. Keller, M. Problems with alcohol: An historical perspective. In *Alcohol and alcohol problems: New thinking and new directions*. Filstead, W. J., Rossi, J. J., & Keller, M., eds., Cambridge, Mass.: Ballinger, 1976, 5–28.

4. Moser, J. Prevention of alcohol-related problems: Developing a broad-spectrum programme. *British Journal of Addiction*, 1979, *74*, 133–140.

5. Ashmore, R. D., & McConahay, J. B. *Psychology and America's urban dilemmas*. New York: McGraw-Hill, 1975.

6. Rieker, P. P., & Suchman, E. A. Prescriptions for evaluation. In *Further explorations in social psychiatry*. Kaplan, B. H., Wilson, R. N., & Leighton, A. H., eds., New York: Basic Books, 1976, 308–320.

7. Trist, E. L. The establishment of problem-oriented research domains. In *Towards a social ecology*. Emery, F. E., & Trist, E. L., authors, New York: Plenum/Rosetta, 1973, 91–102.

8. Cahalan, D. Why does the alcoholism field act like a ship of fools? *British Journal of Addiction*, 1979, *74*, 235–238.

9. Commoner, B. Urban biology: Its ecosystem needs a lab. *Hospital Practice*, 1975, *10*, 110–111.

10. Kennedy, D. A. Community health and the urban environment. In *The effect of the man-made environment on health and behavior*. Hinkle, L. E., & Loring, W. C., eds., Atlanta, Georgia: DHEW-PHS Center for Disease Control (Publ. No. [CDC] 77-8318), 1977, 7–44.

11. Pattison, E. M. Rehabilitation of the chronic alcoholic. In *The biology of alcoholism*, Vol. 3. Kissin, B., & Begleiter, H., eds., New York: Plenum Press, 1974, 587–657.

12. Manis, J. G., & Hunt, C. L. The community survey as a measure of the prevalence of alcoholism. *Quarterly Journal of Studies on Alcohol*, 1957, *18*, 212–216.

13. Selzer, M. L., Vinokur, A., van Rooijen, L. A self-administered Short Michigan Alcoholism Screening Test (SMAST). *Journal of Studies on Alcohol*, 1975, *36*, 117–126.

14. Mayer, J., Filstead, W. J. The Adolescent Alcohol Involvement Scale: An instrument for measuring adolescents' use and misuse of alcohol. *Journal of Studies on Alcohol*, 1979, *40*, 291–300.

15. Jellinek, E. M. "Death from alcoholism" in the United States in 1940: A statistical analysis. *Quarterly Journal of Studies on Alcohol*, 1942, *3*, 465–494.

16. deLint, J., & Schmidt, W. Alcoholism and mortality. In *The biology of alcoholism*, Vol. 4. Kissin, B., & Begleiter, H., eds., New York: Plenum Press, 1976, 275–305.

17. Cleary, P. D. A standardized estimator of the prevalence of alcoholism based on mortality data. *Journal of Studies on Alcohol*, 1979, *40*, 408–418.

18. Westermeyer, J., & Bearman, J. A proposed social indicator system for alcohol-related problems. *Preventive Medicine*, 1973, *2*, 438–444.

19. Gerson, L. W., Preston, D., & Golshani, S. A surveillance system for alcohol and drug related problems. Paper presented at the Toronto meeting of the Society for Epidemiologic Research, 18 June 1976.

20. Seixas, J. Children from alcoholic families. In *Alcoholism: Development, consequences, and interventions*. Estes, N. J., & Heinemann, M. E., eds., Saint Louis: C. V. Mosby, 1977, 153–161.

21. Popham, R. E., & Schmidt, W. The biomedical definition of safe alcohol consumption: A crucial issue for the researcher and the drinker. *British Journal of Addiction*, 1978, *73*, 233–235.

22. Castelli, W. P. How many drinks a day? *Journal of the American Medical Association*, 1979, *242*, 2000.

23. Fisher, A. How much drinking is dangerous? Reprinted from the August 1975 *Reader's Digest* (condensed from *New York Times Magazine*, 18 May 1975).

24. Lieber, C. S., Jones, D. P., & DeCarli, L. M. Effects of prolonged ethanol intake: Production of fatty liver despite adequate diets. *Journal of Clinical Investigation*, 1965, *44*, 1009–1021.

25. Lane, B. P., & Lieber, C. S. Ultrastructural alterations in human hepatocytes following ingestion of ethanol with adequate diets. *American Journal of Pathology*, 1966, *49*, 593–603.

26. Rubin, E., & Lieber, C. S. Early fine structural changes in the human liver induced by alcohol. *Gastroenterology*, 1967, *52*, 1–13.

27. Lieber, C. S., & Rubin, E. Alcoholic fatty liver. *New England Journal of Medicine*, 1969, *280*, 705–708.

28. Rubin, E., & Lieber, C. S. Fatty liver, alcoholic hepatitis and cirrhosis produced by alcohol in primates. *New England Journal of Medicine*, 1974, *290*, 128–135.

29. Rubin, E., & Lieber, C. S. Alcohol-induced hepatic injury in nonalcoholic volunteers. *New England Journal of Medicine*, 1968, *278*, 869–876.

30. Klatsky, A. L, Friedman, G. D., Siegelaub, A. B., & Gerard, M. J. Alcohol consumption and blood pressure: Kaiser-Permanente Multiphasic Health Examination data. *New England Journal of Medicine*, 1977, *296*, 1194–1200.

31. Klatsky, A. L., Friedman, G. D., & Siegelaub, A. B. Alcohol consumption before myocardial infarction. *Annals of Internal Medicine*, 1974, *81*, 294–301.

32. Hennekens, C. H., Willet, W., Rosner, B., Cole, D. S., & Mayrent, S. L. Effects of beer, wine, and liquor in coronary deaths. *Journal of the American Medical Association*, 1979, *242*, 1973–1974.

33. Smart, R. G., & Fejer, D. *Drug education: Current issues, future directions*. Toronto: Addiction Research Foundation of Ontario, 1974.

34. Globetti, G. Teenage drinking. In *Alcoholism: Development, consequences, and interventions*. Estes, N. J., & Heinemann, M. E., eds., Saint Louis: C. V. Mosby, 1977, 162–173.

35. Mendelson, J. H., & Mello, N. K. Biologic concomitants of alcoholism. *New England Journal of Medicine*, 1979, *301*, 912–921.

36. Barnes, G. E. The alcoholic personality: A reanalysis of the literature. *Journal of Studies on Alcohol*, 1979, *40*, 571–634.

37. Harper, F. D. *Alcohol and blacks: An overview*. Alexandria, Va.: Douglass Publishers, 1976.

38. Zelhart, P. F., & Schurr, B. C. People who drive while impaired: Issues in treating the drinking driver. In *Alcoholism: Development, consequences, and interventions*. Estes, N. J., & Heinemann, M. E., eds., Saint Louis: C. V. Mosby, 1977, 204–218.

39. Dekker, E. Elements for an alcohol control policy. *International Journal of Health Education*, 1979, *22*, 14–24.

40. Schmidt, W. Cirrhosis and alcohol consumption: An epidemiological perspective. In *Alcoholism: New knowledge and new responses*. Edwards, G., & Grant, M., eds., London: Croom Helm, 1977, 15–47.

41. Kendell, R. E. Alcoholism: A medical or a political problem? *British Medical Journal*, 1979, *1 (6160)*, 367–371.

42. Editorial. Action on alcohol. *British Medical Journal*, 1979, *1 (6160)*, 361–362.

43. Breslow, L. A positive strategy for the nation's health. *Journal of the American Medical Association*, 1979, *242*, 2093–2095.

44. Kristein, M. M. Economic issues in prevention. *Preventive Medicine*, 1977, *6*, 252–264.

45. Cottrell, L. S. The competent community. In *Further explorations in social psychiatry*. Kaplan, B. H., Wilson, R. N., & Leighton, A. H., eds., New York: Basic Books, 1976, 195–209.

46. Poust, M. A., & Tumulty, B. The Bronx battles the cancer of decay. *The* (Port Chester, N.Y.) *Daily Item*, 3 December 1979, 1.

47. U.S. sending aid to Bronx: $20 million fulfills Carter housing promise. *The* (Newark) *Star-Ledger*, 11 October 1978, 35.

48. Straus, R. Alcohol and society. *Psychiatric Annals*, Vol. 3, no. 10, 1973. (Reprint, not paginated.)

# INDEX

Abad, V., 109–111
Abstinence, 32n, 192, 204n
  *See also* Example cases; Sobriety
  among non-alcoholic blacks, 94,
  96
Accidents and alcohol, 205
Adaptation
  *See also* Maladaptation
  as measure of disease, 34–35, 51,
  54–55, 68, 85
  and sobriety, 186
  and treatment outcome, 75
Addiction, 124, 136
  *See also* Dependence, alcohol;
  Example cases
Addiction Services Agency, 118
Adolescents. *See* Youths
Advertising of alcoholic beverages,
  211
After-hours clubs, 28, 94
Afternoon-only drinkers, 130, 135,
  162, 182
  *See also* Zenia
Age
  of black alcoholics, 154
  of first drink, 98–99, 106; and
  prevention, 209; and prognosis,
  184–185; of study subjects,
  127, 155, 157
  and prognosis, 177–178, 183–185
  of study subjects, 119, 135–136,
  154, 157
Agent of disease, 63–67
  alcohol as, 70–72, 74, 81; and
  prevention, 204–205, 209–211
Albahary, R. S., 183–185
Alcohol
  *See also* Agent of disease, alcohol
  as; Consumption, alcohol;
  Dependence, alcohol;
  Withdrawal states, alcohol

  and accidents, 205
  attitudes toward, 79, 81, 89, 208
  availability of: to blacks, 28,
  94–95; and prevention, 25,
  209–210
  and black culture. *See* Blacks
  in blood and the diagnosis of
  alcoholism, 152
  effects of: on the central nervous
  system, 72–73, 80, 205–206;
  on the liver, 86, 206–207
  fatal overdoses of, 205–206
  and Hispanic culture. *See*
  Hispanics
  and legislation, 25, 87, 210–211
  vs. other drugs of abuse, 87–88
  questionnaires on use of, 107, 203
  tolerance to, 53, 152–153
Alcoholics
  *See also* Alcoholism; Example
  cases; Patients; Subgroups,
  clinical; Subjects of this study
  black, 99–107
  choice of treatment by, 188–189,
  195
  essential vs. reactive, 184–185
  rights and duties of, 75
  skid-row, 153–154
  and social competence
  measurement, 183–187,
  194–197
  and surveys, 86, 96–99, 202–203
Alcoholics Anonymous (AA), 75,
  172, 204
  *See also* Example cases
  and clinical subgroups, 181, 188,
  194
  model of alcoholism of, 69
  role of, in the MLKHC program,
  173
  and sobriety, 186

243

Occupation
and alcohol problems, 86
of blacks in alcoholism treatment,
106
and prognosis, 175–178
of study subjects, 121, 122,
154–155, 157, 170, 182
Osmond, H., 32n, 59, 69, 76–77
Outpatients, studies of, 175–176,
182, 189, 196–197
cross-cultural, 29, 100–105,
115–136


Pancreatitis, 52
Parents. See Families
Pasteur, L., 50n, 64
Pathogenesis of disease, 73
Pathways in alcoholism treatment,
174–175
See also Subgroups, clinical
and social class, 176, 188
Patients
See also Alcoholics; Inpatients,
studies of; Outpatients, studies
of; Subgroups, clinical;
Subjects of this study
importance of choices by,
188–189, 195
and the scope of individual
medicine vs. social medicine,
78–79
treatment-seeking behavior of,
188–189
variability of, 36–37, 45–47,
52–53, 174, 192
Pattison, E. M., 32n
on abstinence, 192
on clinical subgroups, 174, 175n,
181; defined by field
dependence/independence, 179;
defined by treatment-seeking
behavior, 188–189
on community epidemiology, 202

on deviant behavior and
responsibility, 58
Pediatricians, 27
Peer pressure
among blacks, 95
and prevention, 208, 210–211
among study subjects, 131
Permissiveness of heavy drinking. See
Tolerance of heavy drinking and
drunkenness
Personality inventories, 179
Personality theories of alcoholism,
81
Phenobarbital, 141
Phenomenological characteristics of
alcoholics, 180–185
Phenomenology, 180n
"Phenomenon" and alcoholism as a
disease, 47–50
Phenytoin (Dilantin), 138, 141–142
Phillips, L., 183–186, 194, 196
Physical dependence. See
Dependence, alcohol;
Dependence, drug
Physicians
See also Example cases
and alcoholism as a disease,
52–53, 59, 69
as an alcoholism treatment
resource, 69, 194
and "individual medicine," 78
and the "medical model," 50–51
and referrals to the Alcoholism
Unit, 118, 166
views of disease of, 39–41
Physiological dependence. See
Dependence, alcohol;
Dependence, drug
Pittman, D. J., 97–99
Places of Drinking. See Drinking,
places of
Planning, program
and choices by patients, 189, 195
and clinical subgroups, 174–175,

INDEX 259

Roebuck, J. B., 63, 81, 82, 85
Rogler, L. H., 160
Roman, P. M., 177
Rorschach tests, 179
Rosen, B., 186
Rosenblatt, S. M., 177
Rudie, R. R., 184

Saenger, G., 175–176
Safety, highway, 205, 209
Saint Louis, Mo., 97
Sampling of subjects of this study,
  115–116
Santo, 149–150
Scale, Essential-Reactive Alcoholism
  (ERA), 184–186, 195
Schizophrenia, 160, 168
Schmidt, W., 176, 188
School
  See also Education
  problems in, and future alcohol
  problems, 98
Science
  and conceptual evolution, 38
  and interest groups, 61
  and reification, 50
Scientists
  communication among, 32, 50
  and inner-city alcoholism,
    213–215
Scotch (beverage), 91, 95, 143
Screening
  for alcoholism risk, 208
  for alcohol problems, 202–203
Seeley, J. R., 44, 56
Seixas, F. A., 52
Seizures, 53, 105
  See also Example cases
Self-esteem and *machismo*, 108
Sex
  of blacks in alcoholism treatment,
  118
  comparisons by, 108; of study

subjects, 119–136, 153, 157
  female, and program planning,
    178–179
  and prognosis, 178
Sherman, R. E., 192
Sick role, 57–58
Siegler, M., 32n, 59, 69, 76–77
Significance level used in this study,
  117
Skeet, 145–146
Skid-row alcoholics, 23, 153–154
Slavery, 93–94
Sleep, disturbances of, 127,
  138–139, 144, 150
Smart, R. G., 88n.2, 176, 188
Sobriety
  See also Abstinence; Example cases
  in Alcoholics Anonymous, 186
  reported by study subjects, 125
Social Class. See Class, social
Social disorganization, 84–85
Social drinking, 110, 207
Social medicine, 78–79
Social problems due to drinking,
  98–99
Social service agencies, 118,
  170–171, 196, 203
Society
  and alcoholism etiology, 70–72,
    74–78, 81, 83, 85–86
  and disease etiology, 63–68,
    84–85
  industrial, 68, 77
  and medicine, 78–79
  position of Puerto Ricans in,
    111–113, 160
  and responsibility for alcoholism,
    25–26, 76, 198–202, 210–215
Sociology, 72, 78, 82, 85
Source of referral of study subjects,
  118
South Bronx, 26–28, 85, 163,

non-whites, 85
and black history, 93–94
drinking and alcohol problems of:
vs. blacks, 96, 98–106, 155; vs.
blacks and Hispanics, 108
Wholistic Theory. *See* Holistic
Theory
Whybrow, P. C., 50–51
Wine, 117, 127n, 152, 156
*See also* Example cases
and blacks, 97, 108
and Hispanics, 108
and study subjects, 135–136, 158
Winokur, G., 169
Withdrawal states, alcohol, 75, 80
*See also* Example cases
of study subjects, 116, 127,
131–135, 152, 158–161
Wolff, II. G., 68, 84
Women, 110, 157, 178–179
*See also* Blacks, male-female
differences among; Example

cases; Sex
Work. *See* Employment
World Health Organization, 37, 200

Yates's correction for continuity,
157n.1
Youths, 135–136, 212
*See also* Age, of first drink;
Families
black, 98–99, 209
Hispanic, 111
and the prevention of alcohol
problems, 88n, 205–206,
207–208
screening questionnaire for, 203

Zenia, 147–149
Zigler, E., 183–186, 194, 196
Ziglin, A. L., 176
Zimberg, S., 99, 154, 155, 170, 173
Zwerling, I., 175